# A COUPLE'S
## —GUIDE TO—
# M$NEY

✓ **Grow Closer** ✓ **Dream Bigger**
✓ **Thrive Together**

## By Prudence Zhu

CPA, CFP®, CFT™

Published by Jumpstart Publishing PO Box 6, Roseville, CA 95661, (916) 872-4000 www.JumpstartPublishing.net.

**DISCLAIMER AND/OR LEGAL NOTICES**

ISBN: 979-8-9932038-0-5

PRINTED IN THE UNITED STATES OF AMERICA

# Voices from Those Who Followed the Guide

*"It's a life-changer realizing our own fears and money beliefs were holding us back and splitting us apart. But what's been most surprising is how much our experience has changed when navigating through difficult conversations. We talk more openly about money and our feelings, understand each other a lot more, and we're making plans together for the first time in years. It feels like a fresh start!"*

**— David, Toronto, Canada**

*"Ever since I started the program, I've noticed that I've been more present with my partner and more patient with myself. I'm no longer scrolling down my phone out of boredom when I'm sitting in the passenger's seat with my kids in the back seat when my husband is driving. Instead, I pay attention to the music or conversation in the car and add to the energy that's developing. I feel more connected. My financial outlook has shifted too—I'm no longer just getting by while hoping things would change one day; I'm actively creating it with my partner."*

**— Laura, Chicago, USA**

*"The exercises in this book have been eye-opening. The moment I read through the first one, I'm already filled with guilt, seeing clearly where I've fallen short all those years. I'm starting to realize how much I ignored and have taken for granted for years. I've already started to change, and my wife is happy to see my change. She's now filled with excitement for where the journey would take us!"*

**— John, Calgary, Canada**

*"I thought I had everything figured out, but after going through the process, I realized how much more I could gain by having regular and deep conversations with my partner, and align my personal goals and actions with my partner's. The insights I've gained about love and money have not only brought us closer but have also sparked new ideas for our financial future. I'm so grateful for this!"*

**— Ashley, Seattle, USA**

For Wyatt,
my best friend and mentor.

For my parents,
who instilled in me the values of frugality and hard work.

For my clients,
whose journeys remind me each day why I love what I do.

# CONTENTS

# FOREWORD

*By Sheryl Garrett, Founder of Garrett Planning Network and Renowned Financial Planning Pioneer*

After nearly forty years as a personal financial planner, consultant, coach, and author, I've realized that much of the core practices we advise on is not rocket science. Far from it. It's basic stuff. But we don't stay on track. We may know what we need to do, but we can't stick with it for some reason or another. Some of us self-sabotage. How to overcome it, you wonder.

We all can benefit from someone to hold us accountable. Our life partner, financial advisor, or coach can dramatically enhance our success along the journey. But that advisor or coach is not as vested in or dependent on the outcome as you are. If you share your life with a partner, that individual just may be your greatest ally or detriment to your ambitions. You don't want to achieve "your dreams" only to find out that your life partner is unsatisfied.

For instance, very early in my relationship with the person I'd later marry, we discussed living abroad. After months of research and discussion, the island of Roatán, off the coast of Honduras, was our selection to explore.

Much to my fiancé's surprise, I bought a plot of land during that trip.

On the flight home the next day, my partner shared that they could not live there, or even move far from their parents in Kansas.

Oops! What the heck happened? At that time, my partner was willing to support any daydream I had. They didn't realize I was serious.

Nearly twenty years later, we still own the lot. However, we've never been back and we've had no luck selling it. This was an enormous financial mistake that could have been avoided simply by working through the exercises laid out in this book.

I wish that all of my clients would have had this resource available and worked through it before we met.

# INTRODUCTION

It was a regular weekday afternoon, but I was anything but at ease. Tucked away in the windowless storage room at work, I balanced my laptop on my knees while pumping breast milk. The cold plastic flanges clamped to me, and the pump hummed steadily. Every few minutes, the 'ping!' of new emails pulled me back to work, but my eyes kept drifting down to the two nearly empty bottles hanging from my chest. Panic crept in. *Why isn't there more milk? What am I doing wrong?*

Longing for comfort, I grabbed my phone and played a shaky video of my three-month-old giggling. I hoped his soft coos would spark the release I desperately needed. Anything to feel closer to him! Instead, I felt lost, heartbroken, and out of sync with the very family my husband and I were building.

That evening, after rocking my baby to sleep, I faced the relentless bottle-washing routine, tiny breast pump parts scattered across the counter in an endless assembly line. By ten o'clock, my body felt hollow. I collapsed into bed but soon found myself scrolling through YouTube videos at double speed, grasping for a moment of escape from the overwhelm of work and childcare. When sleep finally claimed me around 1:00 a.m., it was restless. I felt vacant and foggy, like a ghost. Then, at sunrise, my son's cries jolted me awake and the cycle repeated.

From the outside, everything looked flawless: a steady job that paid the bills, a loving husband who stood by me through it all, an elegant home in a neighborhood bursting with character and charm. And, of course, our chunky, eighteen-pound baby boy who made every sleepless night worth it. But behind the smiles and the perfect photos, I felt trapped in a job I didn't love, watching the days slip through my fingers like grains of sand. I couldn't fully enjoy the small, precious moments with my family. The pressure of mortgage payments and childcare costs weighed heavily on me, and giving up the career and vibrant city life my husband and I dreamed of felt like losing a fight I didn't want to quit.

Fast forward six years, and *everything* had changed. I had built financial freedom, launched two businesses I truly cared about, and regained energy and clarity I never thought possible. I began taking eight full weeks off every year to travel and make memories with my family. Work stopped being just a paycheck. It became passion, purpose, and joy.

On this new journey, I realized that wealth means so much more than just a number. My relationships deepened not only with my husband and kids, but most importantly with myself. I learned that true freedom comes from building a life that matches what matters to you, not just piling up assets. I only wish I'd known this and seen it sooner!

Working with couples from all walks of life only deepened this truth. I saw partners open up, build trust, and unite on their dreams, creating plans that brought them closer both emotionally and financially.

Once I had these breakthrough realizations, I knew I couldn't keep them to myself. I saw that others could bypass years of confusion and overwhelm with the right tools and support. That's what inspired this book. My mission is to walk alongside you, sharing the clarity, guidance, and genuine excitement that transformed both my journey and those of my clients, so you can start making life-changing shifts right now. Why spend years struggling when you could begin your transformation today?

## What You'll Get

This book is for couples ready to transform not just their relationship but their financial future. It's designed to help you grow closer, dream bigger, and confidently build a thriving life together. Inside, you'll find practical tools, relatable stories, and meaningful exercises that make conversations about money (and life) a little easier, and a lot more fun!

I'll guide you every step of the way as you decode dreams, tackle doubts, and uncover the strengths that make your partnership unique, no matter where you start from. Building an amazing financial life together begins with a simple yet powerful foundation: understanding what truly matters to both of you, and taking those first real steps, side by side.

## Chapter 1: Love Is the Foundation

Let's start by rewinding to the heart of your partnership: your connection! Reignite what brought you together, infuse your days with joy and gratitude, and discover why love is the secret sauce for real "money talks."

## Chapter 2: Face Fear—Lean In to Move On

Money can bring up all kinds of emotions: fear, guilt, even old family baggage. We'll gently explore those feelings and turn them into fuel for rewriting your future together.

## Chapter 3: Live Fully with Tomorrow in Mind

Dream a little, or a lot! Picture what a stress-free, joy-filled life truly looks like for you both. This chapter will help you envision your perfect day, week, and year, and empower you to live fully starting today while preparing for an even brighter tomorrow.

## Chapter 4: Envision Real Change

Is there a big change calling your name? Maybe it's starting that dream business, spending more time with family, or finally putting your own well-being first. This chapter is your launchpad. We'll help you let go of what's holding you back by focusing on what really motivates you, and then plan the steps to make those changes happen together.

## Chapter 5: Master Money Basics

Money doesn't have to be complicated! We'll break down the essentials, guide you through a simple financial wellness flowchart, and share easy tips to help you build a solid foundation for a brighter financial future.

## Chapter 6: The Hidden Secret to Freedom

True freedom is about much more than just hitting the right number! Learn to think through a comprehensive plan, including investments, taxes, and your wildest dreams. This brings clarity, confidence, and peace of mind for you and your partner through the entire journey.

## Chapter 7: Keep Going—Momentum for Life

You've started building a shared vision and healthy new habits. Now, let's keep that momentum going strong! Get the practical tools to stay motivated, track progress, and support each other, no matter what life throws your way.

## Chapter 8: Two Sides, One Coin

This special bonus chapter is for cross-cultural and immigrant couples. We'll celebrate your stories, address the unique challenges you face, and explore the amazing possibilities that come from blending different backgrounds and dreams.

*Above all, I hope this book helps you build healthier, happier relationships—with each other, with money, with your dreams, and with life itself. Combining love and money is a true superpower. As you begin this journey, may you create a life together that is deeply fulfilling and uniquely yours!*

## How to Get the Most out of This Book

This book is very different from most self-help books. Let me be blunt: reading it alone won't change your life. The last thing I want is for you to feel like you've made progress by simply flipping through the pages. Real change happens when you take the insights and knowledge here and apply them to your daily decisions. Whether those decisions are big or small, turning them into good habits is what creates lasting results.

That's why I strongly encourage you to do the exercises at the end of each chapter with your partner. These aren't just for reading—they're for doing! They're designed to help you grow and experience the kind of transformation I've seen in the couples I work with, both in my group coaching program and in one-on-one sessions.

When you actively engage with this book and commit to doing the work alongside your partner, you'll start to see real changes in your relationships and money. That's where the magic happens. Start the journey, apply what you learn, and watch your life transform!

## Adaptation for Other Relationships

Even though this book and its activities are mainly for couples, they work great for other close relationships too, like with siblings, parents, grown kids, or best friends. The real magic happens when two people who trust each other join forces and figure out how to make their money fit the kind of life they really want.

# CHAPTER 1

# Love Is the Foundation

John was the first to join my Couples and Money group coaching program. He's in his early forties and chats with me on Zoom from his home in Calgary. The computer light glows on his glasses, and he looks calm but focused. John has a good job, but there's a big challenge: every twenty-seven days, he has to travel for work and spend two weeks away from home, leaving his wife and three kids—aged fourteen, nine, and six—behind. Even though his career is going well, his heart feels heavy, burdened by the distance that's growing between him and his family.

John and I have never met in person. Our conversations have all been online, but even through the digital screen, I can feel his sincerity, his longing for something more. He came to me with two clear goals: to improve his relationship with his family and to get better at managing his finances. He wants to live a better life, one where he has more time to enjoy the things he loves, like spending time with his family, pursuing his passions, and having the freedom to truly enjoy life.

## The Spark of Love

As John talks to me, I ask him to share more about his relationship with his wife, whom he has known for over two decades. He smiles as he remembers the early days of their relationship, back when everything was exciting and new. When they first met, there was an undeniable spark between them. They would spend hours talking, sharing dreams, and making plans for a future together. Those were the days filled with passion and possibility. But now, with the demands of life, work, and raising children, that spark feels dimmed.

He tells me that over the years, he's become so focused on providing for his family that he's unintentionally neglected his emotional connection with his wife. The long weeks away from home have left him with little energy to invest in the relationship that once felt so alive.

As we talk, John expresses his regret. He doesn't want his children to grow up with the memory of a distant father or a mother who feels alone. He doesn't want their memories of him to be marked by missed moments or the frustration that often accompanies his absence. "I want my kids to remember me as a present father who's always there for them, not someone who was always out working," he says, his voice thick with emotion.

## A Wake-up Call: The Christmas Card

The wake-up call came when his youngest daughter made him a Christmas card. As he prepared for another work trip on December 24, she handed it to him with a simple but powerful message: "Please, Daddy, don't fight with Mommy anymore. I love you so much, and I want you both to be happy."

John recalls that moment with a deep sense of guilt. "I drove away that day with the card in my hand, and I cried. I couldn't believe the impact my absence and our arguments were having on my kids. It was like a punch to the gut." He tells me how his daughter's words echoed in his head for days, and how he realized that if he didn't make a change, he would lose the opportunity to make connections with his family. The thought of his children growing up without seeing the love and partnership between their parents broke his heart.

For John, that card became a symbol of everything he needed to change—a reminder that his family needed him not just as a provider, but as an engaged, loving father and husband.

## Commitment to Change

"I need to change for them," John says. "For my wife and kids. I don't want them to think of me as someone who wasn't there or didn't show enough love. I want to be a better husband, a better father, and a better person."

As we continue our work together, I help him explore ways to rebuild his connection with his wife, rediscovering the intimacy they once shared. We focus on one small but meaningful step: making time for them to reconnect. Later on, we also discuss his financial plan, which has been pushed to the back burner in the midst of life's chaos (as it has for many of us). John recognizes that while he's worked hard to provide for his family, he's not been proactively planning or visualizing long-term wealth and their future. Together, we discuss how he can handle his money better. This way, he can not only secure his family's future, but also free up time to enjoy the life he's worked so hard to build.

But first, we need to lay the groundwork for rekindling the spark in his marriage.

## The Path Forward

Now John is committed to improving his relationship with his wife, engaging more with his family, and getting better at managing his finances. Paving the path forward is where I come in, but I don't jump right in, as the work is first on him to reignite the spark within himself and rebuild the connection with his wife. At this point in the process, I give him his first homework assignment: a set of small exercises (see the end of this chapter) that he can do with his wife. Then he'll come back online with the group to discuss what they learned.

## Love Is the Foundation

When it comes to family finances, we often think about numbers—budgets, investments, and savings goals. And a lot of times, those numbers can come with judgments, past history, or conflicting priorities. These issues can quickly escalate to clashing values and misunderstandings. It's becoming a common phenomenon: more than 45% of people admitted privately that they sometimes argue with their significant other about money. And for one in four couples, money is the biggest problem in their relationship, according to the 2024 Couples & Money Study[1].

This is no surprise since money quantifies your differences, and you have to make a decision one way or another. What if there's a way to turn things around and switch your communication

[1] https://preview.thenewsmarket.com/Previews/FINP/DocumentAssets/660835_v4.pdf

to start from a jointly shared sentiment: the feeling that first brought you together? Love is the bedrock that holds couples together, and it plays a crucial role in shaping both relationships and financial decisions within a family unit.

## Love Fosters Open Communication

The foundation of every strong family is built on trust and communication, and love nurtures both. When family members feel secure in the love and care they give and receive, they are more likely to share openly about their financial concerns, dreams, and aspirations. This transparency helps couples align on their goals, whether that's saving for a home, sending kids to college, or preparing for retirement. Without open communication, financial decisions can quickly become sources of stress and conflict.

The importance of open communication was brought into sharp focus for me through a story shared by Brandyn Caires, co-founder of Parent Team and my trainer in the collaborative divorce process. To truly understand something, I tend to explore extremes, and relationships are no different. I needed to see both ends of the story. Brandyn shared that many couples, by the time they reach the end of their guided divorce journey, tell her, "If we had known how to communicate like this years ago, we wouldn't be here today." This powerful truth highlights just how vital communication is, not only to avoid conflict but to build a stronger, deeper connection from the very start. It's a reminder that learning to talk openly and listen deeply can transform a relationship long before it reaches a breaking point.

## Love Encourages Shared Goals

When family members are united by love, they can approach financial decisions with a shared vision. Love allows couples to compromise and work together towards common financial goals. For example, if one partner is focused on paying off debt while the other wants to invest in real estate, love helps them find common ground and work out a strategy that honors both priorities. In a family where love and mutual respect are present, financial decisions feel less like sacrifices and more like steps toward building a better future together.

Warren Buffett once said, "The most important decision you make is who you marry." He credits much of his success not just to his financial savvy but to choosing the right life partner. Buffett's unconventional marriage to his first wife, Susan, meant staying emotionally close even though they lived apart for decades. Later, he welcomed a close friend into his life with Susan's blessing. This relationship reflects how love and mutual respect can build a strong shared vision. Despite the complexity, Buffett and his partners stayed aligned on their goals, proving that love grounded in trust enables couples to navigate challenges and build a future together. His wisdom reminds us that when love and respect guide your partnership, you create a strong foundation for making decisions together and building a future that reflects both your values and dreams.

## Love Drives Long-Term Financial Security

Financial choices aren't just about today's wants or quick thrills. They're about something much deeper. Often, what matters most is resisting the urge for instant rewards so you can build a stronger, more secure future for your loved ones.

When you care for your family, sacrifices like skipping a luxury purchase, paying down debt, setting aside money for your child's education, or saving for retirement don't feel like burdens. Instead, they become acts of devotion.

- Every dollar you save or invest is a way of saying, "*I want you to be safe and well, not just today, but always.*"
- Every sacrifice is powered by the hope that your family can thrive—not just get by.

At its core, making wise financial decisions is less about denying yourself and more about providing room for those you love to flourish. When love is the motivation, every tough choice becomes a step toward a brighter, more abundant future together.

## Love Cultivates Financial Creativity

When love guides financial decisions, there's often greater creativity in the family's financial approach. Love teaches patience and understanding, allowing couples to adapt as life circumstances change, growing stronger through challenges and adversity. Whether it's a change in income, a job loss, or an unexpected expense, families driven by love are better able to weather financial storms together. They work together, support one another, and keep the bigger picture in mind, rather than reacting out of fear or frustration. Taking a loving approach makes it easier to brainstorm creative solutions to financial problems and see unique opportunities.

One couple I worked with faced a sudden job loss that cut their household income drastically. Instead of falling into panic or shame, they leaned into their love and commitment. Sitting down with patience and openness, they brainstormed ways to stretch every dollar and tap external resources. They explored ideas like switching to a single car, starting a small side business at home, and temporarily cutting non-essential expenses without sacrificing family time or joy. Through their creativity and mutual support, not only did they survive the tough financial patch but they also discovered new areas for growth. They realized they could thrive on less and recognized the importance of financial preparedness. This adversity became a catalyst for growth, sparking more creativity and building a stronger foundation for the future. Their story shows how love fosters resilience and innovation, helping families face financial challenges united and stay focused on the bigger picture.

## The Bottom Line

At its core, love is what allows couples to make thoughtful, balanced, and empowering financial decisions. It creates a space where all voices are heard, where differences are respected, and where everyone is working towards a brighter future. When couples approach financial decisions with love, they build not just wealth but stronger, more resilient relationships. At the end of this chapter, I'll share an exercise that can help you and your life partner reground your communications in love.

## Navigating Personalities and Money

Another amazing couple in my program, Hannah and Matt, both in their late twenties, are navigating a completely different kind of financial and emotional journey. While they've only been married for a few years, they've already tackled some huge milestones: buying a home, investing in real estate, doing their own renovations, managing an Airbnb, and working hard to advance in their careers. And now, they're stepping into one of life's biggest adventures: planning to have a baby! But like many couples, they're finding that balancing finances and their personal relationship is no easy task.

Matt, a typical guy in the tech industry, is a "straight shooter." He's all about getting to the point. No fluff. He isn't the type to talk much about his feelings or display emotions openly. Instead, he finds comfort and security in a steady, uncomplicated life. His motto: "Spending less is making more." He's the type who'll optimize everything from credit card rewards to coupons, prioritizing practicality and spending wisely.

Meanwhile, Hannah is a bit more adventurous. She loves exploring new experiences, enjoying life, and indulging in some quality moments. The challenge comes because while she craves a little extra spice in life, his reserved, frugal side often leaves her feeling disconnected from his approach.

As they approach the exciting (and a little scary) milestone of parenthood, financial stress has become a real concern. Between the high cost of living, the upcoming expenses of raising a child, and their need to save for the future, she wishes her partner would take a more comprehensive approach to their finances. But being the practical type, his focus remains on advancing his career and expanding his AI side hustle.

Now comes Hannah's real challenge: how to soften his approach and invite him into dreaming and discussing their future without it feeling like a burden. As two IT professionals with similar backgrounds but contrasting personalities, it's hard for either to step outside their comfort zones when it comes to money talks.

Hannah isn't just focused on the numbers. She's also thinking about the bigger picture. She wants connection, partnership, and clarity as they enter this new chapter of life. She doesn't want to go through the unknowns of parenthood alone. She wants to feel secure in their finances and relationship, knowing they have a clear, aligned plan to meet their goals, tackle uncertainties, and ensure both of their needs are met. It's not just about money. It's about building a future that reflects both of their dreams and values.

## Why Financial Conversations Are Particularly Hard

Sometimes, talking about money in relationships can feel like trying to defuse a bomb. One wrong word and things can blow up! That's because financial conversations are rarely just about dollars and cents. When someone gets upset about money, they're often not just upset about the immediate issue (the tip of the iceberg). There is a lot more going on underneath, like frustration, stress, past problems, and things that led up to it. Emotions can take over, making it easy to get angry, defensive, or even shut down completely.

To make things worse, when we're on the listening side, it's tempting to jump straight into "fix-it" mode, offering solutions before our partner has even finished sharing. We want to save the day. But if someone feels unheard, ignored, brushed aside, or isolated, the real issues may stay buried and resentment can start to build. Most people won't open up about what's truly bothering them unless they feel safe and understood. So, while it might seem like you're just talking about a purchase or a bill, these conversations are really about building trust and creating a space where both of you feel valued.

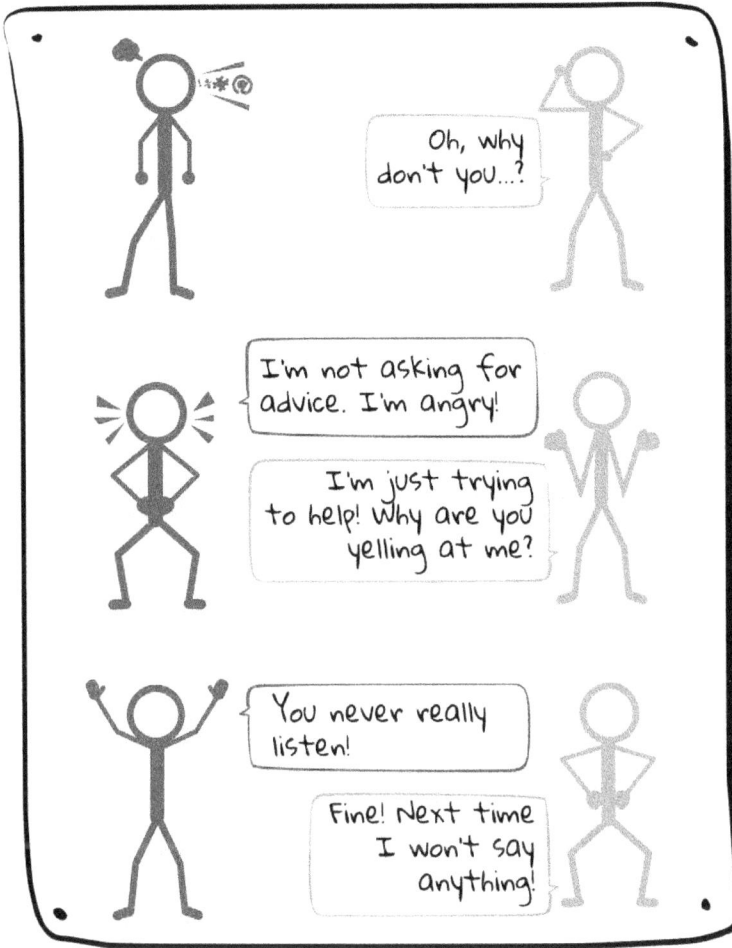

Figure 1: The Art of Not Listening

Have you had one of those moments when you are upset and just want your partner to really listen, hoping for a simple nod or a gentle word while you pour your heart out? Instead, your partner interrupts with, "Here's what you should do," and suddenly a list of solutions takes over the conversation. In that moment, you might feel invisible, as if your emotions are shortcomings to be fixed rather than simply understood. The air gets heavier, voices sharpen, and what started as a plea for understanding

11

becomes a tense and disappointing exchange. Instead of comfort, both of you end up feeling unheard, unappreciated, and strangely far apart, even though all you wanted was to connect.

## You Could Save Thirty-five Cents

Hannah shared with me a moment that really stuck with her, one of those everyday conversations that reveals deeper feelings. One evening, after a long and draining day at work, she came home frustrated and just wanted to vent. She turned to her husband, Matt, and said, "Can you believe it, the price of gas is now $4.27 a gallon!" But before she could even catch her breath, he jumped in with, "Was it at Costco? It's usually thirty-five cents cheaper there."

But here's the thing—Hannah's frustration wasn't really about the gas price. It was the culmination of a day filled with stress. She'd been dealing with a bug at work (remember, she's in IT) that she thought she had fixed, only to find out it wasn't resolved. The commute was terrible, and a driver cut her off in stop-and-go traffic, almost causing an accident. By the time she got to the gas station, the price hike felt like the last straw.

What Hannah truly needed wasn't a solution; it was simply to be heard. She wanted the space to express how everything had piled up and to feel understood, not to have someone fix it for her. Instead, Matt immediately went into problem-solving mode, thinking that by pointing out a cheaper gas station, he'd quickly resolve the situation. However, he missed an opportunity to connect with her on a deeper level and to help her process the emotions she was carrying from the entire day.

The truth is, she wasn't asking for a solution. She wasn't looking for a way to save money on gas. What she wanted was for him to see that the stress she was feeling wasn't just about the price of fuel, but the emotional weight of everything else that had been happening. Behind that frustration were larger issues: the strain of a tight budget, the uncertainty of job security, and the self-doubt that often creeps in when she feels like she's falling behind on both her dreams and the needs of her growing family.

*It wasn't about the solution. It was about being listened to.*

While Matt's intention was to help, he missed the opportunity to truly connect with Hannah. He didn't take the time to understand what was truly bothering her beneath the surface. Jumping straight into problem-solving instead of listening is a common trap in financial and emotional conversations, particularly when things feel overwhelming.

## What's Really Going On

Ever had a conversation where you felt like your partner just wasn't hearing you? Maybe it wasn't that they weren't listening, but rather that they were listening to respond—ready with a solution or trying to fix things before you even finished speaking. This happens all the time, especially when the topic is something as sensitive as money. Financial stress can bring out personal fears, insecurities, or external pressures, and if we're not really listening, we miss the full picture.

Now, let's add another layer to the challenge: pause and listen to yourself. I know, it sounds a little deep, right? But it's vital! When we're emotionally triggered (like during a heated discussion about money), it's easy to react immediately, often without fully understanding why we're upset. The trick is to pause, step back, breathe (possibly try to mimic your partner's breathing pattern for a few seconds to develop empathy and be fully present with them), and separate your emotional response from the situation. Then, ask yourself: What's really bothering me here?

This is where real growth begins! Imagine being your own guide, taking the time to truly listen to your thoughts and feelings, then digging deeper to understand what's really going on beneath the surface. It's not easy, but the more you practice, the better you become at recognizing what you need and why you react the way you do. This kind of self-awareness can change not only how you connect with others but also how you treat yourself.

Making a habit of checking in with yourself is one of the most powerful things you can do. It helps you grow stronger, feel more connected, and build the kind of life and relationships you really want.

## It Takes Two

Okay, now return your attention to your partner. It's hard enough to listen to ourselves, but listening to our partner with active care can be an even bigger challenge, especially when emotions run high. The key is to create space to process feelings together, rather than jumping in with an immediate fix. There's no rush here, and you can take turns, like we do in the exercise at the end of this chapter. Let your partner speak freely about their frustrations or concerns, and you get the chance to listen without judgment. When both of you participate in this exchange, magic happens.

This is where you and your partner start to grow closer, helping each other understand your feelings and what really matters, creating a space where you both feel heard, loved, and supported. Active listening isn't about fixing or solving—it's about understanding and being present. This is the first step to the real solution. It's the foundation for better decision-making, especially about money. If you and your partner can listen with empathy, you will have a much stronger emotional and financial connection, allowing you to tackle challenges together and build the future you both dream of.

## Growing Closer

Here's the good news: You already have the best asset to unlock growth and connection—each other. A trusted partner who listens without judgment and reflects your thoughts back to you can help you see what you really need and give you strength and clarity. When you share feelings and needs, it's also easier to understand and support your partner. And the best part? You can then focus on what truly matters.

In relationships, especially when it comes to discussing finances, having a partner who listens with patience and care is priceless. It's about creating a safe space for each person to express their feelings, process emotions, and understand the deeper motivations behind their actions.

When you and your partner listen to each other this way, you build deep trust. That trust becomes the strong foundation for aligning your dreams and financial goals, bringing you closer than ever. By opening up and truly listening with care, you unlock the wisdom to make smarter money decisions together. Exploring what truly motivates you helps reveal your fears, hopes, and aspirations. This helps you create a bright financial future that fits both of you perfectly.

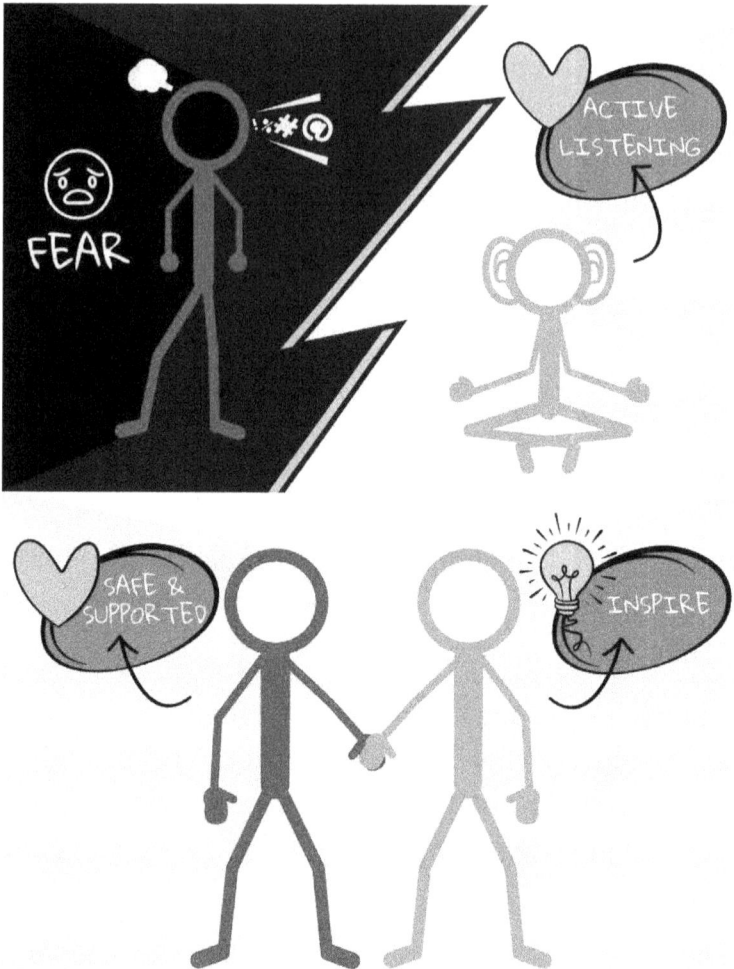

Figure 2: Listen Up, Then Lift Up

## What If Matt Responded Differently?

Let's go back to Hannah and her husband for a moment. Here's where things could have gone differently. Matt immediately jumped in with a solution, "Oh, was it at Costco? It's usually thirty-five cents cheaper there!" Imagine if instead he had paused for a moment and responded with both feeling and presence.

Using a simple, heartfelt structure we'll explore in later exercises, he could say: "That's crazy! I'm surprised too. But mostly, I'm just happy you're home."

By doing this, he would have taken a step back and realized there might be more to Hannah's frustration than just the gas price. He could have given her space to express her emotions without rushing in with unsolicited advice. Knowing that one of her primary love languages is physical touch, he could have also reached out for a hug and said, "How was your day?"

This simple response would have given Hannah the space she needed to release her emotions and process her day. Only after that could they address what could be done about the gas price, or anything else that was bothering her.

When I mentioned this idea to Hannah, her face lit up with excitement. She smiled and said, "Ah, I get it now! Maybe next time, instead of just complaining about the gas price, I could just say, 'I had a really bad day, I need a hug!'"

Hearing her response, my heart filled with delight. It wasn't just a realization for her—it was a shift. Hannah was becoming her own active listener, tuning into what she truly needed emotionally, instead of reacting impulsively to the day's frustrations. By taking a moment to process her feelings, she was able to clearly identify her needs and express them in a calm, direct way. She would also give her husband the chance to respond in the most loving and supportive way possible in the future. And that, my friends, is a win.

She laughed and added, "This is such an amazing realization! I'm going to tell him as soon as I get home. When I say, 'Please say you love me,' or 'Give me a hug,' I'm not being needy or simply seeking attention. I'm trying to gather warmth and strength from him so I can cheerfully face the challenges for the rest of the day!"

I couldn't be prouder of her. It was a beautiful moment of growth for both of them. Hannah had learned to recognize her own needs, and her husband now had the chance to support her in a way that would strengthen their bond. This moment perfectly illustrates how love, understanding, and active listening can transform even the most mundane situations into opportunities to grow closer.

## Small but Meaningful Moments

In relationships, the smallest moments of connection can be the most meaningful. These moments don't always require grand gestures, but rather, an understanding and acknowledgment of each other's needs. Jessica, another member of my program, shared with the group a moment with her partner that really stuck in her head.

Not long ago, Jessica had spent a long day at work with kids (she runs a small home daycare near Los Angeles), taking them for a field trip to the zoo. By the time she got back home, she was exhausted, and the thought of cooking dinner felt over-whelming. So she suggested to Ethan, her boyfriend, that they grab a quick bite out. When they sat down, she told Ethan, "Can we just eat and not talk during dinner? I'm really tired and just need some time to myself."

Ethan's response was a pleasant surprise that totally changed the dynamic during the meal and the energy for the entire evening. Instead of being hurt or withdrawn, he responded with understanding and love. "Okay," he said, "I just want to let you know, I had a really nice day today. And I'm happy to see you. I'm here for you whenever you need me."

It was such a simple interaction, but for Jessica, it was a moment of love and connection. Not only did Ethan agree to her request for space, he also expressed his feelings in a way that acknowledged her tiredness, while also sharing something positive from his day. It wasn't a long conversation, but it was meaningful and inspiring. The understanding and the ability to express authentic self in just a few words brought them closer.

This is a perfect example of what I call the power of active listening—the skill of building strong and loving connections by communicating simply and clearly. Jessica's story highlights how powerful it is when partners can express their needs, and even more so when they can reciprocate with understanding and affirmation. Ethan not only acknowledged Jessica's feelings but also showed her that he was emotionally attuned to her needs. This gave her a safe space to process her stress without feeling pressured to entertain, and it enhanced her trust in Ethan.

## It's Not All Roses

David is another member of my group coaching program. He met Jennifer, his wife, twenty-four years ago. At that time, they both felt like they had finally found their soulmate. But after two decades of marriage and having a daughter together, their initial passion had transformed into something all too familiar to many long-term couples: politeness and shared family responsibilities.

Having read many books on marriage but still struggling over the years, David found himself reflecting on his relationship, eager to find a way to revive the connection and passion they had once shared. Despite all the years they'd spent together, there was still emotional distance that needed to be bridged and trust to be rebuilt as the foundation of his marriage. He joined my program to start this process and was excited to see the first exercise, which focused on expressing feelings of love and appreciation for one another.

However, Jennifer had endured many life changes and repeatedly expressed a great deal of pain and resentment over the years. She was especially hesitant to revisit painful memories of their move from a comfortable life in China to start over in Canada seven years ago. The thought of reopening old wounds terrified her. When David first suggested doing the exercise, Jennifer was resistant.

"I don't know, David," Jennifer said softly, her arms crossed. "I don't want to talk about all that stuff again. We've been through so much. What's the point of bringing it up now? It just hurts."

David noticed her hesitation and tried to reassure her. "I know this isn't easy," he said. "But if we don't talk about how we're feeling and face what's hurting us, we'll stay stuck. I want us to feel close again, and I really want to know what I can do to help us get closer."

Jennifer's face softened, but her frustration was clear. "It feels like we're just going around in circles. I don't want to dig up everything again. It's a waste of time and only makes me feel bad."

David paused, reflecting on her words. He had sensed the same sentiments many times before, but this time felt different—he didn't argue back or drop it there. He would try again; he wasn't giving up.

## Second Try

The next weekend, while they were walking in the park under the warm sun, David tried again, this time with a more gentle approach.

"Jennifer, do you remember the day I failed that licensing exam? I was really hard on myself, and I felt like I had let everyone down. But when you saw how upset I was and just held my hand, I realized how much you care about me. You didn't have to say much, but that act of kindness meant everything to me."

Jennifer paused, looking at the trees around them. She didn't respond right away, but David could see the small shift in her expression. She was thinking, processing.

"I just want to know if we can be happy together again," David continued. "I know I've made mistakes. But I'm trying to understand your needs better. I want to listen."

Jennifer turned to face him, her eyes welling with tears. "I've been carrying so much of this anger and sadness around. Sometimes, I feel like I'm invisible to you. Like you don't see me anymore." Her voice trembled slightly. "It feels like I'm a burden to you."

David felt the weight of her words, and for the first time, he didn't rush to comfort her or move to a happy subject. He just listened, allowing her to express herself fully.

"I'm sorry," he whispered, his voice thick with emotion. "I didn't realize how much I was shutting you out. I'm here for you now."

## The Power of Being Present

Even though David and Jennifer didn't finish the whole exercise, David's efforts were a good reminder that in relationships, it's not about having no problems—it's about how we face them together. Every couple's journey is unique. We all want to avoid pain and uncertainty, but those moments can actually be opportunities for healing. By choosing to listen without judgment and making space for vulnerability, David created a real moment of connection with Jennifer that helped rebuild their trust, even if things didn't go perfectly.

Jennifer's breakthrough wasn't instantaneous, and there were still deep emotional layers to unpack, but the key was that she finally felt heard. And that's all it took: space to share, to express, and to have her feelings acknowledged.

David's experience highlights the core message of this book: life is not always easy, and both relationships and wealth require work over a long period of time. But when we're willing to face the challenges, embrace vulnerability, and actively listen to one another, we can overcome the history that holds us back and keeps us apart.

David's initiative is a powerful reminder that, even when things feel difficult, the courage to love yourself and your partner deeply is where the transformation begins. It's not always about having the perfect conversation or solving every problem right away. Sometimes, just being there, listening, and holding space for each other is enough to take that crucial first step toward healing and growth.

## What Love Gives

Lao Tzu, the famous Chinese philosopher, once said, "Being deeply loved by someone gives you strength, while loving someone deeply gives you courage." In Chinese, it's just four characters—"慈故能勇"—and the translation truly captures the meaning perfectly. Love has this incredible power to spark strength and courage inside us, pushing us to do things we never thought we could. But here's the important part: love isn't about grand gestures or big sacrifices. It's something we build every day through simple acts like truly listening and making space for each other to be ourselves.

When you're loved, you get to be your true self, with freedom and courage. And when you love, you get to help someone else do the same. Love is the kind of bond that's strong enough to carry you through life's ups and downs, letting you stay true to who you are and grow into who you want to be. It's the key to a happy, fulfilling life.

So, how do we really love? By listening, accepting, and inspiring. It's simple but powerful, and it's one of the most effective ways we can love someone else . . . and ourselves.

## The Spark Within You

If you are holding this book, it is no accident. Something inside you has sparked a quiet nudge to strengthen your relationships, take charge of your money, or simply grow into your best self. This is your promise to create the life you really want, a life where love, money, and personal growth all come together. Choosing this path takes courage, and I truly admire you for taking the first step.

Figure 3: From Emotion to Intention, Finding Your Superpower

The fact that you have chosen to take this step and invest in yourself and your partner is the strongest sign of your success. Growth and improvement are not just about mastering money skills or being the perfect partner. They are about being willing to keep evolving no matter where you begin and staying committed to the journey. This commitment, the desire to be better for yourself and those you love, is the foundation for everything that comes next.

## A Game Changer

Before we dive into the exercises of this chapter, I first want to share John's feedback, which really captures the transformative power of this work. For John, the exercise wasn't just a routine task—it became a profound moment of self-reflection and realization. Here's what he shared:

"Before I started the exercise, I looked it over and immediately felt a sense of guilt and realized that I had some real work to do. When it came to questions about love languages, appreciation, and trust, I had to search my memory for answers instead of just responding to them quickly. This exercise felt like a checkpoint for me to reflect and even apologize to my wife for the things I've neglected."

He admitted, "With three kids and a demanding career, I was so focused on tasks, work, and responsibilities. And I overlooked the simple but important acts of love, such as buying gifts, celebrating birthdays, or even acknowledging each other's efforts on a daily basis. We both deeply love and trust each other, but I realized we hadn't been actively showing it. As a result, our marriage had become routine, even stale."

John's realization was powerful. We can't just rely on trust as a foundation and hope for a healthy relationship ever after. We have to actively work to maintain the bond, express our love, and remind each other how much we care. It's easy to take these things for granted, but the exercise helped John see where things had slipped. And more importantly, it gave him a path to rekindle the connection with his wife.

As he put it, "My wife is so happy to see me expressing my feelings this way. She's excited about the changes I'm making, and I'm excited too."

## Something New

Starting something new can feel a little awkward, and it's completely normal to feel that way, especially when you've never tried the exercises like synchronized breathing or yoga before. I've seen people show up to a new practice so many times and feel like they're "not getting it" right away. Sometimes, one person might burst into laughter, while they are supposed to focus on the breathing. And that's totally okay! It was the same for me and my husband when we first tried it, too. The keys are patience and persistence. It might take a few minutes to get used to, but I promise, *you will get it*. If you stay sincere and caring in the exercise, progress will come naturally.

## The Secret Sauce for Thriving Together

Trust and authentic connection are the ultimate ingredients for a couple who wants to thrive—not just in love, but in life and money too! Think of these exercises as your relationship booster pack. They are not just "nice to try" but powerful tools to help you both build real skills and experiences that lead to a deeper, lasting connection. Ready to get started? Let's dive in!

## 1. Synchronized Breathing

The first exercise is synchronized breathing. Now, before you think this is "just another relaxation thing," hear me out. Synchronized breathing is like your relationship's reset button. When you both slow down for a moment, breathe deeply together, and sync up, you're doing more than calming your nerves. You're tuning in emotionally and physically with each other. It's like pressing "refresh" on your relationship, where you both just become more present, connected, and ready to listen.

Imagine this: You're both calm, breathing together, and all the noise of life just melts away. It's like creating your own little bubble of peace and connection where empathy, understanding, and presence happen naturally. There's no need for big gestures. All it takes is a couple of minutes of deep breathing, and bam! Instant emotional alignment, ready to tune in to each other's feelings and needs.

## 2. Active Listening

Now that you and your partner are literally on the same wavelength, breathing together and creating a calm, connected space, it's time to level up with true active listening. This exercise isn't just about nodding along or letting what your partner says pass through your ears. It's about giving your full attention, listening not just to the words, but also to the emotions behind them. You're putting aside your own agenda, truly showing up for your partner, and making sure they feel heard and valued.

As you practice this, you're not just learning a powerful communication skill that makes you grow closer. Active listening isn't just about words. It's about the energy of being fully present and open. It's about creating an environment where both of you feel comfortable expressing your feelings without fear of judgment.

David Augsburger, a well-known relationship counselor, says, "Being heard is so close to being loved that for the average person, they are almost indistinguishable." Think about that for a moment. What if truly hearing your partner is the most direct way to make them feel loved? Active listening is an expression of love. When you practice active listening, you are not just getting through the conversation; you are truly connecting—emotionally, intellectually, and beyond!

## 3. Authentic Connection

Let's take it one step further into authentic connection. This is where the magic happens. It's not just about using the right listening techniques, it's about being vulnerable and showing up with an open heart, genuinely willing to be changed by what your partner shares.

You've probably heard about "listening without judgment," but what does that really mean? It means setting aside your story and focusing on your partner's experience. It's all about hitting pause on your own thoughts, jumping into their shoes, and really soaking up what they're saying. There's no need to plan your reply while they're talking! Just be there, listen, and see the world from their eyes.

True connection happens when both of you feel seen, heard, and valued. It's not just the techniques that matter, but the emotional openness and sincerity behind them. When that shows up, trust, love, and understanding naturally follow.

At the end of the day, it all comes down to this: When both partners feel understood, the relationship grows stronger, and the emotional walls come down. So, get ready to embrace open communication, empathy, and vulnerability through these exercises. This is your chance to connect more deeply than ever before.

## 4. Your Roles

In most exercises in this book, you'll take turns playing two important roles: the empowered narrator and the empowering listener. As the narrator, your job is to share your thoughts and feelings openly and honestly. As the listener, your role is to give your full attention to the narrator without interrupting or taking notes, showing respect and trying to tune in emotionally.

Active listening means both people have to put in effort. The listener keeps natural eye contact—not staring, but showing they're fully present. Simple sounds like "um," "wow," or "ah," plus intentional body language like putting a hand on your heart, giving two thumbs up, nodding, or smiling, encourage the narrator to open up emotionally. Most importantly, the listener avoids interrupting, taking notes, or thinking about their response while the narrator is sharing. The goal is to create a calm, welcoming space so the other person can really feel and share what's on their mind freely.

This approach gives the narrator room to be truly heard and the listener the chance to really understand. Listening for two minutes without jumping in can feel a little awkward at first, but it's actually crucial. It's okay if there are a few quiet moments. These silences give the narrator time to process their feelings and gather their words. Even though we often rush through talks or interrupt each other, making space for uninterrupted listening is what leads to real conversations and genuine connection.

Both roles matter. When the narrator shares openly, it invites the listener to join in the journey. And when the listener pays full attention, it helps build a genuine connection. Working together this way makes conversations richer and more meaningful.

A lot of the times, people breeze past their feelings when things seem fine. You hear short answers like "I'm fine" or "Nothing much" because we're used to moving on quickly. If you and your partner are new to active listening, you can help each other explore deeper feelings. When you get short answers, gently ask things like, "Tell me more," "What makes you feel that way?" or "Where do you feel that in your body? Does it feel light or heavy?" Then just be quiet and listen. These simple prompts can help reveal layers of feelings and bring clarity.

In my training to become a Registered Life Planner®[2] I once paired up with another financial planner in an eight-minute exercise that started with "Why are you here?" She said, "Oh, I'm here to get the training so I could better help my clients. Personally, I'm all good." I literally followed the rule of eight minutes of listening with no interruptions while keeping eye contact. You can imagine the embarrassment, unease, and boredom with each second that passed by between us. Finally, we survived the staring contest and it was my turn.

I answered with an expansive response including why I moved from China to the US by myself in 2012, why we moved from Chicago to Phoenix in 2020, and how I started a family and now have two kids. I even talked about what I'm struggling with while trying to find my passion and align it with my work. It was a lengthy answer, but after hearing me, she said, "Had I known you'd answer it this way, I wouldn't have stayed silent and

---

[2] A Registered Life Planner (RLP®) is a financial professional trained through the Kinder Institute of Life Planning, founded by George Kinder, known as the father of life planning. Rather than just managing investments or budgets, life planners help clients clarify their deepest life goals and align financial strategies to support them. The training emphasizes active listening, structured inquiry, and relationship-building, enabling advisors to guide clients through major life transitions with a focus on the "human side" of financial planning.

wasted my eight minutes." That was a very important lesson for me. The goal is not sticking to the rules of the exercise itself, but *building a connection and creating the space for your partner to feel comfortable* expressing whatever is on their mind. If the prompt doesn't provide enough direction, a little guidance from the listener can make all the difference.

For this book, we'll stick to two-minute exercises with different questions. When the narrator starts, the listener sets a timer and listens without interruptions, maintaining eye contact and paying attention to how feelings shift in the body—where do you feel it when different emotions are expressed? Are the feelings light or heavy? Tense or relaxed? Even if what's shared is hard or vulnerable, stay fully present. This dedicated time lets the narrator process their thoughts and emotions fully while strengthening your understanding and bond.

At first, open communication may take extra effort. But as you practice these exercises, it will start to feel natural. Along the way, you'll understand yourself and your partner better and grow closer together.

## Now, It's Your Turn!

Do you have something you've always wanted to discuss but never quite found the right moment for? How do you bring your partner into the conversation in a way that feels positive and collaborative?

Let's kickstart meaningful conversations around love with the first set of exercises from the book. It will help set a solid foundation for more difficult topics that are essential to your relationship and money. This exercise may take thirty minutes, but trust me, it will likely lead to an hour of connection and understanding, deepening your bond in the best way possible.

Here's the thing: it might feel new and a little strange at first, but stick with it. Over time, these exercises will help you rekindle the connections that might have gotten lost in the hustle and bustle of life. You deserve the time and attention to be connected, to work toward something truly meaningful and lasting.

Ready to get started? Here's the first set of exercises to help you reconnect with your partner in love:

# Exercises for Chapter 1:
# Love Is the Foundation

## Exercise 1-1: Sync Your Breath

1. Sit comfortably facing each other. Feel free to lean back if that helps you feel more at ease.

2. Close your eyes or soften your gaze.

3. Breathe in slowly and deeply through your noses together, counting to four.

4. Hold your breath gently for a count of four.

5. Exhale slowly through your mouths together, counting to six.

6. Once you feel comfortable with this rhythm, set a timer for two minutes.

7. Keep repeating this breathing cycle—breathe in, hold, breathe out—focusing on syncing your breaths with each other.

## Exercise 1-2: Love Language

1. Take a moment to think about your main love language, based on Gary Chapman's book *The 5 Love Languages: The Secret to Love that Lasts*. It might be: words of affirmation, acts of service, receiving gifts, quality time, or physical touch.

2. You and your partner will take turns to share and listen. Decide who goes first. The listener pays full attention,

making eye contact and not interrupting or taking notes. It's okay to use sounds like "um" or "wow" and body language.

3. When the narrator is ready, set a timer for two minutes.

4. Share with your partner: "My primary love language is . . ."

5. Once the narrator finishes, the listener shares their feelings with: "When you said (repeat their specific words), I felt (an emotion) in (a part of my body)."

For example:

- "When you praised my efforts, I felt a smile come to my face and warmth in my heart."

- "When you noticed the chores I did, I felt deep gratitude in my chest."

6. Switch roles and repeat the process.

7. Optionally, you can do this again to share your secondary love language.

## Exercise 1-3: Being Touched

1. Again, set a timer for two minutes each.

2. Take turns to open up and share with your partner: "You recently did . . . (a specific thing) and it touched me."

3. Decide who goes first. The listener pays full attention, keeping eye contact and not interrupting or taking notes. It's okay to use sounds like "um" or "wow" and body language.

4. Once the narrator finishes, the listener shares their feelings with: "When you said (repeat their specific words), I felt (an emotion) in (a part of my body)."

   For example:

   - "When you said you were grateful for the things I did, I felt a soft warmth in my cheeks."

   - "When you mentioned that you missed me, I felt a tender flutter on my skin and a quiet happiness in my heart."

5. Switch roles and repeat.

## Exercise 1-4: Trust

1. Take two minutes each to share with your partner: "The last time I felt I could completely trust you was . . . (specific situation)."

2. Decide who goes first. The listener pays full attention, keeping eye contact and not interrupting or taking notes. It's okay to use sounds like "um" or "wow" and body language.

3. Once the narrator finishes, the listener shares their feelings with: "When you said (repeat their specific words), I felt (an emotion) in (a part of my body)."

   For example:

   - "When I heard you saying you completely trust me, my eyes felt wet."

   - "When you spoke about our future, I felt a joyful lightness spread through my body."

4. Switch roles and repeat.

## Exercise 1-5: Ideal Date

1. Take two minutes each to share with your partner: "What would your ideal date be like, what would we do, where would we be, and what other details would you notice?"

2. Decide who goes first. The listener pays full attention, keeping eye contact and not interrupting or taking notes. It's okay to use sounds like "um" or "wow" and body language.

3. Once the narrator finishes, the listener shares their feelings with: "When you said (repeat their specific words), I felt (an emotion) in (a part of my body)."

   For example:

   - "When you mentioned a sunset picnic in Maldives, I felt a wave of happiness and excitement in my heart."

   - "When you mentioned exploring a new city together, I felt a thrilling energy in my legs, ready to go."

4. Switch roles and repeat.

5. Discuss how you can incorporate elements of what you shared into future interactions.

## Adaptation for Other Relationships

For Exercise 1-5 (Ideal Date), you can adapt it to "Ideal Moment" to fit any close relationship, not just romantic ones. Instead of asking, "What would your ideal date be like?" you could ask:

- "What does a perfect moment together look like for you?"

- "If we could spend quality time anywhere, doing anything, what would you choose?"

- "Are there any small details that would make it extra special?"

This set of exercises works whether you want to connect with a sibling, a parent, or a friend. By focusing on what makes time together meaningful, you open the door to deeper understanding and genuine connection.

Have fun with it, let it flow naturally, and see where it takes you!

# Your Reflection

Take a moment to jot down your thoughts and experiences from the exercise. Use this space to capture any insights, feelings, or ideas that came up.

_____

_____

_____

_____

_____

_____

_____

_____

_____

_____

_____

_____

_____

# CHAPTER 2

# Face Fear—
# Lean In to Move On

It was a typical Sunday afternoon. The sun streamed through the living room window, casting a warm glow over the space, while David and Jennifer relaxed on the couch. Their conversation had started casually enough, but as often happens, the topic shifted. David's mind wandered to something deeper—the ongoing exercises in the program, this time, around fear.

He glanced over at Jennifer, feeling the weight of the thought he'd been carrying for a while. Something about the quiet afternoon made it feel like the right time to speak up. He didn't follow the exercise's exact structure, but instead, let the conversation flow naturally.

"Hey, do you remember that commercial property we bought in China about ten years ago?" David asked, his tone a bit hesitant, as if he knew exactly where this was going. Jennifer paused, raising an eyebrow. She could sense a shift in the air. "I've been thinking about it a lot lately," David continued, ". . . it's kind of worthless now."

Jennifer looked at him, her expression softening as she absorbed his words. David's voice carried a mix of frustration and regret.

He went on, recalling how they had paid for the property in full with cash. At the time, it seemed like a good decision, but now, looking back, it felt like a mistake. "I felt a little uneasy about it back then, but we had the money, and I trusted your judgment. But now, I wish we'd picked a different property, one that would be easier to sell. It would help ease a lot of our cashflow stress right now."

Jennifer sat quietly, listening intently, her mind clearly working through his words. She took a deep breath before speaking, her voice barely above a whisper. "I've never told you this," she began, her eyes downcast, "but when we bought that property, I was afraid—not just about the big move to Canada, but about our future. I wasn't sure about our marriage, either. I thought paying in full for something we could afford would give me some kind of security."

David froze. He had never expected this. He had no idea that Jennifer had been carrying that fear all these years. As she finished speaking, David could almost feel the weight lifting off her shoulders. The relief in her voice was palpable. In that moment, he realized that the honesty they'd just shared was worth far more than any financial loss.

The regret would no longer hold him back, and he had gained a deeper appreciation for the strength of their relationship. He sat quietly for a while, allowing the moment to sink in, then gently took Jennifer's hands, offering her the comfort and support she needed in that vulnerable moment.

This was the beauty of the conversation: it wasn't just about regret over a financial decision. It was about understanding and processing each other's fears and finding common ground. David didn't interrupt her, didn't offer solutions, and didn't try to fix things. He simply listened, giving Jennifer the space to share her feelings.

This wasn't just a breakthrough about money. It was a moment of emotional connection, a moment where fear, when shared, had the power to bring them closer together.

## Breaking the Cycle

David had an aha moment about his and Jennifer's financial decisions after moving to Canada. Looking back, he realized that they had been making bold decisions based on past successes, not comprehensive analysis. "We weren't thinking them through," he shared with the group in our coaching. "We were relying on what worked before, but we were so overwhelmed by all the changes in our new life in Canada that we didn't have the same clarity we had back in China when we had time to reflect."

This feeling isn't unique to David. I hear similar stories from clients who experience major life shifts: rapid decline in the industry where they'd worked for decades, a business that stops making money, losing a high-paying job, dealing with legal troubles, or becoming the primary caregiver for a sick loved one. These changes can be tough on money, but even tougher on emotions. If those feelings aren't talked about, they eventually spill over into money decisions, often in ways we don't notice right away.

We can't control everything—market crashes, life happens, and surprises come when you are least prepared. But what we can control is how we handle things when life is good. We can create a solid financial foundation that helps us stay steady when the world feels like it's spinning out of control. I'll dive into more detailed strategies on this in Chapter 6. And here, we will focus on the emotions first.

Thankfully, David and Jennifer faced their emotional and financial challenges before it was too late. They had a candid conversation, and as they discussed their past mistakes and future plans, David said, "It's not just about the financial decisions we've made. The real problem is that we've been making decisions without clarity or alignment. Once we address the emotional side of things, I'm confident we can start thinking more strategically about what's next."

David discovered that it's not just about the numbers. It's about clearing the emotional fog to make better decisions that are aligned with their long-term goals. That's where the real transformation happens.

## A Path Forward

After this realization, David and Jennifer began to form a new approach to their finances and their relationship. They agreed that it was time to let go of certain assets, mostly the ones in China, and focus on increasing their earned and passive income. They also committed to spending more time together as a family, traveling and experiencing new things—just as they had done earlier in their relationship. Those times of closeness and experiencing new things together led to creative business ideas and smart investment decisions.

David shared the new approach they developed: "The key to moving forward was to recognize our fears and our patterns, so we could break free from the financial pitfalls. We decided that going forward, we would make decisions based on clear communication and mutual trust. When it comes to investing, we would ask ourselves, 'Do we truly understand this opportunity?' If the answer wasn't clear, we would rather not invest."

## Facing Fear Together

Laura joined our program while she was navigating a new chapter in her life. She's in her late twenties and had lost her job a few months prior to joining. Even though she wasn't very happy with that job and had thought about taking a break, being suddenly unemployed for the first time in her life made her feel lost. She wasn't sure where to go next.

"I thought I was ready to take a break and explore new things, but after losing my job, it felt like the ground shifted beneath me. It wasn't as freeing as I thought it would be," Laura shared during a group coaching session. "I was feeling anxious about the future and whether I could still meet the financial goals I had set with my husband for the year. What was supposed to be a gap year had suddenly turned into chaos and uncertainty."

Her husband, Chris, also in his late twenties, was a self-employed freelancer. Together, they had always had a steady flow of income, despite some ups and downs. Now, without Laura's salary, they had to reassess things. They sat down to go over their savings and monthly cash flow to determine what adjustments needed to be made. Despite Chris's decent earnings, the unknown still loomed large for Laura. The fear of the future, of possibly not reaching their goals, began to weigh on her.

In an effort to ease their financial strain, they sold an investment property they had been holding onto, a decision that, while painful, would give them a bit more breathing room. Laura also began freelancing, though the unpredictability of her career shift added to her anxiety. "The first week went well. I felt productive and regained some control. But soon, the fear crept in. I started questioning myself, wondering if I could make enough to sustain this new lifestyle, and whether I was even making the right decision."

Laura found herself caught in a cycle of doubt, questioning whether she should just look for another full-time position. "I keep thinking, 'Maybe I should just go back to a nine-to-five job. That will fix everything.' But then I remind myself that I wanted this break to figure things out. The fear keeps coming back, though. I'm scared I won't live up to my potential."

During the coaching sessions, Ashley, another member of the group, shared her own story to cheer Laura up. "I completely get where you're coming from. A year ago, I quit my job that was paying half a million dollars when you include the stock compensation. At first, I had a lot of the same fears you're feeling. But I had to shift my mindset and remind myself that I gave up a lot to find a path that truly resonated with me. Your time right now is precious. This gap year isn't just about what you achieve; it's about discovering what makes you happy. You might be scared of not making enough money, but take it from me: not everything in life can be measured by money."

Ashley added with a laugh, "And I realized I'm truly happy when I'm dancing at the YMCA on a Monday morning with a bunch of retired ladies in their sixties and seventies. I'm grateful I don't have to wait until I'm old to enjoy life."

Her words stuck with Laura, who had been focused on financial goals but never fully considered the value of personal growth and enjoyment. "Ashley, you're right," Laura said. "I've been so focused on financial security that I forgot about the joy in living. I need to give myself permission to enjoy this time and stop overthinking everything."

Another member chimed in, "As someone who decided to quit law school and left a career path many people dreamed of more than ten years ago, I can tell you that sometimes it's okay to just enjoy life. Society and family might judge you, but it's your life. You deserve to live it the way that feels right for you."

That conversation sparked something in Laura. She realized that she had been so caught up in financial fear that she'd forgotten the bigger picture. "I'm starting to embrace the uncertainty," Laura said. "I'm not going to let fear control me. I'm going to use this time to explore, learn new things, and see where it takes me."

I also shared my perspective with Laura: "Now's the perfect time to be creative and open to new opportunities. Go explore new places, try something new, and talk to people who inspire you. It's all part of the journey. If you feel anxious about what's next, use the exercises we've been practicing in the program with Chris. Trust that your heart will lead you to the right path."

Laura smiled, feeling a renewed sense of hope. "I'm not going to worry about having everything figured out right now. I'm going to make the best use of my freedom and see where it takes me."

For Laura, and many of us, the path to personal growth and success isn't always a straight line. Sometimes, it's about embracing the unknown, facing our fears, and trusting that the future will unfold as it's meant to. Through this experience, Laura learned that fear doesn't have to hold her back—it can be the catalyst for change and growth.

As Laura continues to explore her new career path, her financial goals may shift, but she's no longer overwhelmed by fear or restricted by comfort. Instead, she's learning to be more in tune with her feelings, accept them, and use them as guidance for something greater. And in doing so, she's found the courage to open up to her partner, trusting herself, and finding joy in the journey.

## Am I What I Make?

After the webinar, Laura sat down with Chris to go through the exercises on fear together. They unpacked their feelings, especially around the emotional ties to money and the fears they had about the future. The conversation flowed naturally as Laura reflected on the past: the property purchase that drained their savings, the soul-crushing job she's ready to leave behind, and the opportunities they had missed.

Laura admitted that, on a deeper level, the financial stress was rooted in a fear of not being enough. She wanted to feel secure not just with money, but emotionally as well. She explained how her gap year felt like both a gift and a curse, as she didn't want to waste any time but feared she wasn't using it productively.

As Laura spoke, Chris remained silent at first, simply listening. His presence was reassuring, his gaze steady and warm. When she finished sharing, Chris finally responded, "When you mentioned you didn't want to be a burden to me, my heart cringed. I just wanted to hold you tighter. I'm happy to support you while you figure things out. There's no pressure. You deserve the freedom and time to be yourself and find your own path. Succeed or fail, I trust you no matter what. You'll shine in your own way."

Laura, overwhelmed with love by his words, started to cry. "I never really felt worthy unless I was making progress in school or at work," she said, as tears dropped down her cheeks. "You gave me strength. I'll cherish every minute I have, I promise. And I'll check in with you regularly to see if I'm on the right track or just distracting myself again!"

This shared moment of vulnerability was a breakthrough. They hadn't connected this deeply in a long time. By acknowledging their fears instead of avoiding them, they cleared the emotional fog and grew closer. Laura realized that this wasn't just about her career or financial goals; it was about supporting each other through the uncertainty and making decisions from a place of trust.

Together, Laura and Chris decided to focus on what they could control. While they couldn't predict everything, they could move forward with intention and love. Laura felt more empowered to navigate her career break with confidence, knowing she had Chris's unwavering support. They would face the fears and uncertainties together, using this time to grow both individually and as a couple.

The group session had given Laura the space to be more at ease with her feelings and draw strength from others' experiences. The exercise allowed Laura and Chris to discuss their fears openly, and more importantly, shifted their mindset from uncertainty to opportunity. The power of facing fear together gave them a sense of unity, not just for their financial situation, but for their relationship as well.

As Laura later shared with me, "When we face our fears and understand them, it allows me to finally move forward. This has not only changed how I approach financial stress; it's changed how we approach our relationship. And that, to me, is priceless."

## Fear as a Source of Strength

When was the last time you had a meaningful conversation about money with your loved one where you really felt connected? And if you were to have a conversation where you reveal your deepest fear, what emotions would arise? What is holding you back from having that conversation?

As a numbers person, I'll admit it's not easy for me to write this chapter. Yet, time and again, I've learned that some of the most revealing insights and invigorating moments come from facing our deepest fears and sharing them with someone who cares. It takes a lot of courage to be vulnerable. But I have seen firsthand how vulnerability can become one of the most powerful and rewarding experiences loved ones share.

In our everyday lives, we don't often face fear head-on. We can usually manage it through emotional regulation and logical correction. But when left unheard and unprocessed, fear tends to come out in the least ideal moments: when we're stressed, when a string of unfortunate events pile up, when we're hungry, exhausted, or sleep-deprived. Sadly, it's often our closest loved ones, the ones we feel most comfortable with, who end up bearing the weight of these emotions, which hurts both them and ourselves.

Fear often lies beneath other emotions. Many times, the small arguments we have are just the surface of deeper feelings like fear of failure, anxiety about not being good enough, or fear of being hurt. These fears usually go unspoken and unnoticed until they suddenly come out, and by that time, some damage may have already happened. Understanding that fear is often at the root of these feelings can help us respond with more compassion and awareness instead of reacting to just what's on the surface.

This chapter isn't about healing trauma or forcing you to relive painful moments. It's about creating a safe space to recognize and process those emotions. When we acknowledge and face our fears, we open the door to courage. We gain clarity to move forward. It might sound a little "out there" now, but you'll see how it works through real-life stories and practical exercises. For now, just remember that there are many ways to deal with fear, and becoming aware of it and talking openly are the crucial first steps.

As Marianne Williamson so beautifully writes in *A Return to Love: Reflections on the Principles of "A Course in Miracles"*:

*"Our deepest fear is not that we are inadequate. Our deepest fear is that we are powerful beyond measure."*

The idea that we are powerful beyond measure might be hard to imagine. But it's in confronting this fear and finding the courage to face it head-on that we can unlock a future where we thrive in both love and financial freedom.

## Let's Get Real

Now it's time to level up! After practicing active listening and open communication in Chapter One, we're now going to tackle fear. I know, it sounds a little intimidating, but trust me, facing your fears together as a couple can be a game-changer. Especially when it comes to money, fear is often tied to deeper feelings like regret, shame, and the uncertainty of what lies ahead.

But here's the kicker: *fear doesn't have to control you*. When you confront it head-on with your partner, you'll discover that it can actually strengthen your bond and bring you closer.

Sure, talking about finances can feel a bit like walking through a minefield, with lots of pressure and emotions tied to those numbers. But money isn't just about cold, hard cash. It's about what those numbers represent: *security*, *safety*, *success*, or even failure.

The good news is: once you acknowledge those fears and share them openly, you're already on the path to a brighter future. The exercise at the end of this chapter is designed to guide you through that emotional minefield. By leaning into your fears, you can transform them into stepping stones that help you grow emotionally and financially.

When you share your fears with your partner, it opens up the opportunity for them to support you. And guess what? The more you support each other, the stronger your partnership becomes. That's what this chapter is all about: finding strength in vulnerability and embracing your financial fears together.

## New Skills for New Challenges

As challenges get bigger, so do our skills! Here's a secret weapon when things get tough: mirroring. Remember when we used it in exercises in Chapter One using and repeating your partner's own words? Well, it's time to bring it out again. This time, when active listening feels hard (maybe because you're dying to fix the problem or change the subject), you can use mirroring to help you stay grounded. When your partner opens up, listen closely and repeat what they say back to them, using their words, their tone, and even their body language.

It's not about getting the words *perfect*; it's about making your partner feel heard and understood. It's also an opportunity for you to be more aware of your own emotions and reactions. This simple tool does wonders for your connection and helps both of you feel validated in a conversation about fear and money.

## The "Fix-It" Pause Button

Here's a bonus tool for when you *really* want to jump in with a solution but know it's time to just listen. It's a trick I learned from Patrick Kelley, a Tools[3] coach who helped me feel the urge and get into the flow to finish writing this book. When your partner is sharing something deep or vulnerable, try this mental exercise. Imagine these four sentences as playful checkpoints; each gives you a new superpower for connection:

1. **"Wow, I'm so glad I don't have this problem."**

   *Take a breath and let out a small sigh of **relief**. This helps stop their stress from piling onto your already busy mind. It lets you listen without feeling overwhelmed, like putting on an emotional raincoat that keeps you dry inside.*

2. **"I know that you can handle it."**

   *This is like quietly handing your partner a gold trophy of confidence. You're showing your **belief** in their strength without needing to control or doubt them.*

---

[3] *The Tools* is a bestselling self-development book by Phil Stutz and Barry Michels, both experienced therapists. The book introduces a set of practical psychological techniques called "The Tools," designed to help people overcome common obstacles such as fear, anxiety, procrastination, and negative thinking. These tools are actionable exercises you can use in real time to transform problems into courage, confidence, and creativity.

3. **"It's just gonna take a little bit of time to get there."**

   *Picture a clock gently ticking. Give each other patience and **grace**. Growth and solutions don't happen instantly. They need time to develop and grow.*

4. **"I'm glad that I'm here to listen."**

   *Take a moment to appreciate the **wonder** of simply being present. This is where the real magic happens. Your presence turns an ordinary conversation into a true partnership.*

## Why This Works (and How to Make It a Game)

By channeling your energy with these phrases, you become an emotional support ninja: present, tuned-in, and delightfully not-judgy. You create a safe zone for your partner to feel heard (instead of hurried), and you sidestep the urge to barge in with your "fix-it" cape flapping.

Want a pro tip? Practice these sentences out loud (or in your head) during low-stakes moments. When your partner's venting, for example, about their weird co-worker's lunch choices, try running through the four phrases. It's like level one of a video game: no pressure, just building your skills for the bonus round when deeper stuff comes up.

Now imagine using these in a money talk. Maybe you're sorting out your new spending goals, or juggling some unexpected expense. Instead of tension, you anchor yourselves in empathy and support. Teamwork unlocked!

*Listening with wonder is the ultimate power move in love, life, and even stressful money talks. Give yourself permission to just be there, and let the magic happen.*

So next time you feel the itch to rescue or "solve," repeat these four sentences: *"I'm so glad I don't have this problem. I know that you can handle it. It's just gonna take a little bit of time to get there. I'm glad that I'm here to listen."* You might just find your conversations, even those stressful ones about money, getting a lot lighter, a lot faster.

## Take It Beyond Money

Not everyone feels uncomfortable talking about money. If you're one of the lucky ones who feel excited or confident about money, you might want to explore fear or regret in a broader way.

Maybe you see limited resources as a chance to be creative or a puzzle to solve. If this sounds like you, congratulations! Being able to adapt and solve problems is a valuable skill for life, not just for money.

You can still use this exercise to learn more about yourself and build connections with your partner. For Exercise 2-4, take two minutes to share one of these: "The most painful experience I've ever had is . . . ." or "My biggest fear is . . . ."

The goal here isn't to dwell on the negative but to get in touch with your feelings and explore your hidden emotions. It's about uncovering the untapped potential within you (trust me, everyone has it, and the deeper you dig, the more you find). Sometimes, it's the hidden parts of ourselves that hold the key to our next breakthrough. So, take a moment to dive into your own emotions, explore the fears or pains that may be lingering, and open the door to new growth together. You might be surprised at what you discover about yourself and your relationship.

## My Biggest Regret

I'll never forget the early days with my first child when I depend-ed on the nanny to do her job. There I was, sitting anxiously in the living room, laptop on my lap and headset ready for a meeting, while my son crawled around at my feet, waiting for the nanny to show up—she was already fifteen minutes late! The stress was overwhelming, and I was just hoping my baby wouldn't start crying right in the middle of the meeting.

We were in a nanny share arrangement with another family in our neighborhood, thinking it would be a cost-effective, practical solution. But by month two, the nanny started to be unreliable: arriving late, taking time off, and not giving the two kids the level of attention they needed.

So, we switched to a new nanny, only to discover that our expec-tations for childcare were completely different from the other mom's. For me, it was unacceptable for a nanny to spend more time on the phone than with the kids. But for her, everything was fine as long as the kids were safe and fed. She wasn't willing to spend more to hire anyone who would do better.

I'd find myself sneaking away to the bathroom during breaks at work, checking the baby monitor to make sure my son wasn't being ignored or left to cry. After three months of going back and forth and trying to make it work, we finally transitioned out of the nanny share and found a solution that actually worked for our family. But those six months, spanning my busiest work seasons, were a stressful nightmare.

Looking back, I see how much I let my worry take over instead of enjoying those precious early moments with my child. I didn't understand the true value of peace of mind at the time, but now

I know that having a reliable, trustworthy caregiver would have been worth any amount of short-term savings.

With our second child, I decided to take a different approach. We budgeted to hire a postpartum caretaker for two months, a professional who provided around-the-clock care for both baby and me, and also helped with cooking for the whole family. I also worked with a personal trainer to support my recovery. I took sixteen weeks of maternity leave and added four weeks of vacation time I had saved over two years. Before returning to work, I made sure a reliable caregiver was lined up to take over. This time, I wasn't rushing back because I knew this period was too important to cut short.

The difference was night and day. I didn't just "get by"—I thrived. My recovery was much quicker, I bonded more with my baby, and most importantly, the time away from work allowed me to start planning the next phase of my life. When I returned to work, I was excited and energized, ready to execute my plans.

That experience taught me a valuable lesson about investing in peace of mind. Sometimes, it's worth it to prioritize your well-being and make choices that support your long-term happiness, even if it means spending a little more upfront.

## Healing Through Honest Money Talks

Earlier this year, I created an opportunity to travel with my mom (in her mid-sixties) and my four-year-old daughter. On the flight back, while my daughter was on her iPad, I decided to take the moment to bond with my mom. I pulled out some exercises from my Couples and Money program to practice with my mom (even though these are designed for couples, I promise they work wonders with anyone you trust and care about!).

Here's where things got real: I told her the prompt, "Financially, the thing I regret the most is . . . ."

Her answer? "No regrets, really. Some investments made money, some didn't. But most of what we have today came from our real estate gains. However, your dad always blamed me for . . . ."

And then the floodgates opened. She started telling me about how my dad never really collaborated on big financial decisions, leaving her to take the blame when things went south.

While this wasn't the first time I'd heard the story, in that moment, I really listened, and then said, "It breaks my heart to hear this. You don't regret your decisions, but you've carried so many of Dad's regrets and negative emotions for years."

That's when my mom went silent . . . and then broke down in tears. In that moment, I could feel the weight lifting off her. My daughter and I dropped everything in our hands and embraced her tightly.

I also shared something personal with her that I'd been carrying for a while: "My biggest fear is that you get depressed, and Dad gets dementia, and I have to leave everything behind: my kids, my business, my husband, my life, and fly back to China to take care of you both."

She looked me in the eyes with deep understanding and said, "I will stand up for myself from now on and live the life I deserve—for me, for your dad, and for you." I had been waiting to hear those words for a long time.

This conversation was a powerful reminder of how important it is to have these hard, honest talks about money, about feelings, and about what we carry inside. When we lean in, listen, and share with loved ones, we create space for healing and find the courage to move forward.

## My Journey to Open Communication

Some of my readers have told me how much they admire the way I have these open, honest conversations with my mom. But here's the truth: it didn't come naturally, and it definitely wasn't built overnight.

My mom is a classic tiger mom (which makes total sense since her zodiac sign is literally the tiger). Tiger moms are known for their strict discipline, high expectations, and relentless drive to push their kids toward success, both academically and in life.

She's the kind of mom who sent me to school with a fever, secretly changed my college applications to a "more prestigious" major, and even tried to be my matchmaker by searching for "qualified" partners online and chatting with them while pretending to be me. In her mind, getting married before twenty-seven wasn't just a hope—it was a non-negotiable life goal for me.

Naturally, I grew up fiercely independent, always fighting for the space to be my own person. I moved across China for college and wasn't exactly counting down the days to come home. And right after graduation? I hopped on a plane to work in West Africa without telling either her or my dad, only calling once I landed in Nouakchott, the capital of Mauritania.

Life has a funny way of working itself out, doesn't it?

But my mom's relationship with my dad hasn't exactly been a picture of bliss either. For over twenty-five years, their relationship has been filled with constant fighting and emotional stress. I've lost count of the late-night phone calls where my mom would tell me every hurtful thing my dad said, hoping I could help her find relief. Of course, this was affecting my sleep and work, while I grew more impatient and frustrated with her.

During the COVID lockdown, when they joined me in the US and we all lived together, it got even worse. The fighting intensified, and my dad's behavior became even more unpredictable. That's when I decided to start focusing on my own mental health. In early 2023, we helped my parents purchase a winter home near us, so they could have space, while still being able to visit us when they are in the US.

## Letting Go of the Fixer Role

I've always been the type who jumps right into solving problems, especially when it comes to family. So, when I realized something deeper was going on, I dove headfirst into research. I read every book I could find about families and personality disorders. Looking back, maybe I went a little overboard, but each story and study helped me connect the dots.

Determined to help, I teamed up with a cognitive-behavioral therapist in the US, reached out to psychiatrists in China, and tried everything I could to get my parents the support they needed. But no matter how hard I pushed, I kept running into the same wall: for their generation, mental health is a taboo topic, surrounded by stigma and silence. Still, I refused to give up.

Then, something shifted when I attended Barry Michels'[4] Shadow Work[5] retreat. Barry didn't sugarcoat it. He told me straight up that my dad's health and my parents' relationship were beyond my control. As much as I wanted to "fix" things, I had to accept that some problems aren't mine to solve. That realization was both tough and freeing.

I finally realized that my constant expectation of "making" things better became the root of so much disappointment and misery. I thought if I just tried harder, read more, or said the right thing, I could change my parents.

But here's what *really* happened:

- **My efforts were met with defensiveness.** Instead of feeling lifted up, my parents often doubled down on their old habits.

- **Change felt threatening to them.** My attempts to help sometimes made me an intimidating dictator, the polar opposite of an empowering listener.

- **I felt drained and frustrated.** The more I pushed, the more I realized I was fighting a losing battle.

Here's what I've learned:

- **Letting go isn't giving up**. It's about accepting fully and allowing your loved ones to be their authentic selves, for better or worse.

---

[4] Barry Michels is a psychotherapist and New York Times bestselling author known for co-writing *The Tools* and *Coming Alive* with Phil Stutz. Practicing since 1986, he works with high-profile clients in Hollywood and focuses on psychological and spiritual transformation.
[5] Shadow Work, as Michels describes it, involves engaging with the "Shadow," the hidden, often negative parts of ourselves identified by Carl Jung. By developing a compassionate relationship with this Shadow, it transforms from a source of shame into an ally that fosters confidence, authentic self-expression, and deeper connection.

- **True acceptance empowers**. When you let go of the need to control others, you create the freedom to find your own happiness, and you lay the groundwork for open, honest communication.

- **Your energy is contagious**. Instead of being impatient and irritated, invest your time in creating moments you could enjoy together.

Letting go of the fixer role is the first step to open communication. Only then can you truly accept and listen to your loved ones fully. When you stop trying to change someone, you create space for real understanding and honest conversation.

All those hard-won lessons became the building blocks of my Couples and Money program. The biggest takeaway? Stop trying to change your partner, and start focusing on what you can control: your emotional well-being and your shared quality time together.

If you've ever felt stuck trying to "fix" someone else, be it your partner, your parents, or kids, know this: you're not alone. Sometimes the bravest thing you can do is to step back, find your own peace, and focus on creating good memories and moments together.

## A Breakthrough Conversation

When I took a step back, something surprising happened. After celebrating Chinese New Year with my cousin's family in Los Angeles to spend quality time with my family, my mom suddenly said to me on the drive back to Phoenix, "You know, what you said yesterday really made sense."

**Pru**: "What do you mean? What made sense?"

**Mom**: "You said I was too anxious. Our whole family—my mom, my siblings, me—we're all anxious."

**Pru**: "Wow, I'm impressed that you can see this. What do you think is the cause of the anxiety?"

**Mom**: "It must be from your grandpa."

**Pru**: "What do you think caused his anxiety?"

**Mom**: "Must be his family."

**Pru**: "So, why was Grandpa, even with a good job, so anxious?"

**Mom**: "In the 60s and 70s (in China), everyone was struggling to survive. No one dared to relax."

**Pru**: "And now, why are you still so anxious, even though things are much better?"

**Mom**: "I guess because I want an even better life."

**Pru**: "When will it end? And is the price we are paying worth it?"

**Mom**: "Maybe it's time to slow down. I'm going to try not to be so anxious and learn to relax. I'll be less controlling and take it easy with you, your dad, and the grandkids. I'll start by taking better care of myself."

I was genuinely moved. That conversation felt like a breakthrough for us.

Then, my mom said something that really struck me: "If your dad starts getting angry again, I'll just leave the house." I nodded and said, "That's a great idea, but your mindset is also important: don't think of it as running away because you're avoiding the pain. You chose to leave because you deserve a better path for yourself. If you know what's coming, leave before things get worse. This isn't about escaping; it's about taking charge of your life."

She looked at me and smiled, "You're right. I've always passively accepted things, but I can choose differently now. And I deserve better."

Her recognition of this shift was huge. A few years ago, this conversation would've seemed impossible. But now, after all the effort, we were finally reaching a new place of understanding. This enlightening conversation wasn't easy or quick. It took twenty-five years of misunderstanding, a couple of years of working on it, and a lot of letting go.

Our later conversation on the plane about regrets and fear was proof that change is possible. It's not about fixing everything at once. It's about showing up, being open, and moving forward—together. The progress we made was worth every bit of effort.

## The Four F's: How We React to Fear and Stress

When we're faced with a perceived threat or trauma, our brains activate deep-rooted survival mechanisms that help us react quickly to avoid danger. These are known as the "Four F's"—Fight, Flight, Freeze, and Fawn. These instinctive responses were essential for survival in the past, allowing humans to quickly respond to physical threats. However, in modern life, these responses are often triggered by psychological stress or emotional trauma, and they can show up in ways that hinder our growth, especially in areas like finances.

**Fight** is the tendency to take immediate action, often in a confrontational or aggressive way when facing danger. In financial situations, the "Fight" response might manifest as defensiveness when discussing money, particularly if there's been conflict or chaos in the past. You might find yourself arguing over every purchase or decision, or becoming irritable when discussing financial plans. This reaction can lead to tension, miscommunication, and poor decision-making when emotions are running high.

**Flight** is the tendency to escape or avoid the situation altogether. In the context of finances, this could look like ignoring bills, avoiding conversations about money, or putting off major financial decisions because they feel too stressful. People who are prone to the "Flight" response may prefer to bury their heads in the sand rather than deal with their financial challenges head-on.

**Freeze** is when we feel paralyzed by fear, unable to take action. Financially, this might appear as feeling stuck or overwhelmed by the magnitude of financial goals, such as saving for retirement or paying down debt. People who freeze may procrastinate or avoid making any decisions at all, hoping the situation will resolve itself on its own, even though the problem may continue to grow worse over time.

**Fawn** is when we try to appease others or conform to their wishes to avoid conflict. In financial matters, this might involve agreeing to a partner's financial decisions even when it doesn't align with your own values or goals, just to keep the peace. People with this tendency may struggle to assert themselves in money matters and find themselves in financially unhealthy situations because they haven't communicated their needs or desires.

Does any of the above sound familiar? How do you tend to respond when facing financial stress or a big financial decision? Write the way(s) you react down here to remember so you can learn how to move on:

## The Importance of Recognizing Our Patterns

These instinctive responses can be helpful when we're in immediate danger, but when triggered by emotional stress or fear, they can create roadblocks in our relationships and financial decisions. Understanding our patterns is key because it allows us and our partners to see and understand how fear, stress, or past trauma can influence how we react.

In financial decision-making, recognizing when we're reacting with Fight, Flight, Freeze, or Fawn is the first step toward correcting harmful behaviors. By identifying our default response in moments of stress, we can take proactive steps to shift our mindset and behavior, make more intentional decisions, and build healthier financial habits.

In this chapter, we've focused on the courage of facing fear. By understanding and embracing our emotions, managing our emotional responses, and openly communicating with our loved ones, we can get clarity and gather strength to move forward, creating a more prosperous path to money and life.

## Now, It's Your Turn!

Ready to face your fears and transform them into something powerful? Fear, regret, and all those other messy emotions don't have to hold you back. They can actually be the keys to building a stronger, closer relationship. When you work through these feelings about money together, you'll feel that you are emotionally connected and your financial future brighter.

So, are you ready to face your fears and unlock your potential? Here's the exercise to try with your partner!

# Exercises for Chapter 2:
# Face Fear—Lean In to Move On

## Exercise 2-1: Sync Your Breath

1. Sit comfortably facing each other. Feel free to lean back if that helps you feel more at ease.

2. Close your eyes or soften your gaze.

3. Breathe in slowly and deeply through your noses together, counting to four.

4. Hold your breath gently for a count of four.

5. Exhale slowly through your mouths together, counting to six.

6. Set a timer for two minutes.

7. Keep repeating this breathing cycle—breathe in, hold, breathe out—focusing on syncing your breaths with each other.

## Exercise 2-2: Regret

1. Share with your partner: Financially, the thing I regret the most is . . . .

2. You'll take turns to share and listen. Decide who goes first. The listener pays full attention, keeping eye contact and not interrupting or taking notes. It's okay to use sounds like "um" or "wow" and body language.

3. Once the narrator is ready, set a timer for two minutes.

4. After the narrator finishes, the listener shares their feelings: "When you said (repeat their specific words), I felt (an emotion) in (a part of my body)."

   For example:

   - "When you talked about missing that opportunity, I felt your disappointment in my chest."
   - "When you shared your regret about not telling anyone about it earlier, I felt a deep pressure behind my eyes and sadness in my heart."

5. Switch roles and repeat the process.

## Exercise 2-3: Shame

1. Again, set a timer for two minutes each.

2. Take turns to open up and share: The time I felt ashamed (or embarrassed) because of money was . . . .

3. Decide who goes first. The listener pays full attention, keeping eye contact and not interrupting or taking notes. It's okay to use sounds like "um" or "wow" and body language.

4. After the narrator finishes, the listener shares their feelings: "When you said (repeat their specific words), I felt (an emotion) in (a part of my body)."

   For example:

   - "When you described that moment of being judged, I felt a burning heat rise to my cheeks and a sinking feeling in my stomach."

- "When you shared your fear of disappointing others, I felt an ache in the back of my neck."

5. Switch roles and repeat.

## Exercise 2-4: Fear

1. Take two minutes each to share one of these: The most painful money-related experience I've ever had is . . . or: My biggest financial fear is . . . .

2. Decide who goes first. The listener pays full attention, keeping eye contact and not interrupting or taking notes. It's okay to use sounds like "um" or "wow" and body language.

3. After the narrator finishes, the listener shares their feelings: "When you said (repeat their specific words), I felt (an emotion) in (a part of my body)."

   For example:

   - "When you admitted the difficulty of stepping into the unknown, I felt a trembling in my hands and a rush of adrenaline through my body."

   - "When you shared your worry about what could go wrong, I felt a chill run down my spine."

4. Switch roles and repeat.

## Exercise 2-5: Breaking Patterns

1. Take two minutes each to share: The financial behaviors of my parents that I do not want to repeat are . . . .

2. Decide who goes first. The listener pays full attention, keeping eye contact and not interrupting or taking notes. It's okay to use sounds like "um" or "wow" and body language.

3. After the narrator finishes, the listener shares their feelings: "When you said (repeat their specific words), I felt (an emotion) in (a part of my body)."

For example:

- "When you mentioned your parents didn't have enough saved, I felt a tightness in my throat and sadness washed over me.

- "When you described your desire to let go of familiar ways, I felt goosebumps all over my body."

4. Switch roles and repeat.

## Exercise 2-6: Our Behaviors

1. Take two minutes each to share: Financially, the things I'd like to keep doing are . . . .

2. Decide who goes first. The listener pays full attention, keeping eye contact and not interrupting or taking notes. It's okay to use sounds like "um" or "wow" and body language.

3. After the narrator finishes, the listener shares their feelings: "When you said (repeat their specific words), I felt (an emotion) in (a part of my body)."

For example:

- "When you talked about staying on top of the bills, I felt a sense of calm wash over my shoulders and a gentle steadiness in my breath."

- "When you mentioned your commitment to the family, I felt a surge of motivation in my stomach and a steady focus in my mind."

4. Switch roles and repeat.

## Moving On from Fear

By working through these exercises, you and your partner will not only build better communication, but also take actionable steps toward understanding and transforming your financial mindset. Embrace the discomfort of talking about emotions and fears, lean into the vulnerability of sharing your experiences, and celebrate the small wins—this is how transformation begins!

Talking about money can be tough, especially when negative emotions are involved. But the payoff is immeasurable! By confronting not just the financial issues but also the underlying emotions and fears, you're building stronger bonds, greater trust, and a more aligned decision-making process.

In the next chapter, we'll look at how to build on this newfound clarity, work together with your partner, and create a vision for a thriving financial life. Keep going, and keep up the great work!

# Your Reflection

Take a moment to jot down your thoughts and experiences
from the exercise. Use this space to capture any insights,
feelings, or ideas that came up.

_____

_____

_____

_____

_____

_____

_____

_____

_____

_____

_____

_____

_____

_____

# CHAPTER 3

# Live Fully with Tomorrow in Mind

John's life was always about routine and getting things done. For the past three years, he had been working fifteen days on and thirteen days off. He traveled far from home and worked long hours in the oil fields. His wife, Melissa, didn't have a full-time job, but she was busy managing their rental properties and taking care of their three kids, ages fourteen, nine, and six. Each child was involved in different after-school activities. Their life was always busy. Every day was filled with tasks neither of them could avoid, and they quickly lost time just for themselves.

When John sat down to work through the "your ideal life" exercise, he wasn't prepared for the emotional depth it would stir up. His ideal day, week, and year had been defined by what he accomplished. "As long as the tasks on my long to-do list are completed, I feel good," he had always told himself. It was simple—finish work, check things off the list, and life would move on smoothly. "If I didn't have any financial pressure, my ideal day would be to have no plans, completely free to do whatever I want. An ideal week would include time to do some exercise and sports, read some good books, learn about some industries and companies that I am interested in, and chat with some good friends. An ideal year would be repeating ideal weeks, and adding more travel, living in different countries and cultural environments for longer periods of time, and experiencing this colorful world."

But when Melissa said, "Mine would be similar, but I will also need a good mood every day and every moment!" John was perplexed; he couldn't understand why she put so much emphasis on having a "good mood." To him, mood was secondary to the things they do. If things were accomplished, then life was good.

So John dug deeper, "Why is having a good mood so important?" Melissa's tears began flowing, and for a moment, John didn't know what to do. He had never seen her so vulnerable, and it shook him to his core. They had been together for years, but this moment revealed things he had never fully understood. Melissa wasn't just crying because of their shared conversation—it was a release of years of unspoken pain.

As she wiped her tears, Melissa began to speak, her voice shaking, but steady enough to share the painful truth she had never spoken aloud before. "You know, when I was in second grade, something happened that changed me," she said quietly. "I was a good kid, always trying to do the right thing. But one day, my teacher called me out in front of the entire class. She mocked me, made the other kids laugh, and I was left standing there, humiliated. I didn't understand why it happened, but it crushed me. I was just a child, and that shame has haunted me ever since."

John listened as Melissa continued. "That feeling of shame followed me for years, but it didn't stop there. When I went to college, I made a big mistake. I helped a friend during an exam, thinking I was just being kind. But I got caught. I was terrified—terrified of being expelled, of not graduating, of failing everything. I feared I would let my parents down, especially since they had such high hopes for me. Being the first to go to college in my family from a small town, it felt like the weight of my entire family's dreams rested on my shoulders. I spent years in fear of ruining my future and disappointing everyone who believed in me."

Melissa paused, her eyes searching John's face as if to see whether he was really hearing her this time.

"Those fears . . . they never really went away," she said softly. "Even after I started working, the struggles didn't stop. And when we got married, I hoped I'd finally feel safe and steady. But it hasn't been easy. Our differences have weighed heavier on me than I've ever admitted. Most of the time, John, I've felt like nobody really cared how I felt, and I carried that weight alone.

As a mom, I pushed myself to be strong, to hold it all together. But while I was doing that, you were out chasing your goals . . . and I felt invisible. No matter how much I did, it never felt enough."

John sat frozen, her words slicing through his defenses. His chest tightened with regret as the truth hit. He had been so blind to Melissa's pains. Even worse, he didn't realize how his choices made those pains deeper. For years, he told himself that working harder, earning more, and building wealth was the way to give his family a better life. But now he finally saw how much he had been missing.

All those times he brushed off Melisa's emotions as her being "moody" or "too sensitive," he now realized were signals he ignored, pleas for support he never answered. What she had wanted all along wasn't a bigger paycheck or another investment. She had wanted him. His attention. His care. His presence.

Melissa looked down, then lifted her eyes back to his, her voice steadier now.

"All these years of feeling pushed aside, of not being enough, of not being fully accepted . . . they've worn me down. That's why being light and cheerful hasn't come easy. What I need—what I've always needed—is to feel safe and loved by the people closest to me. By you. I can't carry that alone anymore."

John's mind was racing as he absorbed her words. He had always thought that mood was something you could control on your own. But Melissa was showing him something he hadn't truly understood until now. For her, mood and happiness weren't just about mental resilience. They depended on the people and environments around her.

As Melissa spoke, John realized that he had unintentionally added to her burdens. He thought about the times he had been absent, focused on his work, and not truly present with her. He had been so focused on getting things done, on checking off boxes, that he hadn't noticed how much Melissa needed him—not just physically, but emotionally, to help lift her spirits.

"I'm so sorry," John said quietly, "I had no idea. I've been so focused on work and our finances that I didn't see what you've been through. I never realized how much you've suffered in silence. I see it now, Melissa. And I'm here for you. I'm here to help carry that burden with you."

John squeezed her hand, feeling a renewed sense of understanding and commitment. This wasn't just about making sure the tasks were completed or the goals were reached. It was about supporting Melissa, about helping her heal.

In that moment, as they sat there together, John understood something crucial. The life they were building wasn't just about financial success, completing tasks or making progress. It was about love, understanding, and supporting each other through the ups and downs. And for the first time, he was truly ready to embrace that, wholeheartedly.

John wanted to create a perfect moment for Melissa, a vision of love and connection that would bring their family even closer. He began, "In a few weeks, it'll be your birthday. I haven't forgotten, and I've planned a surprise for you with the kids. While you're out on your grocery run, we'll decorate the living room, turn off the lights, and set everything up. When you come home, we'll time it so that as soon as you open the door, we'll be walking toward you with a cake and candles, singing 'Happy Birthday.'"

He paused for a moment, letting the image sink in, and then continued, "You'll blow out the candles and make a wish. Then, we'll turn on the lights. Avery and Oliver will take your hands and lead you to the living room, where you'll see two dozen photos— starting from when you were little, to you holding the kids when they were babies, and then some of our more recent trips. We'll go through each one, reliving the memories together."

John smiled at the scene in his mind and said, "While I put away the grocery bags, the kids will come over, give you a big hug, and say, 'We love you so much, Mommy!' Then I'll come over to hold your hands and tell you how lucky I am, that I love you, and that I want to share more with you, and be there more for you." He paused, then asked "How would that make you feel?"

Tears welled up in Melissa's eyes. "I've never dreamed I'd hear those words from you," she said, her voice trembling with emotion. "I'd be so happy."

John smiled warmly, "Would you add anything to make it even more meaningful?"

Melissa wiped away the tears, smiling. "Yes, please make sure that it's a mango cake—that's Oliver's favorite."

John grinned. "That's also my favorite!" But as he thought about it, he realized there was still a lot to plan to make sure this birthday celebration felt like a true surprise for Melissa. Now, he and the kids would need to brainstorm a way to pull it off.

In the end, this wasn't just about the birthday planning. It was about creating a feeling of love and connection that had been missing from their relationship for so long. And in that moment, John knew that this was just the beginning—a new chapter where emotional intimacy and deep connection would shape their family's future.

## The Silent Killer of Connection

Did you know that about 59.3 million adults in the United States, almost one in five people (23.1%), are living with a mental illness in any given year?[6] And only half of them actually get diagnosed. To make matters worse, many people don't even realize they're dealing with depression, anxiety, or other disorders at all. It's easy to assume that something else is causing the emotional strain, like stress, exhaustion, or just a temporary rough patch. But in reality, mental health struggles often hide beneath the surface, and we might not even recognize them.

---

[6] www.nimh.nih.gov/health/statistics/mental-illness

This is especially common in relationships. Partners may be unaware that their spouse is silently struggling with mental health challenges, especially when symptoms are subtle or not openly discussed. Depression, for example, doesn't always look like sadness or withdrawal. Sometimes, it shows up as irritability, fatigue, or even frustration over the smallest things. When these behaviors go unrecognized, we may misinterpret them as personal rejection or a lack of interest, but they can often be signs of depression that have not been addressed.

One area where this issue is especially relevant is during the transition to parenthood. Many new mothers experience postpartum depression, a condition that is more common than most people realize. The overwhelming emotional and physical toll of caring for a newborn, combined with the stress and exhaustion of daily routines, can contribute to depression. But these feelings are often seen as "just part of being a new mom," making it easy for partners to overlook them, especially if they're busy with work or managing other responsibilities.

The issue of mental health isn't limited to mothers alone. Fathers can also face mental health challenges, particularly when dealing with the pressures of supporting a growing family, managing financial stress, or adjusting to new roles and responsibilities. Yet, fathers' struggles are often overlooked, and their emotional needs can go unmet. This lack of awareness can make it harder for both partners to connect emotionally and support one another during this demanding time.

For example, if a partner seems irritable or withdrawn, it's easy to assume they're just having a bad day or are upset with you. But these emotions could be signs of something deeper, like depression. When we fail to recognize mental health struggles in our partners, it can lead to more conflict, feelings of rejection, and emotional distance. Instead of acknowledging and addressing the root cause—mental health—we might misinterpret our partner's behaviors as personal shortcomings or relationship issues. This can further alienate both partners, making it harder to connect, communicate, and support each other.

## Connection Over Correction

So how can couples navigate mental health challenges together? The key is awareness and connection.

Supporting a partner's mental wellness means more than just noticing when they're "off" or in a bad mood. It requires slowing down enough to really listen, asking with care, and being open to hard conversations. It's about creating a safe space where both partners know they can share—even when the feelings are uncomfortable or hard to put into words.

Here's the thing: emotional distance, irritability, or withdrawal usually aren't personal attacks. Research shows they're often signs of stress, anxiety, or depression brewing beneath the surface. When couples take those signals seriously instead of taking them personally, it changes everything. The dynamic shifts from defensiveness to compassion.

When partners choose connection over correction, they build the conditions for healing. Open communication and genuine support can help couples decide together what to do next. This might include seeking therapy, finding stress relief practices, or simply carving out time for each other in small, intentional ways. In fact, studies from the Gottman Institute show that couples who respond to each other's emotional needs with empathy are far more likely to maintain happy, lasting relationships.

The true strength of a relationship isn't tested when things are easy. It shows up in how well you weather the hard seasons as a team. By recognizing and addressing mental health challenges like postpartum depression, work stress, or everyday pressures, couples do more than just support each other's struggles. They actually make their relationship stronger and build a deeper foundation of trust and connection. Facing these challenges together helps create a partnership that can weather any storm.

So take the time. Listen without rushing to fix. Be present without judgment. Understand each other's inner world. Because sometimes, the most powerful thing you can give your partner isn't a solution; it's your patience, steady presence, and the reminder that they don't have to go through it alone.

## A Life Worth Living

As we progress through life, one thing often becomes clearer and clearer: the biggest barriers to living our best lives may not be financial readiness, or even health—although they are certainly critical resources. Instead, it's often our mindset, our priorities, and our willingness to embrace the future that matter most. One person who has epitomized this idea throughout his life is George Kinder, the father of financial life planning, who has been a guiding light for many seeking a fulfilling and intentional life.

In George's own words, *"Life planning is the most efficient process for delivering freedom into a person's life that I think exists. It is a process that has been adopted by financial planners because financial planning is so holistic in its concern with all the aspects of money in a person's life. Financial planners, in particular, have gravitated toward it because, in order for us to*

A COUPLE'S GUIDE TO MONEY

*experience freedom in our lives, most of us need to resolve or address financial issues."*

George began his career as a CPA, with a solid academic foundation. He graduated from Harvard as a math major and scored highly on his CPA exam. Initially, he served a niche market of self-employed psychologists and therapists in the Boston and Cambridge area. After working diligently for many years, he noticed something curious: despite being highly educated and financially stable, many of these professionals weren't truly living the lives they wanted. Traditional financial planning couldn't give them the guidance they were looking for. They longed for financial advice that aligned with their deeper values, something that went beyond the numbers.

This realization led George to an important conclusion: financial planning had to be more than just about securing resources. It could be a tool for living a meaningful, values-driven life. He was inspired to create a new approach, one that combined financial wisdom with introspection and holistic planning. In 2003, four years after publishing his groundbreaking book, *The Seven Stages of Money Maturity*, and selling his tax practice, George founded the Kinder Institute of Life Planning. His work laid the foundation for the life planning process that is now widely practiced across the world.

At the age of seventy-seven, George Kinder is still actively pushing boundaries and inspiring others. He has become one of my personal inspirations, both in life and aging. His commitment to continually growing, learning, and contributing is a powerful reminder that there is no age limit to pursuing what matters most to us.

George's life exemplifies the concept that a life worth living isn't just about securing financial stability; it's about aligning your financial strategies with your deepest values and aspirations. His life's work has shown me, and many others, that we have the power to create a fulfilling life by addressing not just what we do with our money, but how we make decisions that lead to greater personal freedom and joy. This is what true financial planning is really about: helping people create the life they want to live, not just the life they think they should live.

## How My Business Grew Beyond Dollars

Fifteen months after I hit my financial freedom goal, I made the bold, life-changing decision to leave my corporate career and venture into entrepreneurship. I was influenced by several mentors, including George Kinder. The approach of strategizing resources as a foundation to build a meaningful life for clients resonated deeply with my own values. So I started the training to follow his approach.

The experience fundamentally changed the way I communicate with my clients. I evolved from someone who was very logic-driven and analytical into a much better listener and coach. I started creating spaces where clients could express their feelings, learned how to accept and guide them through their emotions, and used a vision that's aligned with their core values to bring positive energy back into our engagement.

I quickly realized that while I was good at helping clients clarify their goals and visions, I struggled to help them push past the obstacles that kept them from taking action. Often, those obstacles were emotional and deeply rooted: family drama with parents or partners, regrets tied to loved ones who had passed, or even inheritances that came with strings attached. Recognizing my own limits, I deepened my learning with more training.

After completing the full program, I gained additional skills that have allowed me to help clients overcome their fears, doubts, and insecurities. I've been able to rechannel their energy toward positive actions that are within their control, which then lead to real transformations in their lives.

I have helped people navigate a wide range of money and life situations, including deciding whether to buy a home, whether to have kids or not, preparing for difficult conversations, building trust through open communication with their partners, saving with purpose, spending without regrets, and finding work-life balance. I've supported career changes, starting and growing businesses, amicable divorces, preparing for retirement, and much more. Seeing these transformations has been deeply rewarding and has strengthened my belief in holistic planning as a cornerstone of my practice.

| Couples and Money Program | Before | After | CHANGE |
|---|---|---|---|
| I often worry about my current financial situation. | 2.1 | 2.0 | -6.67% |
| I feel confident in my ability to manage my finances. | 3.7 | 4.0 | 7.69% |
| Financial concerns negatively impact my sleep or relationships. | 1.7 | 1.7 | -2.78% |
| I have a clear plan for achieving my long-term financial goals. | 3.4 | 4.7 | 36.11% |
| I feel stressed when thinking about my retirement savings. | 2.1 | 1.5 | -30.00% |

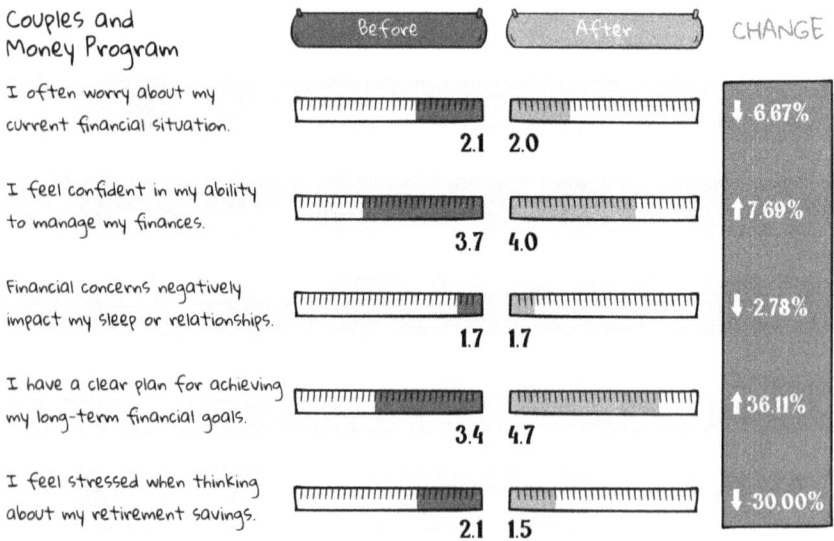

Figure 4: Love + Money = Success

These experiences inspired me to create the Couples and Money group coaching program. This was a major step for my business, expanding from just helping individuals manage money to empowering couples to build stronger emotional and financial bonds. The results were amazing. Within just three months, financial awareness rose by 28%, clarity grew by 36%, and financial stress fell by 30%.

## Why Is This So Significant?

### 1. Confidence and Planning Ahead Matter More Than You Think

It's not just about feeling good. Morningstar's research backs it up: financial confidence and thinking long term, a decade or more, are linked to significantly higher net worth and better financial health scores across all income groups. In other words, building clarity and a positive long-term outlook isn't just comforting; it plays a real role in achieving better financial outcomes.

### 2. Financial Prudence Protects You

Psychologist Brad Klontz's research reveals that being financially vigilant, paying close, thoughtful attention to your money, is very important for doing well with money. When you stay alert and watchful about your money, you're not just becoming more aware; you're putting on the armor. This armor helps you block out distractions and uncertainty, so you and your family can build the life you want and deserve.

## 3. Real Change Happens Fast

The results from our program aren't just impressive numbers for a brochure. They show real growth that points to stronger financial health in the future. Imagine going from feeling overwhelmed and scattered to feeling more in control, clear-headed, and calm about your money, all in less than a few months!

Mindset shifts like those sparked in my group coaching program are about more than optimism or smart plans. They unlock your true potential to build wealth and well-being, proving that with the right tools, everyone can make meaningful progress toward happiness and prosperity.

## Beyond Money: The Real Journey

What surprised me most were the conversations that unfolded in my group coaching program. It quickly became clear the work went far beyond budgets and investments. Together, we explored communication, love, gratitude, fear, career transitions, caring for aging parents, parenting challenges, investment regrets, financial freedom, holistic well-being, and purpose. Money became just one part of a much bigger story, and helping couples navigate that full story has become the heart of my work.

Alongside the coaching program, I began writing my first book, the one you're holding now. It is a natural extension of this work, focusing on emotional connection, open communication, shared goals, and realistic action plans couples need on their journey to financial freedom. Writing this book has given me a meaningful way to share lessons learned both from my own experiences and from the many clients I have had the privilege to guide toward greater financial and emotional harmony.

Meanwhile, as a fee-only financial planner offering one-on-one services, my goal is straightforward: to help clients focus on what matters most to them. Too often, we get caught up in the daily hustle, chasing goals without pausing to ask if those goals truly reflect our core values. That is where true listening and trust come into play. Through personalized planning, I create a clear roadmap that guides clients beyond numbers by connecting their financial decisions to their whole life experience, so every step brings them closer to their most meaningful dreams.

This journey, across coaching groups, writing, and personalized financial planning, has been full of growth, learning, and deep connection. The true beauty lies in aligning your resources with your values. It is about more than managing money; it is about living intentionally, nurturing relationships, and embracing every step of the path with love and clarity.

I'm excited about where this journey will take me, my clients, and my business. Combining the emotional and technical sides of money is a superpower, a gift that keeps on giving. I look forward to continuing to make a lasting difference.

## Trip of a Lifetime

Fatima and Amir, a dynamic couple in their mid-thirties, have always been driven by ambition and a desire to create a meaningful life. Over eight years of marriage and fifteen years of knowing each other, they've built a strong financial foundation through full-time careers and a series of entrepreneurial ventures on the side—selling Halal meat, running an online Hijab store, and flipping houses. Their hard work has paid off: they've built a solid financial foundation to pursue long-held dreams, including career change and the profound journey of Hajj.

Yet, as their financial life planner, I saw that beneath their achievements, Fatima and Amir were wrestling with a familiar uncertainty: when is the right time to truly live out your dreams? Amir, ever thoughtful and responsible, wondered if they should wait for the "perfect" moment—when the projects on hand got to a better place, when they could afford more comfort, when life felt less hectic. Fatima, too, felt the tension between obligations, aspirations, and the desire to leave a legacy of faith, community, and giving.

This is where life planning really started to make a difference. Our conversations went beyond just crunching numbers (which I'll walk you through for your own situation in Chapter 6). We talked about what truly mattered to them: their values, the things that are most important to them, and their biggest aspirations in life. We imagined together: What would you do if money weren't an issue? What if you found out you only had five to ten years left—how would your life change? And then, the toughest one: How would you feel if you only had one day left?[7] Our Zoom meeting fell silent, the soft hum of background noise suddenly noticeable as everyone sat with their thoughts. I could see Fatima's eyes glisten, and Amir leaned in, his hand gently resting on hers. The air felt heavy, charged with meaning. Here's how it unfolded:

**Prudence:** (voice gentle) So, Fatima, you wrote that if this were your last day, you'd wish you'd traveled more, prayed more, given more to charity. Can you tell me what that feels like for you?

---

[7] George Kinder's famous Three Questions of Life Planning are designed to help individuals uncover their deepest values, dreams, and priorities, forming the foundation for a meaningful life plan. For more resources, please go to: www.kinderinstitute.com/books/

**Fatima:** (pauses, then with a small, reflective smile) You know, overall, I'm grateful for what I've accomplished. But there's always this little voice in the back of my mind whispering, "You could've done more." More for others, more for my faith . . . I guess Amir put it best: leaving a legacy. I want to do more of that, not just for me, but for the people around me.

**Amir:** (beaming at Fatima, his eyes warm) She's too humble. At the book club she started, I've seen people light up, find friends, even start their own projects. She's making a difference, even if she doesn't always see it.

**Fatima:** (laughs, a little embarrassed) It's just a small group, really. But I hope it lasts, even if I'm not around to run it. I keep telling everyone, "Rotate hosts, keep it going, don't make it about me." I want it to be something that outlives me, you know?

**Prudence:** That's beautiful, Fatima. If you could expand it, what would that look like?

**Fatima:** (her face brightens, hands gesturing as she speaks) I'd love to rent a little space, somewhere cozy, like a living room or a café. People could come for book club, or financial literacy workshops, or just to feel safe and connected. A real community hub. But . . . (shrugs, sighing) that takes money, and time, and sometimes it feels so far away.

**Amir:** (nodding, his voice soft) We've seen places like that in Chicago. It's inspiring, but yeah, it's a big leap for us right now.

**Prudence**: There are certainly things we can do to get there. And what about travel? What's your dream there?

**Fatima**: (eyes shining, a wistful smile) I want to see the world. All the national parks here, and then everywhere else—experience new cultures, try new foods, see God's creation. But every time

I get a break, I feel pulled to travel to see my family. I love it, but . . . sometimes I wish I could do both.

**Amir:** (grinning, squeezing her hand) She's the adventurer. Me? Give me a fishing pole and a quiet lake, and I'm happy.

**Fatima:** (laughs) I'll join you, as long as there's a boat where I can stretch out and read.

**Prudence:** (smiling) There are beaches and fish everywhere in the world. You two might just have to combine your dreams!

**Fatima:** (laughs) Maybe we will.

**Prudence:** And Hajj—that's something you both want to do soon?

**Fatima:** (her voice softens, turning serious) Absolutely. It's right at the top of my list. If I were to die tomorrow, not having done Hajj would be my biggest regret. But . . . it's expensive, it's complicated. We want to take Amir's mom, too, and that adds another layer.

**Amir:** (sighs, rubbing his forehead) The logistics are a nightmare. Packages sell out, prices keep rising. Sometimes I think, maybe we should wait until we can do it right, comfortably. But then . . . is there ever really a perfect time?

**Fatima:** (quietly, almost to herself) I don't want to wait forever. Life just keeps moving.

**Prudence** (to Fatima): Say, through our work together, we are able to deliver to you a moment, next year, in June. You, Amir, and his mom have just come back from Hajj. It was an experience that you couldn't even describe with words. It's life-changing. So fulfilling. It felt like the essence of life. You stood in unity with thousands, felt the power of your faith, and came home renewed. You're empowered to come back to everything that you've been doing and do it better. You start working with a new company, you have new ideas for building community, starting your own business, and showing other people, young people who are inspired by your story and what you're doing, how to come into the business and build successful lives, and be a cornerstone for their community. It's just incredible, all the things that are in motion, and you can't wait to come back to it. It's just wonderful, and all because of the work you put in to plan and make it happen. Amir is right there with you, he says to you, "It's so wonderful to share this life with you. I'm so excited for everything ahead of us." How would that make you feel?

**Fatima:** (her voice trembling, tears in her eyes) Fantastic. Honestly, stop trying to make me cry, Prudence . . . .

**Prudence:** (smiling) I'm making myself cry now. That would be so wonderful. And I want it for you. Is there anything you'd add to that moment?

**Fatima:** (shakes her head, voice soft) No, I don't think so. You painted it perfectly.

**Prudence:** Then let's make it happen.

**Fatima:** (smiling through tears) Let's do it!

Three months later, Amir called to share some wonderful news: he and Fatima got their official packages for Hajj. They were bringing his mom too. I couldn't be happier for them.

What made this truly special was how their decision came from a place of clarity and alignment. Fatima and Amir began to reimagine their journey: not as a series of postponed dreams, but as a life lived intentionally, with courage and purpose. They committed to pursuing Hajj, recognizing it as both a spiritual milestone and a statement of their values. They envisioned building businesses that not only generated wealth, but also giving back—mentoring youth, fostering community, and giving back.

## Embrace Today, Empower Tomorrow

How many times have you found yourself waiting for the "perfect" moment like Amir? Waiting to ask for a promotion until you get that certificate, planning to start cooking once life slows down, thinking you'll travel more when the kids are older, or waiting for the "right mood" or a special occasion to reconnect as a couple? Maybe you're telling yourself, "Just one more year," or "When the market is right, then I'll retire."

I've been there too, thinking, "As soon as I'm done with this book, I'll resume working out twice a week." But here's the truth: we don't live in the future—we live in the present. Waiting for that perfect time often leads to endless postponing and missed opportunities, and life passes us by. In reality, change doesn't have to wait for everything to align. Starting with a small step today can break that cycle of delay and build momentum for bigger, more meaningful change. Here are some common scenarios where we tend to wait for that ideal moment and how we can start taking action today:

## 1. Traveling More

Many couples dream of taking a big trip, maybe to Europe, a national park, or even just a weekend getaway. They wait for the "perfect" time: when they have more time, when they have more money, or when life is less hectic. Years pass, and the trip never happens because there's always another reason to postpone. In reality, starting with a simple weekend road trip or a day exploring a nearby town can break the inertia and build momentum for bigger adventures.

## 2. Downsizing or Moving

Couples often talk about moving to a dream home, downsizing, or relocating after retirement. They wait for the market to be just right, for the kids to move out, or for "one more year" of savings. Sometimes, the right moment never comes, and they miss out on years they could have enjoyed in a new space. Taking small steps, like decluttering one room or visiting open houses, can help you visualize your ideal home and discover more ways that would make it even more exciting!

## 3. Rekindling Romance

It's easy to put off time reconnecting as a couple, thinking you'll find time when you're in the "right mood" or wait for a special occasion. But busy schedules, family needs, and fatigue can push these plans indefinitely. Instead, couples who intentionally carve out small pockets of quality time—like a daily walk, a coffee together, or a simple picnic—find that intimacy and connection grow through these small shared moments.

## 4. Working Out

Many couples wish they could get healthier or be more active together, but they wait for the "perfect" time when they have more time or more energy, or when they can find the right gym. But that perfect time rarely comes. Instead, starting with something small, like a five-minute yoga session, a short stretching routine at home, or a weekend bike ride, can build momentum. Over time, these small steps can lead to a shared fitness habit and a stronger, healthier relationship.

## 5. Starting a New Hobby or Project

Maybe you've always wanted to learn to cook together, start a garden, or volunteer. It's easy to wait for more free time or the "right" season. But starting with a single recipe, planting one pot, or signing up for one volunteer shift can turn intention into reality and bring new energy into your relationship.

## 6. Having Important Conversations

We've all done it, putting off those big discussions about finances, promotions, retirement, or future goals, waiting for that "perfect" time when things are less stressful. I totally get it. The stakes feel high, and it's intimidating! But here's the thing: the longer you wait, the more those conversations turn into giant monsters in your mind that seem impossible to tackle. So here's the secret: start small. Just setting aside five minutes a week to prepare for an intentional heart-to-heart can make a huge difference.

Now, picture it: When do you want to have the chat? Where will it happen? What are you wearing? How do you feel? What's the key message you want to share? Why is it important to you? The more specific you get about these details, the more prepared and confident you'll feel when it's time to talk. The "perfect" moment might never come, but you can create the right moment anytime, especially if you prepare ahead of time!

## 7. Finally Retiring

Retirement can feel like that distant, far-off dream—a goal that's always "one perfect year" away. But waiting for the ideal time to retire can feel like waiting for a unicorn to appear. Instead of putting off your financial freedom, why not try a mini-retirement? Take a few weeks off, explore part-time work, or dive into a passion project. By taking small steps today, you'll ease the transition into retirement and make the process feel much smoother.

The bottom line? Waiting for the "perfect" moment to chase your dreams or make big changes rarely works out. There's always one more project, one more hurdle, one more excuse to postpone what matters most. Waiting for everything to line up perfectly could mean waiting forever. So, start with small, consistent steps—whether that's trying something new on a small scale, making time for each other, or simply thinking through how to have that tough conversation. It's those little nudges toward your truest priorities that create the momentum for bigger, more meaningful changes.

What's one small thing you can do today to move closer to your dreams together?

## Dreaming Bigger

As you live more proactively in the present and let go of waiting for the "perfect moment," you'll realize that your life partner is not here to perfectly understand your pain or sorrow because they don't live your life. They can't always know what's going on inside your heart and mind. But that's okay, because what they can offer is a mirror, helping you see what you really need and where you can grow and thrive. They show you the parts of yourself you may not be able to see on your own and make the wildest dreams more achievable. Through their presence and the emotional dance you share, you gain clarity. They may not always "get it" right away, but they give you the space to *feel it*. And that's what matters.

So, as you go forward in your relationship and in life, remember that the growth and wisdom you seek comes not from expecting your love to change, or fix everything, or understand every detail of your journey. It comes from finding the clarity and leaning into the emotional space that your partner provides.

That is the true gift of dreaming bigger together: the courage to grow, to understand, to be seen, and to be your true authentic self. And that's where a brighter future becomes real.

**Now, It's Your Turn!**

After exploring others' stories and reflecting on the journey, it's time to take some practical steps to envision your ideal life and deepen your connection with your partner. These exercises are designed to help you get clear on what truly matters to you, while also fostering a deeper understanding between you and your partner. Let's dive in!

# Exercises for Chapter 3:
# Live Fully with Tomorrow in Mind

## Exercise 3-1: Feeling

1. Set a timer for two minutes each.

2. Describe how you feel right now. Think about your emotions, both big and small, and take time to really connect with what's going on inside you.

3. You'll take turns to share and listen. Decide who goes first. The listener pays full attention, keeping eye contact and not interrupting or taking notes. It's okay to use sounds like "um" or "wow" and body language.

4. Once the narrator finishes, the listener shares their feelings with: "When you said (repeat their specific words), I felt (an emotion) in (a part of my body)."

   For example:

   - "When you talked about skipping lunch, I felt hunger in my stomach."

   - "When you talked about your late aunt, I felt sadness in my heart and wanted to comfort you with a hug."

5. Switch roles and repeat the process.

## Exercise 3-2: Ideal day, week, and year[8]

1. Please take five to eight minutes and each write on a piece of paper: How would you spend your ideal day, week, and year if you had enough resources to live the way you want?

2. Decide who goes first. The listener reads the narrator's answers one by one, pausing after each sentence to give them time to add context and details.

3. The listener maintains eye contact, no interruptions or note-taking. You can use sounds like "um" or "wow" and body language.

4. Once the narrator finishes, the listener shares their feelings with: "When you said (repeat their specific words), I felt (an emotion) in (a part of my body)."

   For example:

   - "When you mentioned freedom, my heart lifted."
   - "When you said having no stress and just enjoying life, my whole body felt light."

5. Switch roles and repeat.

## Exercise 3-3: A Perfect Moment

1. Take one to two minutes to envision a perfect moment for your partner and describe it in detail. The more specific, the better!

---

[8] For the full version, please refer to *Life Planning for You: How to Design & Deliver the Life of Your Dreams* by George Kinder, or the free tool on his website www.lifeplanningforyou.com/

2. Vision: "If, through our JOINT efforts, on [specific day within a year], . . . (goal #1 progresses), . . . (goal #2 progresses), . . . (goal #3 progresses). How would that make you feel?" Guide on creating the perfect moment: Sincerity is the first principle. Don't promise anything that's impossible.

3. After your partner answers, ask: "Is there anything else you want to add?" or "Is there anything that could make this moment even better?"

4. Switch roles and repeat.

## Example: A Perfect Moment

*"If, through our JOINT efforts, you wake up on a bright, sunlit morning. It's the day before our big summer trip next year. As you stretch and breathe in the fresh air, a smile spreads across your face. Together, we've made steady progress on our financial goals, with a few delightful surprises along the way. The side business you've been working on is finally starting to bring in steady income—small, but real and promising.*

*You feel confident and happy about your day job, knowing it's more than just work; it's a source of positive change for others, and it inspires not only your colleagues but also our daughter to chase her own dreams with passion.*

*Just then, I walk into the bedroom carrying a cup of hand-poured coffee. You catch the wonderful smell and say, 'Wow, where did you get these new beans? They smell incredible!'*

*Our baby girl, hearing us, bursts into the room with a beaming smile. 'Mommy, Daddy, I've been up since 6:00! I'm so excited for our trip. I can't wait to get on the plane! I love you both so much!' She wraps her arms around your neck and plants a big, warm kiss on your lips.* (Pause.)

*How would that make you feel?"* Then ask *"Is there anything to add, to make it even better?"*

## Sincerity is Key

Creating a vision for your partner is a unique experience. It's about sharing from the bottom of your heart what you truly desire for them and their happiness. When you envision a perfect moment or future for your partner, avoid promising anything unrealistic. The key is sincerity—express what you genuinely want for them, based on their needs, dreams, and values.

And remember, it's okay if things don't work out exactly as you pictured. Often, the details will unfold differently than described, but that's not the point. What matters is that you're helping your partner feel what's truly important to them—whether it's freedom, security, adventure, connection, or growth. By sharing your vision with them, you're giving them the courage and motivation to take action, making their dreams feel possible and real. That's the essence of true support and love.

# Your Reflection

Take a moment to jot down your thoughts and experiences from the exercise. Use this space to capture any insights, feelings, or ideas that came up.

_____

_____

_____

_____

_____

_____

_____

_____

_____

_____

_____

_____

_____

_____

# CHAPTER 4
## Envision Real Change

Hannah's heart fluttered the moment she met Matt. In her late twenties and a bit weary from the endless dating rollercoaster, she never expected to feel this spark. Matt wasn't flashy, but he had qualities that truly mattered: hard work, reliability, and a down-to-earth way of seeing things. Most importantly, he didn't just listen to her wild, sometimes quirky ideas; he embraced them. After just a few months, Hannah felt something she hadn't felt in a long time: she was ready to settle down. She saw in him not just a steady partner, but someone with real potential. She believed in Matt and the future they could build as a family.

Matt felt the same way about Hannah. He would often joke, "You're the brains with all the big ideas, and I'm the guy who makes them happen. We're unstoppable together!" They made a great team, ready to take on whatever life threw their way. But two years into their marriage, as they started talking about having kids, Hannah began to feel a subtle hesitation inside herself, something she hadn't quite expected.

Matt had never been in a serious relationship before meeting Hannah. He didn't fully understand the emotional depth she craved. For her, like many women, marriage wasn't just about living under the same roof. It was about connection, intimacy, and feeling heard and loved. But Matt was a man of action. He was more focused on providing for the family. He expressed his love through hard work, side hustles, and checking things off the to-do list. "I'm working hard for us, making money, and contributing to our home. That's what matters," he'd say.

But Hannah wanted something different. For her, love wasn't measured in tasks completed or boxes ticked. She craved affection, thoughtful words, and moments of romance that weren't tied to responsibility. When conflict arose, Matt's default was a short, awkward, "Oh, I'm sorry," followed by quickly moving on to other things. When she expressed hurt, he struggled to find the words that would comfort her.

Over time, their marriage began to feel less like a love story and more like a business partnership. They ran the household well, but the emotional spark and the feeling of unity were slipping away.

Hannah's worry started to grow. What would their relationship look like if they had a baby? "What if I get pregnant and struggle with postpartum depression?" she thought. "What if he says something insensitive when I'm at my lowest, sleep-deprived state, and overwhelmed by the demands of our newborn?" She had seen how blunt her husband could be with his words, and she feared that his "straight-shooter" approach would only worsen during a vulnerable time like postpartum.

This fear reached a breaking point when Hannah realized the emotional distance between them had become a hidden barrier to their happiness. "On the surface, we're fine," she thought. "But deep down, we're just not as close as we could be." The more she reflected, the more she realized that their differences weren't just about practical matters like spending or logistics—they were emotional too. While Matt focused on career and making money, she longed for emotional connection, adventure, and the kind of deep understanding that only comes from truly hearing each other.

During a group coaching session, something shifted for Hannah. As she shared her struggles openly in the spotlight, a wave of frustration surfaced. But so did a deeper understanding of her relationship with Matt and with herself.

"I really admire Matt's energy. He is always pushing forward, dreaming big, and working hard to make things happen for us. But while he moves ahead, I feel stuck. I have lost my focus, wasting time on short videos and scrolling through social media. I feel my creativity abandoning me, and with AI changing everything, I worry I am falling behind in my career.

Last year, I took a government job hoping it would give me less stress to prepare for pregnancy. Instead, budget cuts have slowed everything down and I am not growing or learning like I hoped. Rather than freeing up my time, I find myself stuck to my phone even more.

What is hardest is feeling like we are living on different tracks. Matt is charging ahead and I am stuck spinning my wheels. I am frustrated with myself but more than that, I do not want this to drive a wedge between us. I want to find my own path again, to grow in ways that bring us closer, not further apart."

## The Power of Collective Learning

The group was quiet for a moment, thinking over Hannah's situation. Then others began to show support by sharing their own stories and ideas, and suddenly, it felt like a weight had lifted for Hannah. She found herself heard, and more importantly, understood. The feedback from others was both practical and comforting, and one after another, the group offered insight that would help her navigate her emotional journey. She wasn't alone in her feelings, and there was a new sense of clarity in her heart.

Jessica was the first to speak up, sharing her own experience with reclaiming her time. "I totally get it," she said with a warm smile. "A few months ago, I was spending hours on TikTok, just scrolling endlessly. I realized I was wasting so much time, so I decided to uninstall all the apps that were draining my energy. I kept just one, an AI app where I can get all the recipes and information I need, and haven't looked back. It's been a game-changer! Short videos rewire your brain and destroy your focus. Do yourself a favor: uninstall social media apps and free up your mind! Then you'll finally be able to work on what really matters."

Hannah smiled, her spirits lifting as she listened. The idea of a clean phone screen sparked a realization: she had the power to take control of her time and stop letting distractions prevent her from growing.

Then, I shared my thoughts: "Absolutely! Another great way to build willpower and energy is exercise. It not only improves your physical strength, but also boosts your mood and resilience, and prepares you for life's upcoming challenges, such as pregnancy and parenthood."

John, one of the group members, spoke up next, his voice full of empathy. "I think you should share both your admiration and your fears with your husband. Postpartum depression is serious. I didn't realize my wife was struggling with it when our kids were young. Years later, I learned from her at a church event how tough it was for her after each of our three kids was born. I was shocked. I hadn't paid enough attention back then, and I deeply regret it. I was so focused on work and providing for the family that I missed the emotional side of things. Don't wait until it's too late. He sounds a lot like I was—too focused on work and not enough on emotional connection. You can share my story with him and encourage him to listen more closely to your needs."

Hannah nodded thoughtfully, feeling her anxiety start to ease. She was beginning to realize just how important it was to share her feelings and to take time to process them herself. By allowing herself to truly feel and express her worries, she was taking the first step toward moving forward. It wasn't just about opening up to her partner. She started to understand her own feelings and found some clarity to move forward. This shift in perspective gave her a sense of relief, and for the first time in a while, she felt a glimmer of hope that things could get better.

I followed up with more reassurance: "John, thank you so much for sharing something so personal. You're all on the right track! Your relationships are strong, and it's clear that all of you are putting in the effort. That's what really matters. You're doing the work with your partner to understand each other better and grow together. Hannah, baby blues might come, but you're not alone. Matt will be there for you every step of the way. There are things you can do to get you better prepared, such as making a list of what brings you joy, clearly communicating it to your partner, and finding ways to stay grounded during tough times. These will make all the difference when you step into parenthood."

Hannah felt deeply moved by all the support she was receiving. She smiled, a new confidence shining in her eyes. That evening, she sat down for a heartfelt conversation with Matt. And to her surprise, he seemed to understand the emotional weight of her words.

## Heart of Dreams

Matt looked at Hannah, his expression softening, and shared something she had only dreamed of: "I've been saving for our babymoon," he said, with excitement in his eyes. "I'm planning to take you to the Maldives, a quiet resort with a private white-sand beach and crystal-clear turquoise waters. We'll stay in an exclusive overwater villa, where you can walk from the beach and see colorful fish swimming beneath you. After a meal prepared by a private chef, we'll visit the Sea of Stars and watch the glowing creatures light up the shore. I'll hold you tight and say, 'You're my star.' My life changed the day I met you. I'm so grateful we're bringing a new life into this world together, and I hope it's a girl, so she can carry your passion and brilliance. I'm here, to learn and grow with both of you. I love you."

In that moment, Hannah's heart melted. She had never imagined her man could be so thoughtful and romantic. It wasn't about the luxurious destination or the extravagant plans—it was the thought, care, and love behind it that mattered most. "I didn't know you had such an expensive taste!" she laughed, trying to hold back her tears. "But honestly, I'd be happy as long as you're holding me tight, no matter where we are."

This conversation marked a turning point for both of them. They realized that it wasn't about grand gestures or solving everything at once. It was about making consistent, intentional efforts to connect, listen with care, and meet each other's needs. It was about showing up, supporting each other, and making small but meaningful steps to strengthen their emotional bond. They both began to understand that love and connection take ongoing effort, and it wasn't just about fixing problems—it was about nurturing their relationship every single day.

From that moment on, Hannah and Matt began taking small but intentional steps to bridge their emotional gap. They started creating moments for connection, like taking day trips, having uninterrupted conversations, and making time for each other despite their busy lives. When she shared her fears and self-doubt, he didn't try to solve everything. Instead, he listened, acknowledged her feelings, and offered support. He was learning to hold back on practical solutions, and instead, create space to process emotions and nurture their relationship along the way.

Through this process, they realized that real change doesn't happen all at once. It's a journey, taken one small step at a time. By showing up for each other, sharing what they needed, and allowing themselves to be vulnerable, they grew closer and started to dream bigger together. The journey wasn't always easy, but it was worth it. As their emotional bond grew stronger, they felt more confident tackling life's and money's challenges side by side, fueled by love, understanding, and fresh energy.

## Real Change Happens When You Take the Lead

Change is inevitable. It happens to all of us, sometimes out of the blue. But there's a big difference between a change that happens to you and a real change that you actively initiate. The starting point of transformation is anticipation. It begins with an inner drive to make things different, to make a lasting commitment that makes your life more aligned with your values and to bring alive what you truly care about.

Take, for example, the experience of starting a new job. If you lose your job due to layoffs and are forced to find a new job, the change is happening to you. Your resistance to this change is likely high, and you might even feel overwhelmed or resentful. The external pressures of that change don't necessarily lead to personal growth. On the contrary, the stress you feel can be often unhealthy and unproductive, since it stems from things outside your control.

Now, compare that to a situation where you make the choice to pursue a new job or career path, knowing exactly what you want. If you are actively seeking change, embracing the uncertainty, and excited about the possibilities that come with a new chapter, real change happens. You are stepping into the unknown, but with a positive mindset and the belief that this journey is an opportunity for growth. It's an inward shift—one that happens because you're ready to make it happen, rather than just responding to external circumstances, feeling you don't have a choice.

This difference in mindset is important because real change starts from within. It's not just about the shifting external environment; it's about your willingness to embrace it and see it as an opportunity rather than an obstacle. Even when change is forced upon you, the way you respond and your internal attitude determine whether it will be a transformational experience.

For instance, when life throws challenges at you, like the loss of a loved one or an unexpected illness, you may not be able to control the external circumstances. But you can control how you respond. Your internal shift from feeling helpless or defeated to choosing to face the situation the best you can and create something new is what leads to real change. By embracing the change and seeing it as an opportunity to grow, to expand your horizon, you empower yourself to move forward and create new possibilities.

Real change is about actively creating the future you want. It begins with your desire to turn things around and your willingness to take the necessary steps. Instead of waiting for things to happen, try taking the lead and deciding that now is the time to create something better for yourself. Once that internal shift happens, everything else follows.

Ask yourself: Do I want to do nothing, or do I want to really change? The journey begins with your courage to overcome discomfort and fear, to take the leap, and to actively shape your future.

## Starting with a Clean Slate

Transforming ourselves to reach financial freedom and emotional well-being isn't always a straight path. For Nicole and Scott, both in their early fifties, the journey had been filled with both highs and lows. Scott, a successful and passionate commercial and fine art photographer, ran his own studio, and Nicole joined him in the business a few years ago. Things were going well until COVID hit, bringing everything to a halt. Their business, which had once been booming, was now struggling, and they found themselves with a $200,000 business loan. As 2024 rolled around, the weight of this debt, paired with mounting credit card bills, left them feeling overwhelmed.

With so many challenges, they reached out to me for help to find a way forward. Like many couples in debt, they were losing sleep over financial stress and their hearts strained. The first thing we did was explore what truly mattered to them. We dug deep into their values and dreams, then made a plan to rebuild both their finances and their emotional connection.

Nicole, in particular, was determined to turn things around. She had always been the one pushing for growth and wanted a better future for herself, Scott, and their family. With a renewed focus on their finances, we started by making adjustments to bring in more income. Nicole had always dreamed of becoming a realtor, but knowing that it takes most mid-career professionals eighteen to thirty-six months to build a reliable income in real estate, she also took on a part-time job at a local grocery store with excellent benefits and a supportive work environment.

Despite their best efforts, a shadow of debt loomed over them. Their credit card balance, which had started at $20,000, had slowly doubled to $40,000. The turning point came, following the passing of Nicole's dad. She had been covering a significant portion of his hospice care costs, expecting to be reimbursed by his life insurance policy. But when the payout came through, it was barely enough to cover her mom's growing credit card debt—another financial setback that hit hard.

Nicole found herself facing a harsh new reality: her mother's financial situation was just as precarious as her own. The weight of debt, coupled with the uncertainty of the future, left her feeling trapped. In the midst of grieving and making funeral arrangements, Nicole's financial world shifted dramatically.

The constant pressure of the numbers weighed heavily on her. She remembered her father's quiet worry in his final years when his health was deteriorating. He'd always tried to shield her from his own financial struggles, something that was never openly discussed in their family. Sitting by his headstone, Nicole realized she was on the same path, and that the burden might one day fall on Samantha, her daughter who was about to graduate college. She thought of the photo Samantha had sent from her cultural immersion trip to Paris, her face beaming with joy and hope. At that moment, Nicole made a promise to herself: she would not let her situation become her daughter's burden. "I don't want Samantha to have to take care of me financially when I get older," she confided in Scott. "I need to break this cycle."

That realization was a turning point. Nicole committed herself to taking control of her finances, not just for her own sake, but for her family's future. She created a budget, focused on saving, and began contributing to her Roth IRA. She even encouraged Samantha to put $100 a month from her internship earnings into her own Roth IRA, planting the seed of financial independence in her daughter.

The road to recovery wasn't easy. With Scott's support and encouragement, Nicole made some sacrifices. She traded dinners out for home-cooked meals, canceled subscriptions she didn't need, and took on extra shifts at work. She learned to say "no" to things she couldn't afford yet, sold things she no longer needed, and started tracking every dollar. The hardest part was confronting her own habits—shopping for comfort, ignoring statements, and hoping that things would magically improve. But each step, no matter how small, brought her closer to the financial freedom she craved. Soon, the debt began to shrink. Nicole discovered a strength she hadn't realized she had. Slowly, the shame began to fade, replaced by pride in every small victory.

Nicole and Scott's financial journey was about more than numbers. It was about moving past their history and building a future they could be proud of. Every effort they made brought them closer to a life of independence and stability, for themselves, their family, and especially their daughter. It wasn't easy, but it gave them strength. And they were finally on the path they had always dreamed of.

A year later, Nicole stood proudly as Samantha received her diploma. She felt pride for her daughter's achievement, and for the new path she'd forged for both of them. Nicole knew there was still work ahead, but she no longer felt trapped. She had taken control of her money and life, and that made all the difference.

"Mom, thank you so much for taking care of me all these years. I know it hasn't been easy, especially with everything going on with the business and grandpa. Your strength and resilience have inspired me to do better every day," Samantha said, her voice full of gratitude.

Nicole's heart swelled with pride, her chest tight with emotion. She never imagined that all the sacrifices and struggles could lead to such a moment of connection and understanding. She smiled, holding back tears, "I'm so proud of you, and I can't wait to see the incredible life you're going to live!"

It was a beautiful moment—a reflection of how far they had all come. This journey wasn't just about managing debt; it was about shifting their mindset and embracing a new path. Nicole and Scott learned the power of emotional honesty, shared goals, and small, actionable steps toward financial freedom. Much like Hannah and Matt, their transformation was about more than just money. It was about embracing real change, facing challenges together, and building a life that truly felt meaningful to them.

## To Live or to Get By

As I reflect on my journey over the past forty years of life, I can't help but think of the many pivotal moments in my life—decisions that forced me to step out of my comfort zone and really live. These moments weren't always easy, but they shaped me into who I am today. The difference between simply existing and truly living comes down to one thing: *the desire for change.*

Oscar Wilde famously said, "To live is the rarest thing in the world. Most people exist, that is all." How often do we find ourselves just getting by, doing what we're supposed to do and meeting expectations, but not fully embracing the life we truly want?

## Low-Stakes Life: Going with the Flow

Growing up, my life followed a script that was set by my parents. They were teachers, dedicated to stability and tradition, and I was the product of their hopes and ideals. From childhood through college, everything was planned out for me—after-school tutoring, chosen extracurricular activities, and constant reminders to stay on the "right" path and not to get "distracted." The goal was clear: excel academically, get a respectable job, settle down, and live a predictable, comfortable life.

When I was growing up, I didn't have much chance to explore who I really was or enjoy the things I loved. At fourteen, my dad took away all my games, comic books, novels, and even my Japanese study materials. He thought the only languages that mattered for school were Chinese and English. He didn't give them back until I passed my middle school exams a year later. My mom chose my university major based on job opportunities, not what I was passionate about. Even my friends and relationships were chosen to fit what my parents thought was best.

I got really good at meeting everyone's expectations, but deep inside, I felt like a scared hamster trapped in a cage that gave me safety but no freedom. That cage didn't lock me up forever, though. My desire to get out pushed me to learn what it truly means to live life on my own terms.

## High-Stakes Life: Choosing My Own Path

The more I followed the script, the more I realized how much I resented it. My parents' choices for me, from my major to my relationships, felt suffocating. The turning point came when I told them I wanted to study abroad. They vehemently opposed the idea, fearing the financial strain and the uncertainty about my future. They also worried I'd get "lost at sea" without the safety of my family. But their resistance only made me more determined. I began saving for my plan, took on part-time jobs, and pushed forward, even when things felt uncertain and people doubted me.

The real leap came in 2010 when I accepted a private equity job in West Africa, a place few of my peers had even considered. I knew it would be met with skepticism and concern from my parents, so I waited until I had already landed in Nouakchott, Mauritania, to tell them about my new job. The challenges were immediate: navigating a new culture, dealing with unreliable infrastructure, and the loneliness of being far from home. But there was also something incredibly freeing about it. The experience challenged me to negotiate deals, present to investors, build relationships, and solve problems. It was demanding, yes, but it was also exhilarating.

Had I stayed in China, I would have followed the same predictable path: a stable job, an old apartment and a mortgage, marriage, and kids. I would have continued to live under the weight of my family's expectations, gradually losing my freedom and dreams. Moving to Africa was the first of many high-stakes decisions that set the course for everything else to come.

## The United States: Reinventing Myself

After two years in Africa, I had saved enough money to chase my dream of studying in a developed country. But then I arrived at another crossroads: stay in China with my high-profile career or take a leap and start fresh in the US. Staying would have been the safe, easier path, building on what I already had. But I felt stuck and unhappy. I knew I wasn't reaching my full potential, and it was time for a new breakthrough.

Studying in the US was more than just earning another degree—it was about reinventing who I was. The American education system, with its focus on critical thinking and innovation, was the complete opposite of the hierarchical, male-led environment I had known. I was determined to surround myself with people with different backgrounds and to challenge myself both in my mind and heart. It wasn't easy: I felt homesick, faced cultural differences, and struggled with the pressure to prove myself. But each challenge became a chance to grow stronger.

## Saving and Investing: The Road to Freedom

Armed with new knowledge, I entered the workforce with a fresh perspective on money. I realized that financial security wasn't just about having enough to get by—it was about having the freedom to make choices without being bound by fear. I committed to saving aggressively, putting away 40% of my income even if it meant living frugally. This discipline paid off over the years, as the stock market and real estate markets surged. The journey wasn't always smooth—there were tenant issues, market downturns, and moments of doubt. But the habit of saving and investing gave me a sense of control over my life and my future.

Looking back, I realize that if I hadn't made the decision to prioritize saving and investing, I'd still be stuck in the cycle of making ends meet, with no clear path forward. Financial freedom isn't just about building wealth. It's about having the power to choose your own path. It's about walking away from situations that no longer serve you and creating the life you want.

## Entrepreneurship: Breaking the Shackles

When I finally reached financial freedom, I faced a big choice: keep my comfortable remote job with a great boss or take a risk and become an entrepreneur. The job was stable, the pay was good, and failure wasn't likely. But deep inside, I knew I wanted something more. The idea of spending years stuck in the same routine felt suffocating.

Quitting my job was terrifying. I gave up security for a future full of unknowns. My parents thought I was making a huge mistake, and my husband wanted me to have a clear plan, a timeline, and a backup plan. He was smart, but it also added a lot of pressure on me. The beginning of my entrepreneurship journey was tough. I worked long hours, felt the constant pressure to make money, and kept trying new ideas, knowing most wouldn't work. I was always solving problems and learning new skills, building systems, and navigating a fiercely competitive market. But with every challenge, I grew stronger. I discovered a sense of purpose and fulfillment I'd never felt in a corporate job. Through all the ups and downs, my husband and I grew closer, and I became an inspiration for others wanting to change careers, proving it's possible to build a business and life on your own terms.

The rewards went beyond business success. Entrepreneurship reignited my ambition and reminded me that the future is full of possibilities for those willing to take the leap.

*Are you really living your life to the fullest?*

The biggest changes we face can be scary, but they are also what make life truly meaningful. My journey has taught me that real strength comes from leaving comfort behind and accepting the unknown. Every bold step I took, even when it was incredibly hard, brought me closer to the life I've always wanted. The truth is, it's not about waiting for the perfect moment—nothing will ever be perfect. It's about deciding to take control and live fully, with the future in mind.

Ask yourself: Am I just going through the motions, or am I really living? How big are my dreams, and how much am I willing to risk? The choice is yours.

## The Wisdom of Master Jinghui (净慧禅师)

Life can have many setbacks, hardships, and moments of uncertainty. However, some of the most profound transformations come, not from dodging life's tough times, but from facing them head-on and letting them shape us. Master Jinghui, my Zen teacher, showed me that even the hardest moments can become turning points, teaching me how to find meaning and strength in the midst of adversity.

My journey with Master Jinghui began just before I moved to Africa, during one of the toughest times in my life. On the personal side, I was stuck in a rocky, on-and-off relationship that brought out the worst in me—anger, bitterness, and ignoring how others felt. Professionally, I was feeling lost after working for a "social enterprise" for months without receiving any pay, despite being promised a salary of 6,000 RMB a month (about $900 USD at the time). With my world turned upside down, I found myself seeking wisdom and peace through meditation, hoping it would guide me to find my path forward.

Master Jinghui's teachings on life and spirituality had a profound impact on me. He often spoke about suffering—not as something to avoid, but as something to embrace and learn from. "Suffering is inevitable," he said, "but how we respond to it shapes our lives." His words resonated deeply with me.

He emphasized that we should strive for enlightenment in life and dedicate ourselves to something bigger than ourselves. His teachings were a constant reminder that much of the suffering in the world stems from the disconnect between our heart's desires and the harsh realities of life. Master Jinghui believed that much of our suffering comes from the stories we tell ourselves about what's happening in our lives. He taught that only we have the power to heal and change those stories from within.

This was a wake-up call for me. I had been blaming the world around me for my unhappiness, but I now understood that I had the power to change my response and action. Jinghui's wisdom helped me see that the results of my choices or not making any were mine to face. It was up to me to take responsibility and find my own way to solve my problems.

He also taught that satisfaction through material things is not the ultimate goal in life. Inner peace and spiritual abundance are the true foundations of happiness. When facing life's impermanence and suffering, we must confront it, not escape it. To transcend ourselves, we must break through our limitations in the present moment. We can only find peace and freedom from our hearts, not from the outside world. True liberation starts with acknowledging our suffering, then training ourselves through practice to overcome it.

You might be thinking, "Why should I listen to him? What does he really know about my life?" Let me share his story with you. Maybe it will inspire you to see things differently.

Master Jinghui (1933–2013) was born into poverty in Hubei Province, China. As an infant, he was sent to live in a Buddhist nunnery and was raised by two nuns. When he was seventeen, political turmoil forced his adoptive mother to leave the monastery and return to regular life. After being apart for three years, they had a deeply emotional reunion that stayed with him forever. While many monks at that time gave up their vows or even married, Jinghui stayed true to his faith. He then made a long journey, mostly on foot, of around 600 miles to Guangdong Province to study under the famous Zen master Xuyun (虚云和尚).

During the political chaos of 1962, leading up to the Cultural Revolution, Master Jinghui was punished for editing the works of Master Xuyun. Local officials labeled his religious work as "counter-revolutionary," and he was sent to labor camps for sixteen years. Even through extreme hardship and isolation,

Master Jinghui never lost faith. In 1978, after years of suffering, he was finally allowed to return to his temple.

Over the next three decades, Master Jinghui not only restored and reconstructed eight major temples across China, but he also served as the editor-in-chief of one of the most influential academic and Dharma journals in Chinese Buddhism. His efforts restored both the physical and spiritual heritage of Chinese Buddhism, ensuring its vitality for future generations. In 1993, he was elected Vice President of the Buddhist Association of China, a role he held until his passing in 2013.

Master Jinghui created and championed the idea of practicing Zen in everyday life (生活禅). He was deeply committed to sharing Zen teachings and helping people grow spiritually. He also founded the first week-long, overnight Zen summer retreat at his temple, which was completely free and open to anyone who wanted to apply and join. This retreat became a cherished tradition, offering hundreds each year the opportunity to deepen their understanding and practice of Zen. His work touched the lives of hundreds of thousands, if not millions, across China and beyond, leaving a powerful and lasting legacy in the world.

What drove him to do all this? He once said, "Because I have personally experienced what it's like to lose my freedom, I know just how precious it is. And I refuse to waste it."

Through his teachings, I learned to embrace my struggles instead of being overwhelmed by them. He showed me that true strength doesn't come from avoiding pain, but from facing it head-on, accepting it, and allowing it to guide you toward growth. This shift in mindset helped me see that challenges aren't obstacles—they are stepping stones toward transformation. Instead of viewing obstacles as walls, I began to see them as opportunities to deepen my practice and pursue freedom in every aspect of my life. Whether it's financial freedom, emotional freedom, or spiritual freedom, that pursuit has become my driving force. It's what keeps me moving forward, even when fear and doubt try to hold me back.

## Turning Adversity into Real Change

Life is full of tough moments like loss, disappointment, fear, and failure. But each of these challenging experiences also holds the potential to change us in a deep and meaningful way. When we stop pushing away the pain and instead lean into it with courage, we make room for healing and growth. This helps us build deeper connections with ourselves and the people we care about, while also seeing the world around us more clearly and with new understanding.

The key is to acknowledge that we don't need to have it all figured out. We don't need to be perfect. By confronting life's struggles with openness, empathy, and a willingness to change, we find that we can grow stronger, more resilient, and more aligned with our deepest values.

So if you are navigating a difficult phase in life right now, remember: it's not about avoiding the pain—it's about learning to move through it. Real change happens when we don't let hardship define us but allow it to refine us.

With this in mind, let's pause and take a moment for you to envision real change in your own life. The following exercises will help you turn adversity into a powerful catalyst for transformation.

## Now, It's Your Turn!

Are you ready to get started on your own transformation? This is where the real magic happens! Deep, meaningful change doesn't just appear overnight—it starts within, sparked by a strong desire to create something better. But turning that desire into action? It takes courage, preparation, and, often, the support of those around us.

The exercises in this chapter are your first steps toward making real changes, both in your relationship and your financial future. The key here is honesty. Be honest with yourself about where you are now and where you want to go. Picture the life you're aiming for. Imagine what your future could look like instead of getting stuck on today's struggles. It might seem out of reach at first, but trust me, this is the crucial starting point for creating the life you've always wanted.

What makes these exercises so powerful is that they go beyond just talking. They are about connecting, understanding, and planning with your partner. This is the foundation for real, lasting change.

So, take a moment to put down your tasks and distractions. Take a break, and really tune into your feelings. Then, share them with your partner, honestly and vulnerably. Be ready to hear their feelings with an open heart, too. There's so much power in just being fully present and supporting each other.

Remember, this isn't just an exercise. It's the beginning of a roadmap for the life you want. In the next chapter, we'll take these insights and turn them into action. We'll create the foundation for positive change in your finances, your relationship, and the life you're building together.

What do you think? Ready to dive in? Let's do this!

# Exercises for Chapter 4: Envision Real Change

## Exercise 4-1: Unity

1. Set a timer for two minutes each.

2. Share with your partner a recent moment that made your relationship stronger.

3. You'll take turns to share and listen. Decide who goes first. The listener pays full attention, keeping eye contact and not interrupting or taking notes. It's okay to use sounds like "um" or "wow" and body language.

4. Once the narrator finishes, the listener shares their feelings with: "When you said (repeat their specific words), I felt (an emotion) in (a part of my body)."

   For example:

   - "When you shared your gratitude for our partnership, I noticed joy in my smile."

   - "When you brought up planning a trip with the kids to cheer me on for the marathon, I felt warmth in my heart."

5. Switch roles and repeat the process.

## Exercise 4-2: Real Change

1. Again, set the timer for two minutes each.

2. Take turns to open up and share with each other: The real change I particularly want to make is . . . .

3. Decide who goes first. The listener pays full attention, keeping eye contact and not interrupting or taking notes. It's okay to use sounds like "um" or "wow" and body language.

4. After the narrator finishes, the listener shares their feelings with: "When you said (repeat their specific words), I felt (an emotion) in (a part of my body)."

   For example:

   - "When you talked about finding balance in life, I felt relief at the back of my neck."

   - "When you mentioned transitioning to a new career, I felt excitement in my chest."

5. Switch roles and repeat.

## Exercise 4-3: Vision

1. Now it's time to picture the change you want to create. Take a moment to reflect on the changes you want and how you'd feel as you are making meaningful progress. Write down and share with your partner: What kind of progress will make you feel happy in one year, six months, and six weeks?

| In A Year | In Six Months | In Six Weeks |
|-----------|---------------|--------------|
|           |               |              |

2. Decide who narrates first while the other listens without interrupting.

3. Switch roles and repeat.

## Exercise 4-4: A New Path

1. Take two minutes each to share: What can you do today to get you closer to your goal?

2. Decide who goes first. The listener pays full attention, keeping eye contact and not interrupting or taking notes. It's okay to use sounds like "um" or "wow" and body language.

3. After the narrator finishes, the listener will make a statement of feeling, and then guide the narrator to answer these two questions: "When do you plan to do it?" and "Who can help you?"

4. Switch roles and repeat.

## Exercise 4-5: Support System

1. Please take two minutes to write down who in your life—friends, family, professional connections, or industry groups—can support you during this transition.

2. Discuss how to make the most of these resources.

3. Discuss when new support might be needed. Maybe there are people you haven't yet reached out to that could help or new networks to explore.

## Exercise 4-6: Partners in Transition

1. What moments or experiences have helped you and your partner understand each other better? These could be small or big, but they've made a real impact on your relationship.

2. Take two minutes to write down the moments that helped you both connect better and share them with your partner.

3. Discuss how you can facilitate these moments in future interactions.

Before you move on to the next chapter, take a moment to jot down your thoughts and insights from the exercises. Reflect on what came up for you. How did you feel? What did you learn about yourself and your partner? Writing down your answers helps solidify these insights and gives you something to look back on as you continue your journey.

# Your Reflection

Take a moment to jot down your thoughts and experiences from the exercise. Use this space to capture any insights, feelings, or ideas that came up.

_____

_____

_____

_____

_____

_____

_____

_____

_____

_____

_____

_____

_____

_____

# CHAPTER 5

# Master Money Basics

In 2016, during my second year working in the US, I calculated my financial freedom number using the 4% rule[9]. By 2021, I had hit that milestone. I didn't overthink it at the time, but since then, I've been asked by many people how I did it. Here's the simple truth: when it comes to managing money and creating a secure, fulfilling life, I've always kept a few core principles close to my heart. These principles have guided every decision I've made and every action I've taken. They're not just good advice; they're guiding principles that keep me grounded, confident, and moving forward no matter what life throws my way.

## 1. Live Below Your Means

Spending less than what you make is the foundation of financial stability. It doesn't matter how high your salary is if you're constantly overspending. The key is simple: spend less than you make, or follow a plan so you know where your money is

---

[9] The 4% rule is a popular guideline to help plan for retirement. It states that in your first year of retirement, you can safely take out about 4% of your investment portfolio. In the following years, you just adjust that number for inflation. If you stick to this rule, there's a good chance your money will last for 30 years.

going. Life can get chaotic, and unexpected expenses will eventually pop up. Having a cushion for those bumps in the road is essential.

Think of living below your means as your personal safety net, and the best way to build that net is to "pay yourself first." This is especially crucial if you're an entrepreneur. Paying yourself first means automatically setting aside a portion of your income for savings before you spend a single dollar elsewhere. It's a form of forced savings that ensures your future self is always covered.

No matter where life takes you, whether you're changing careers, raising a family, going back to school, or launching new ventures, having savings set aside gives you the freedom to handle life's curveballs without unnecessary stress. It's more than just filling up your piggy bank; it's about building real confidence and peace of mind for whatever comes next.

The key isn't making one-off good decisions; it's building smart habits. Saving should be as routine as your morning coffee—automatic, reliable, and part of your daily rhythm. Many of us, though, are on autopilot when it comes to spending. Here's a quick reality check: Can you recall what you bought online last week? Or last month? If you're curious, scroll through your order history and see how many purchases are actually still in use today. In 2024, the average US household spent about $2,700 on Amazon, making seventy-one purchases a year[10]. Imagine if even a fraction of that spending became automatic saving instead. Small changes, repeated over time, can completely transform your financial future.

---

[10] www.chainstoreage.com/news-briefs/2024-09-12

*"Do not save what is left after spending, but spend what is left after saving."* — *Warren Buffett*

My husband and I used to save an impressive 40% of everything we made each year. Then I left my corporate job to start my own business, and our savings dropped to 25%. But I'm determined to get back to saving 40% within the next three years! So how did we manage to save so much in the first place? Getting creative with our housing and cutting back on other expenses helped us start strong early on.

Our first home was a two-flat building in Chicago, where we lived in one unit and rented out the other. The rental income covered 70% of the mortgage while allowing us to live in a prime location. This made it easier for us to save more each month. We still own that property today, and with both units rented out, it continues to generate positive cash flow.

When it came to travel, we made the most of work trips by planning weekend getaways before or after business commitments. We'd explore new cities for minimal extra cost, making the most of our time and money.

I also love high quality pre-loved and pre-owned items. Most of my kids' clothes in the early years were hand-me-downs from friends and family. And some of my favorite things I've bought were from estate sales. Buying gently used items saved us money and was better for the environment, too!

We both worked hard to move up in our careers, and as our family grew, our paychecks grew too. That helped us keep up with rising costs while still saving 40% of what we earned. It wasn't about giving things up. Instead, it was about being creative, making smart choices, and spending money in ways that matched our goals for the future.

We also pay attention to what and where we shop for groceries. Having a list written down is now a habit that's been passed down to my eight-year-old son. He takes so much pride in going down the shopping list and finding them at WinCo Foods every weekend!

Living below your means doesn't mean you have to miss out. It's about being thoughtful and sticking with good habits. When you save on things that don't really make you happy, you build up money that gives you more options and freedom later on. This way, your finances are ready to handle whatever surprises life or your income might bring.

## Snapshot 1
### (My LinkedIn Post on 10/22/2024)

Thirteen years ago, I was wrapping up my career in private equity in West Africa and preparing for my MBA in the US. New country, new start. So, of course, I needed to look the part!

I treated myself to an Italian tote for $400—coated canvas, just like Louis Vuitton bags. It symbolized my dream to keep traveling the world in style.

Naturally, I paired it with a $1,500 MacBook Air, because my bulky ThinkPad wasn't fitting in that sleek new bag. I thought I was all set!

But reality hit fast. Coated canvas? Just a fancy name for plastic. And plastic stretches. Soon, my world-traveling tote looked like an inflated balloon. And Excel on a Mac back then? Let's just say it's like trying to teach a cat to do your taxes—adorable but completely useless. 🐱 💸

Both the bag and the Mac soon ended up in the back of my closet, reflecting on their poor performance.

Fast forward to today, and I've been to over twenty countries and lived on three continents. I've realized that connections and memories are worth far more than how things look. Now, I'm a financial life planner helping others avoid these same mistakes and focus on what really matters. True freedom comes from what works long-term, not just what looks good in the moment.

That's why I carry a $20 backpack (over ten years old already) and a Dell from Costco (on sale, of course!) that handles everything I need. Function over fashion, every time! 🤓

So, what's a purchase you regret? And how did it change your perspective?

(Photo: Me enjoying my brief moment of style with that Italian tote while traveling through Europe— before I learned to focus on substance over surface.)

## 2. Keep Investing

The stock market is probably the easiest investment most people can get their hands on: it's accessible, with standard-ized trading systems, minimal transaction and holding cost (if you buy low cost index funds, not actively managed funds or mutual funds), and doesn't require your attention most of the time. There's one downside though: investing in stocks can feel like a rollercoaster ride. And many of us have experienced that first-hand over the years. But here's the thing: the rollercoaster never stops. The market will always have its ups and downs, but the key to building wealth is *staying committed to investing, no matter how wild the ride may seem*. Whether stocks are soaring or crashing, sticking to the right investment strategy is key.

Making money may seem simple. Just buy low and sell high. But many people do the opposite! When a stock is doing well and everyone is talking about it, it is easy to jump in out of fear of missing out, not realizing they are buying at the peak price. Then, when the market drops, like during the 2007 to 2009 financial crisis or COVID, panic takes over. Investors often sell at a loss, worried prices will fall even more, and wait too long to get back in until prices recover. It feels natural emotionally, but these choices can cost a lot of money in the long run.

Instead, think long-term: If you had invested just **$100** in the S&P 500 index forty years ago, with dividends reinvested, it would have grown to **$4,526** today, assuming the historical average annual return of 10%. That's far more than a savings account, which would have turned $100 into just $221 over the same time period with a 2% annual interest rate.

Figure 5: Investor's Emotional Ride—Buy, Panic, Regret, Repeat

Here's what's even more amazing: Imagine you invested just $100 each month for twenty years, starting forty years ago. With an average 10% return, your $24,000 total investment would be worth about $486,269 today. This isn't magic—it's the power of sticking with your investments over time and letting compound interest work for you.

Even if you started a little later, the difference is still huge. For instance, if you invested $100 a month for twenty years starting twenty years ago, your $24,000 would be worth about $72,352 today. That's triple what you put in! The main point is this: the sooner you start, the more your money can grow for you.

So don't panic or try to time the market. Just keep investing, and you'll reach your goals over time. *Investing early and regularly* is one of the best ways to build wealth. It helps you handle market ups and downs without worrying about every little drop. Even when the market crashes, if you keep investing, your money will grow steadily over time. Stay calm, stick with it, and the rest will fall into place!

Also, we'll dive deeper into details of asset allocation and risk management in the next chapter.

## 3. Skills + Passion = Freedom

Most people don't figure out their true passion right away. Finding it takes time, sometimes years or even decades. In the meantime, you'll need to make a living to support your lifestyle until you can fully follow your passion. Interests and money can come and go, but skills stick with you for life. When you invest in learning skills, especially ones that are in demand, you boost your earning power for the long haul. The more you build your skills, the more valuable you become, making it easier to find life-changing opportunities. It's like upgrading your personal software, helping you stand out at work and unlocking doors others might not reach.

So, what should you focus on? Two key skills: selling and net-working, plus how to provide real value.

Sales and networking are important for any kind of business or making a difference, no matter your industry. Knowing how to sell yourself, your ideas, or your products, and how to connect with people the right way, can create a lot of opportunities and help you get noticed. But it's not just about talking to the right people. It's about understanding how you can help and bring value to others too!

Once you've mastered these two essential skills, it's time to build upon them by aligning your work with your passions. When you truly love what you do, work doesn't feel like work anymore. It becomes fun and creative, and that enthusiasm leads to better performance, increased satisfaction, and higher rewards in the long run. It's a win-win-win for your boss, your heart, and your wallet!

The alignment may not happen overnight, and may not be a straight path. It's an iterative process. Whether it's deciding to pivot in your career, gaining new certifications, or starting a side hustle, the goal is to keep evolving, adapting, and creating the work that lights you up. The more aligned you are with your passion, the more enjoyable it will feel. And before you know it, you'll find yourself achieving the kind of freedom that goes beyond just financial success.

And here's the secret: You don't need seven digits in the bank to achieve freedom from work. Sometimes, it's the pursuit of what excites you and the willingness to harness your skills that can give you the freedom to walk away from the traditional grind. If you do it right, you might even reach that freedom long before you become a millionaire (but if you follow the flowchart I'm about to share with you, you'll be a millionaire sooner or later!).

# Snapshot 2
## (My LinkedIn Post on 8/12/2024)

Funny story to share: My husband recently canceled an event on our calendar titled, "By this date, Mama must be making $12,000/month revenue @ Mon Mar 31, 2025." 🎯

Quitting my job paying $150K+ in March 2023 was no easy decision, especially with two young kids and three mortgages to support (that's a story for another day). One of the biggest fears we had was not knowing when to call it quits and move to Plan B. Well, that was more my husband's fear. Mine was: What if I failed and had to return to the corporate world?

Fast forward to June 2024—before I went on a long vacation—my revenue was still less than $6K/month, and I had $15K in credit card debt with the interest-free period ending soon.

But after coming back from the Garrett Planning Network annual retreat yesterday, I'm certain there is no Plan B. The only plan is to keep doing what I love and reaching people however I can. I'm committed to making it work, no matter what. 💪✨

I think my husband saw this determination, which is why he canceled the calendar reminder. We both realized that money is just a measure, not the end goal. The real goal is living a life you truly love—and I'm already doing that. At this point, the revenue KPI is no longer relevant. 🩶

(Photo: with Sheryl Garrett and Beth Agnello at 2024 Garrett Retreat)

So, if you're ready to find the work you love and stop "working" for a living, start with finding out where you need to improve by taking baby steps!

## Smarter, Happier Money: The Eleven-Question Adventure

Now that we've covered the principles, let's get practical! I've created a simple flow chart to help you understand where you are on your financial journey. Check it out and see which steps you're currently working on. Once you have a clearer picture of where you stand, we'll dive into why each step matters and explore resources to help you take it to the next level!

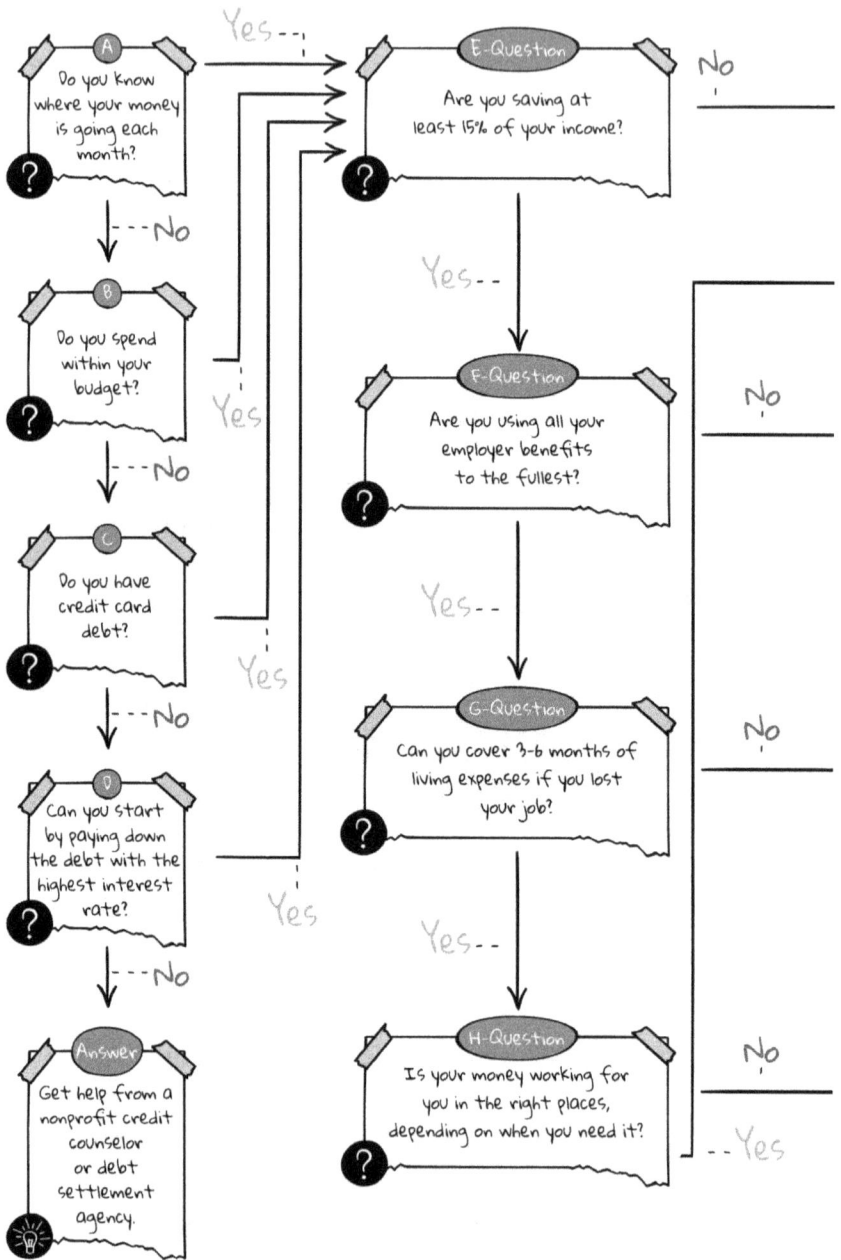

**A** — Do you know where your money is going each month?

Yes → **E-Question**: Are you saving at least 15% of your income?

No ↓

**B** — Do you spend within your budget?

No ↓

**C** — Do you have credit card debt?

Yes →

No ↓

**D** — Can you start by paying down the debt with the highest interest rate?

Yes →

No ↓

**Answer** — Get help from a nonprofit credit counselor or debt settlement agency.

**E-Question**: Are you saving at least 15% of your income?

No ___

Yes →

**F-Question**: Are you using all your employer benefits to the fullest?

No

Yes →

**G-Question**: Can you cover 3-6 months of living expenses if you lost your job?

No

Yes →

**H-Question**: Is your money working for you in the right places, depending on when you need it?

No ___

--Yes

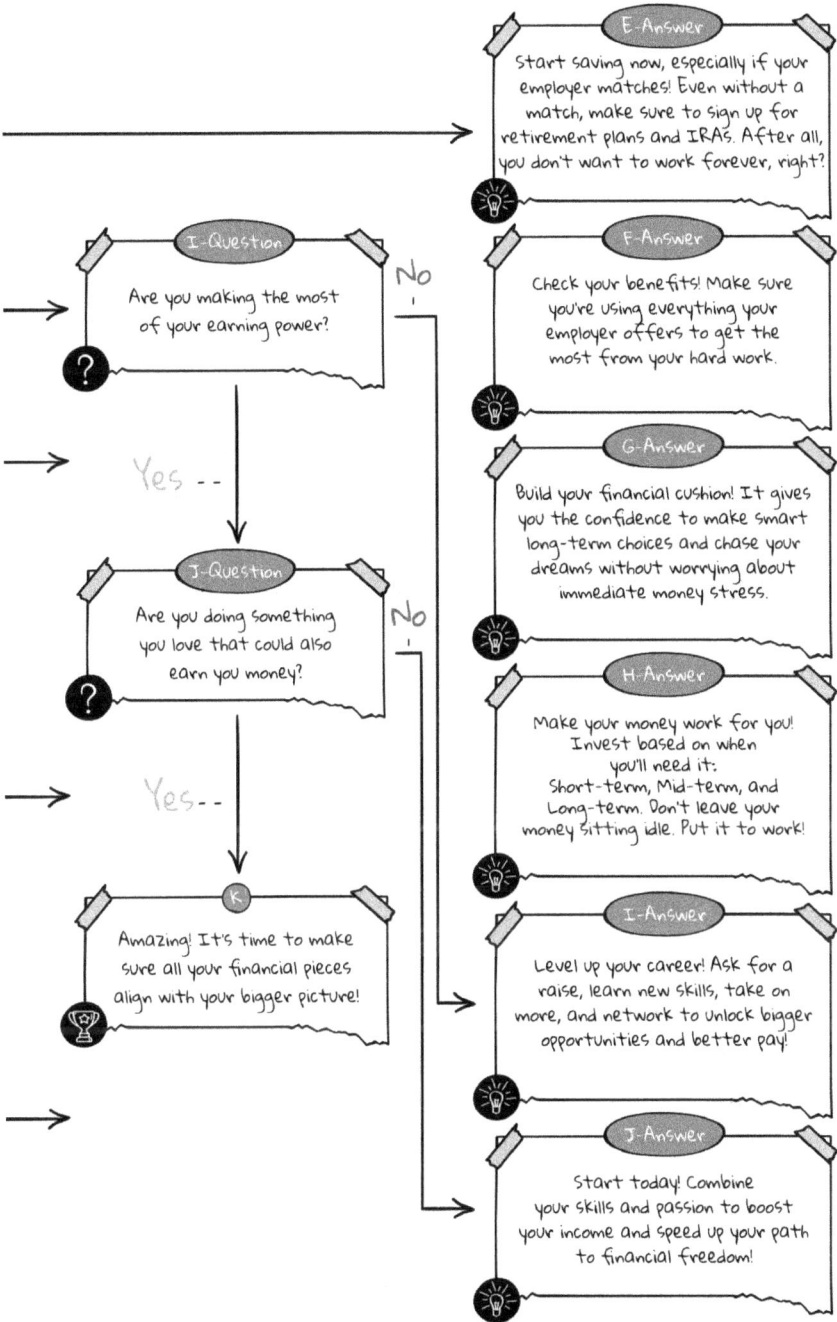

**E-Answer**

Start saving now, especially if your employer matches! Even without a match, make sure to sign up for retirement plans and IRAs. After all, you don't want to work forever, right?

**I-Question**

Are you making the most of your earning power?

No -

Yes --

**F-Answer**

Check your benefits! Make sure you're using everything your employer offers to get the most from your hard work.

**G-Answer**

Build your financial cushion! It gives you the confidence to make smart long-term choices and chase your dreams without worrying about immediate money stress.

**J-Question**

Are you doing something you love that could also earn you money?

No -

Yes--

**H-Answer**

Make your money work for you! Invest based on when you'll need it: Short-term, Mid-term, and Long-term. Don't leave your money sitting idle. Put it to work!

**K**

Amazing! It's time to make sure all your financial pieces align with your bigger picture!

**I-Answer**

Level up your career! Ask for a raise, learn new skills, take on more, and network to unlock bigger opportunities and better pay!

**J-Answer**

Start today! Combine your skills and passion to boost your income and speed up your path to financial freedom!

## How Did You Do?

**A for Ability**: This is your first step toward financial freedom. Do you really know where your money goes each month? A 2023 survey showed that about half of Americans feel confident managing their money—budgeting, tracking spending, and handling debt. Another third are getting there, and 13% admit they don't know much about their finances at all. If you're in that "working on it" group, that's great news! Starting to track your money now is a powerful step that can lead to more control, confidence, and freedom down the road. You've got this!

**B for Budget:** The "B word." Let's face it, no one really loves budgeting. Only one-third of US adults actually create and stick to a written or digital budget. The rest track spending informally or don't budget at all. In the early days, I tracked every transaction, but as time passed, I settled into habits that no longer required close attention. If your spending isn't providing peace and lasting happiness, or if you have no idea where your money is going, following a spending plan could be your next big goal that can be broken down into smaller steps. But trust me, you can get really good at it in just a few months!

**C for Credit Card Debt:** According to recent data from the Federal Reserve and other sources, the average US household carries about $7,321 in credit card debt as of early 2025. Households that carry revolving credit card balances owe even more, typically around $9,000 or higher depending on the state. Credit card interest rates currently average around 21% to 24%, and if your interest rate is about 25%, your balance can grow quickly—potentially doubling in less than three years if you only make minimum payments. To put this in perspective, Warren Buffett's Berkshire Hathaway achieved an average annual return of about 19.9% from 1965 to 2024. That means credit card debt at high interest rates grows faster than even one of the most successful investments in history! If you're not paying your balance off in full every month, it's crucial to act now and pay down that debt before it spirals out of control.

**D for Other Debts: Make sure they work for you!** Not all debt is created equal. Some can help you grow, while others can drag you down. Here's a fun way to think about the different kinds:

- **Bad Debt: The Money Gobbler**

  Think of credit card debt like a hungry ghost chomping away at your wallet! It is usually high interest debt on things that lose value fast, like shopping sprees or fancy vacations. Why avoid it? Because you end up paying way more than what those things are actually worth. There are smarter ways to spend. Check the previous section or see Chapter 6 for more ideas on how to live below your means and start saving!

- **Risky Debt: The Rollercoaster**

  This debt is like hopping on a wild ride—exciting, but hold on tight! It covers things like business or personal loans with high interest and lots of unknowns. Starting a business can be thrilling, but it's risky: about one in four businesses don't make it past the first year, and almost half are gone by year five[11]. If things go sideways, you could be stuck with those payments long after the fun stops!

---

[11] www.lendingtree.com/business/small/failure-rate/

- **Neutral Debt: The Slow Mover**

  Think of this as the turtle of the debt world—not super fast or flashy. It's lower-interest stuff, like a car loan or a condo with high HOA fees. These debts aren't as pricey, but the things you buy might not go up in value much. And extra costs (like those pesky HOA fees) can nibble away at any gains.

- **Good Debt: The Growth Booster**

  Now we're talking! Good debt is like planting seeds for your future. It's low-interest loans that help you build wealth, like a student loan for a degree that opens doors or a mortgage for a home in a great spot. This kind of debt can actually pay you back by helping you earn more or own something that grows in value.

**Bottom Line:**

Think of debt as a tool. Use the growth boosters to build your future, steer clear of the money gobblers, and be extra careful with the risky rollercoaster! Here's a quick chart to help make this easier to understand.

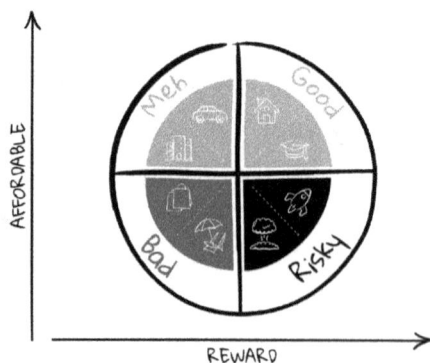

Figure 7: The Good, The Meh, The Risky, and The Ugly

**Taking Action**

Knowing where your money goes is the first step to financial stability. If you're stuck on steps A through D—whether it's budgeting, saving, or reducing debt—it might be time to seek additional help. A financial coach or financial therapist can guide you through the tough stuff and help you create a plan to move forward. Don't be afraid to ask for support when needed, as it could be the key to your financial success!

If you've answered "No" to Step D, or are struggling with debt, consider reaching out to organizations such as National Foundation for Credit Counseling (NFCC), American Consumer Credit Counseling (ACCC), GreenPath Financial Wellness, Money Management International (MMI), Take Charge America, Operation HOPE, InCharge Debt Solutions, etc. for support.

**Step E: Save 15% or more of your income.**

These days, traditional pensions are rare, and Social Security benefits probably won't be enough to cover all your retirement expenses. By saving at least 15% of your pretax income, including any money your employer adds, you give yourself a much better chance of enjoying the lifestyle you want when you retire.

Saving at this rate doesn't just help with retirement. It also helps you build an emergency fund and save for other big goals, like buying your first home or paying for education. Plus, having extra savings means you're better prepared for unexpected expenses and less likely to need to use credit card debt or personal loans.

If you want more than an average retirement, like retiring early, you'll probably need to save more. A series of interviews by ESI

Money[12] with over 400 millionaires aiming for financial independence found most were saving between 30 and 40 percent of their income. These high savers, often in their forties with kids, had an average net worth of $2.3 million.

**The bottom line**: the more you save now, the more financial security and freedom you'll have in the future.

Figure 8: Buckets of Wealth—Grow Some, Use Some!

## Step F: Make the Most of Your Employer Benefits

Getting the most out of your employer benefits means using everything your employer offers to help your finances, health, and daily life. In simple terms, don't leave free money or valuable perks unused.

Start by finding out what benefits are available to you. These can include health, dental, and vision insurance, retirement plans, life and disability insurance, paid time off, flexible work schedules, mental health support, wellness programs, tuition help, legal assistance, Health Savings Accounts (HSA), and

---

[12] www.esimoney.com

Flexible Spending Accounts (FSA) for things like healthcare, childcare, or commuting, and many more.

If you're not sure what you have or how to use them, ask your HR department or benefits administrator. Many companies also have online tools to help you understand your choices.

We'll go into more detail about tax-advantaged accounts like 401(k), HSA, and FSA in the next chapter.

## Step G: Build Your Emergency Fund

Think of your emergency fund as your financial superhero cape. It's there to save the day when life throws you a curveball, like losing a job, facing a medical emergency, or dealing with a surprise car repair. Aim to set aside enough to cover three months of basic living expenses if your household has two steady incomes, and six months if you have kids or your income isn't predictable. By "living expenses," focus on the essentials—rent or mortgage, utilities, gas, groceries—so you can keep your life running if the unexpected happens, even if you have to pause on streaming services or takeout nights.

Why is this so important? Because life is full of surprises like flat tires, leaky roofs, sick pets, sudden medical bills, or even losing your job. With an emergency fund, you won't have to panic, rack up credit card debt, or dip into your retirement savings when the unexpected happens. It could also be your "F* you Money," a cushion that gives you the freedom to make smart choices, like leaving a bad job, starting fresh, or taking the time you need to find the right next step. Having this fund means you're less dependent on stressful situations and more in control of building the life you want.

Getting started is easier than you think:

- Start small! Even $50 or $100 is a great monthly goal.
- Set up automatic transfers to your savings account so you don't have to think about it.
- Toss in any extra cash you get, like tax refunds, bonuses, birthday money—whatever comes your way.
- Keep your emergency fund in a separate, interest generating account so you're not tempted to spend it on non-emergencies.

Remember, the hardest part is just getting started. Even small, regular deposits will grow over time and give you peace of mind when life gets messy.

## Step H: Investments Made Simple

You've worked hard for your money. Now let's make your money hustle for you! Picture your investments as three different buckets, each with its own job based on when you'll need the cash. Here's how to play the "bucket game":

## Short-Term Bucket (Need the money within two years):

This is your "to use" bucket. Put your money somewhere safe, like a high-yield savings account, CDs, or Treasury bills. These options are steady and low-risk, so your money will be there when you need it, with little chance of losing value.

*Examples:* Down payment for a house, emergency fund, upcoming major appliance purchase.

## Mid-Term Bucket (Need the money in three to ten years):

This is your "to balance" bucket. Here, you can blend some bonds (safer but slower growth) with some stocks (riskier but higher potential). This balance lets your money grow while avoiding big swings, creating a happy medium.

*Examples:* Taking a career break, going back to school, saving to start a business.

## Long-Term Bucket (Do not need the money for at least ten years):

This is your "to grow" bucket! Since you won't need this money for a long time, you can take more risk for bigger rewards. Invest in low-cost index funds or diversified stocks, which have a better shot at growing over time (even if they bounce up and down in the short term).

*Examples:* Retirement savings, buying your dream home, generational wealth building.

Figure 9: Money Buckets—Grow, Balance, Use!

## Why does this matter?

The longer you can leave your money invested, the more risk you can afford to take. Markets might go up and down, but over time, they usually trend up. If you need your money soon, keep it safe. If you don't need it for a long time, let it grow!

*Examples:*

- Saving for a house in two years? Keep that money out of the stock market and stick to safer, more reliable options.

- Saving for retirement in thirty years? Index funds are your best friend. You have plenty of time to weather the ups and downs of the market and adjust your investments as you get closer to retirement.

## Pro Tip:

Everyone's situation and goals are unique, so your financial priorities might look different from your friend's or popular advice you hear. If you're unsure about your mix, consider talking with an independent financial advisor—someone who doesn't sell financial products. They can review your investments and build a plan that fits your situation. Many advisors work by the hour, typically charging between $200 and $400 per hour, and don't require a minimum investment. This approach makes professional advice more accessible and lets you pay only for what you need.

## Bottom line:

Don't let your money just sit there. Put it in the right bucket and make it work for you! The bucket approach means dividing your money into different groups based on when you'll need it. Keep some in safe, easy-to-access places for short-term needs, put some in moderate-risk investments for the next few years, and let the rest grow in higher-risk, long-term investments. This mix helps you balance safety and growth, so you can relax knowing your money is ready to help you reach your goals when the time comes.

## Step I: Level Up Your Career!

Ready to supercharge your income and unlock your full earning potential? Let's make this fun—think of your career as a video game, and you're about to hit the next level!

## Power-Up #1: Master Your Current Role

Don't just work hard—work smart! Start by having a conversation with your boss to clarify expectations and set some stretch goals together. This way, you'll know exactly what success looks like and where to make your efforts. Present your progress early and regularly to make sure you're on track and not waste time or energy in the wrong direction. This keeps you focused, efficient, and ready to shine when new opportunities come up.

## Power-Up #2: Learn New Skills

Learning new skills or earning certifications, whether it's vibe coding, data analysis, digital literacy, or some professional designations that lead to greater earning potential. Many companies will even pay for your training and exams, so check with your boss on how to develop your skills and untap new opportunities! The more skills you have, the more valuable you become.

## Power-Up #3: Negotiate like a Pro

Don't be shy—ask for that raise! Do your homework when you get off work: research what others in your field are earning, highlight your achievements, and pick the right time to make your case. Practice your pitch with a coach or mentor so you're confident when the moment comes.

## Power-Up #4: Network like a Millionaire

Networking isn't just for extroverts! Connect with coworkers, join professional groups, attend industry conferences, and reach out on LinkedIn. Building real relationships can open doors to hidden job opportunities and insider info about the best gigs.

## Power-Up #5: Befriend Headhunters

Don't overlook professional recruiters and headhunters—they're career matchmakers who can connect you with positions you might not find on your own. Keep your LinkedIn profile up to date, let them know your goals, and update them on your latest moves. Even if you're not job hunting, staying in touch can keep you in the know on salary trends, in-demand skills, and new openings. A quick chat with a headhunter today could lead to your dream job tomorrow!

**Bottom line:**

Your career is your greatest asset, especially when you're young. So keep leveling up! Learn new things, negotiate for what you're worth, make awesome connections, and don't be afraid to dream big. Every time you invest in yourself and play to your strengths, you're building a toolkit of unique skills that make you stand out from the crowd.

Here's the magic: employable skills help you earn more, which means you've got more money to add to your investments. And guess what? Keep investing is your ticket to real financial freedom down the road. The more you bet on yourself, the more doors (and paychecks) open up, fueling your wealth and your confidence every step of the way. Ready? Game on!

## Step J: Turn What You Love into Extra Cash

Who says you can't make money doing what you love? Picture turning your skills and passions into a side hustle that brings in extra cash. It may even lead to your next big opportunity. Whether you're into baking, fixing bikes, designing apps, or teaching AI, there's a fun way to earn on the side.

Start by looking at where your talents meet real market needs. It's not just about making extra money; it's about trying new things and learning along the way. So when it's time for your next chapter, you'll already be on your way to a meaningful, happy life!

# Snapshot 3
## (My LinkedIn Post on 9/20/2023)

Reimagining Freedom & the Fluid American Dream

**2017, Parisian Vibes:**

I'm sitting in the Left Bank in Paris with a friend before heading to Berlin for work. Over some café and croissants, I'm letting off steam about my seemingly bleak American Dream. The 'checklist'—good job, marriage, big house, growing family—it all felt so prescribed. It made me wonder, 'Is this all there is?'

**2023, A New Chapter Unfolds:**

Fast forward to June 2023, I reunite with the same friend, this time by a lively sandbox in the heart of Paris. And how life has changed! I'm the owner of two more houses, I've claimed financial freedom, left the nine-to-five grind for entrepreneurship, and every day is about learning and impacting the world.

**America: A Land of Transformation:**

I feel incredibly blessed to be in a place that has allowed my dreams to morph and materialize in magical ways. My journey exemplifies the endless opportunities that unfold when one dares to work hard, invest smart, and venture into the unknown. It's remarkable to ponder how different my life would be if I hadn't made the move to the US eleven years ago.

**For the Visionaries Feeling Stuck:**

If you find your life to be a replay of the same old story, or if the future seems blurred, it's time to stop and reassess. Align your actions with your true desires. It might not be easy, and the road may be rough, but there's always light at the end of the tunnel.

Paint Your American Dream:

The American Dream is still alive and thriving, but it's not a one-size-fits-all. For those aspiring to a richer, fuller life, your canvas is ready. It's time to grab your brush and paint your very own American Dream!

Photo 1 taken in 2017: All smiles but kinda feeling lost inside.

Photo 2 taken in 2023: Europe trip with the fam! No makeup, husband's hair all over the place, but who cares! We were creating beautiful, messy memories.

## Step K: The Big Picture

You've gathered your financial building blocks, and now let's make sure all the pieces fit together for a truly comprehensive plan! This is where you zoom out and dive in to make sure every part of your financial life works in harmony with your life goals.

**Insurance:** Protect what you've worked for! Make sure you have the right coverage for the key parts of your financial life: health insurance to cover medical costs, life insurance to support your loved ones if something happens to you, disability insurance to protect your income if you can't work, homeowners or renters insurance for your place to live, auto insurance for your car, and umbrella insurance to cover unexpected major liabilities. These policies help protect you and your family from big financial surprises that could otherwise derail your financial stability.

**Taxes:** Don't pay more than you have to! Smart tax planning starts long before you file your return. Unlike tax filing, tax planning means thinking ahead to find ways to lower your taxes legally. There are lots of strategies tailored to your income and situation, like contributing to retirement accounts, using tax credits and deductions, and timing income and expenses. Planning ahead helps you keep more of your hard-earned money and stretch your wealth further over time.

**Education:** Planning for your kids' (or your own) education? Consider tax-advantaged accounts like 529 plans to save for those big future expenses. More on 529s in Chapter 6.

**Family Support:** Think about how you can support loved ones now and in the future—whether it's paying for family trips, caring for aging parents, or supporting a family business.

**Wills & Trusts:** Secure your legacy. A will and, if needed, a trust ensure your assets go where you want and help your family avoid legal headaches and unnecessary taxes.

**Retirement:** This is where smart planning pays off! We'll go into more details in Chapter 6. Here are some key pieces:

- **Social Security**: The timing of when you claim Social Security can make a big difference in your lifetime benefits. Waiting to claim until age 70 increases both your monthly check and survivor benefit, so if longevity runs in your family, it is often smart to delay. However, it's important to weigh your health, financial needs, and long-term plans when deciding.

- **Medicare**: Make sure to enroll on time and understand the coverage each part offers. Part A covers hospital stays, Part B covers doctor visits and outpatient care, Part C (Medicare Advantage) is an alternative plan often including extra benefits, and Part D helps with prescription drugs. Most people need both Part A and Part B; Parts C and D are optional based on your needs.

- **IRMAA**: The Income-Related Monthly Adjustment Amount (IRMAA) increases Medicare premiums for Parts B and D if your income is above certain thresholds. In 2025, people with the highest incomes will pay about $530 extra per month for Medicare premiums (for Part B and D), compared to those with lower incomes. That's over $6,300 a year, or more than twelve thousand dollars for a couple. These surcharges are based on income from two years prior, so keep this in mind when planning ahead.

- **Required Minimum Distributions (RMDs):** If you were born in 1960 or later, you must start taking RMDs from your tax-deferred retirement accounts. This includes Traditional 401(k)s, Traditional IRAs, SEP IRAs, 403(b) plans, 457(b) plans, and profit-sharing plans. Missing your RMD can lead to a penalty of 25 percent on the amount you should have withdrawn, so it's important to plan ahead and take them on time. The amount you must withdraw each year is calculated using IRS life expectancy tables based on your age and account balance at the end of the previous year.

- **Roth Conversions**: Moving funds from a traditional IRA or 401(k) to a Roth IRA means you pay income taxes on the amount you convert in the year of the conversion. This allows you to make tax-free withdrawals later, which can be a smart move if you expect to be in a higher tax bracket in retirement or want to avoid required minimum distributions (RMDs) from Roth accounts. The timing matters: converting smaller amounts over several years may help keep you in a lower tax bracket and could help you avoid higher Medicare premiums caused by IRMAA in the future.

- **Asset Location**: Where you keep your investments can impact taxes and long-term growth. Tax-inefficient assets, such as bonds and money market funds (since interest income is generally taxed at higher ordinary in-come rates), are often best held in tax-deferred accounts like traditional IRAs or 401(k)s. More tax-efficient assets, like index funds or stocks, work well in taxable and Roth accounts. Using this approach can help you reduce taxes and boost your after-tax returns over time.

- **Withdrawal Strategy**: A common guideline for retirement withdrawals is to start by taking out about 4 percent of your savings each year. Those who retire early some-times use a lower rate, like 3.3 percent. Optimize your withdrawals across taxable, tax-deferred, and tax-free accounts to help minimize taxes and make your sav-ings last. The best strategy depends on your lifestyle, investment returns, and tax situation. We'll look at some real-life examples in the next chapter.

A good holistic financial plan brings all these elements together so your money supports your life today and your dreams for tomorrow. Regularly review your plan as life changes. Think of it as keeping your financial engine running smoothly for the long haul. Let's get comprehensive and make sure your wealth is working for you and your loved ones. We will go into more details on investment, tax, insurance, and estate planning in the next chapter.

## Additional Resources

Now if you're aiming to level up on E through H, it's time to educate yourself and take control of your money. Resources like 3rd Decade, Savvy Ladies (where I volunteer), Financial Beginnings, and Banzai offer great tools to sharpen your financial skills and knowledge.

For tackling I or J, you might need a mentor, or a few. Mentors can help you grow in your career and business, but if you're feeling like you need more support and accountability, consider hiring a result-driven career coach or startup coach to give you the extra push.

If you're stuck on K because you keep putting it off or don't have time, working with a fee-only, advice-only, or hourly comprehensive financial planner can really help. You can find trustworthy planners at places like the Garrett Planning Network and NAPFA (I'm a proud member of both) or Advice-Only Network. A good planner gives you structure and helps you with the implementations of recommendations, so you can effectively and efficiently tackle those holistic financial topics and be successful.

Money management is a life skill. It's about mindset, strategy, and consistently taking small steps toward bigger goals. Financial freedom is a marathon, not a sprint. Live below your means, invest with a long-term plan, and grow into your passion. With these principles, you'll be ready to handle the ups and downs with confidence and clarity. Start today, and make sure every financial decision you make brings you and your partner one step closer to the life you want and deserve!

## Break Big Goals into Small Steps

Big goals can feel like staring up at a mountain and wondering, "How am I ever going to make it to the top?" The simple answer is: one step at a time. Whether it's your financial goals, personal growth, or that dream venture, taking small steps makes big dreams achievable.

Let's break it down one by one, starting with retirement planning.

Thinking about how much money you need to save for a comfortable retirement can feel overwhelming, but here's a simple trick: start small and focus on the numbers one at a time.

First, grab your Social Security statement to see how much you'll receive each month at the age you want to retire. You can request your official benefits estimate online by creating a free account at the Social Security Administration website: www.ssa.gov. Keep in mind that setting up the account might take some time if you haven't done it before, since they may send information by mail for security reasons.

Next, look at your current monthly expenses and subtract those you won't have in retirement, like mortgage payments (if you've paid it off by then), kids' expenses after they're independent, and costs related to work (such as commuting, lunches, and work clothes).

Now, take your monthly expenses after subtracting what you won't have and minus your monthly Social Security benefit. Multiply this number by 12 to find your total annual cash need, then multiply by 25. Why 25? It's based on the four percent rule, which estimates how much money you need saved to safely withdraw four percent a year for about thirty years of retirement.

That final number is your nest egg goal—the amount you want saved before you retire, in today's dollars, to cover your living expenses comfortably for the next few decades.

Finally, break that big number down into smaller monthly savings goals. Instead of stressing over the entire sum, focus on manageable monthly contributions. Set it up to come right out of your paycheck and invest automatically. Voila! You're on a simple path to your dream retirement.

## Example:

Let's say your household spends $7,500 each month. Of that, $2,500 goes to your mortgage payment (not including escrow for homeowner's insurance and property taxes, since you'll still pay those after the mortgage is done). When you retire, you'll receive a combined $3,500 per month from Social Security. So, the amount you'll need to cover each month in retirement is:

$$7500 - 2500 - 3500 = \$1,500$$

Multiply by 12 months:

$$1500 \times 12 = \$18,000 \text{ per year}$$

Multiply by 25 to find your savings goal:

$$18,000 \times 25 = \$450,000 \text{ (in today's value)}$$

You would need to save $450,000 to maintain your current lifestyle in retirement. But because prices go up over time, you'll actually need more. For this example, we'll use a 3% increase each year to keep it simple.

Here's how much you should save monthly based on your years to retirement and a 7% return for simplicity.

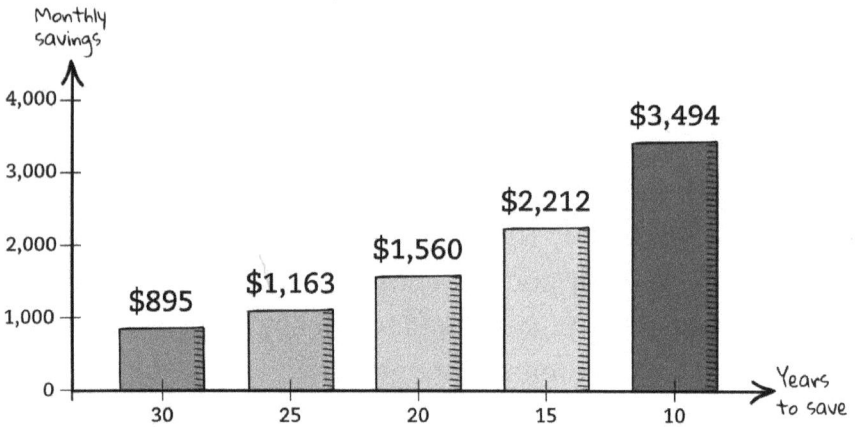

Figure 10: Savings needed to reach $450,000 in today's money.

## Save Smart, Save Early!

**Bonus**: When you invest for the long haul, especially more than ten years ahead, historical returns can be higher than seven percent. That means you could reach your goals sooner than you think. It all begins with starting early!

Next, let's talk about paying off bad debt, the common money gobbler that often feels impossible to beat. It's normal for couples to feel overwhelmed or anxious when facing a large credit card balance like $40,000. Take a deep breath and remember you're in this together. Instead of letting those feelings hold you back, break the debt down into bite-sized chunks. Start by reviewing your credit card statements together to understand the balances and interest rates.

At first, you both might feel frustrated or even angry about the size of the debt. That's completely normal. Decide together whether to focus on paying off the card with the highest interest rate or the smallest balance first—whichever keeps you motivated as a team. The snowball method, paying off the smallest balance first, offers quick wins that boost confidence. The avalanche method, tackling the highest interest rate first, saves the most money over time, even if progress feels slower.

Aim to pay $250 every week, and add extra payments whenever you can. It's common for couples to feel discouraged at times, but the key is to pay more than just the interest as often as possible. This will save money in the long run and help shrink your balance faster.

Over time, you will feel the weight of that debt begin to lift. Along the way, expect moments of relief, pride, and even excitement as your progress builds with each small step. Remember, paying off debt is both a financial and emotional journey. Having open communication and support in your relationship is just as important as a solid plan. A good financial coach can also help you navigate the ups and downs and guide you toward making the most of your options.

You can use the same approach of breaking big goals into smaller steps in other parts of your life. The skills you build by doing this will help you reach goals not just with money, but with anything you want to achieve in life.

For example, if you want to learn a new skill like vibe coding, painting, or even write a book, *start with a small, specific step.* Instead of trying to take on everything at once, watch a short introductory video or write a few sentences a day. The same goes for health goals: if running a 5K feels overwhelming, start by standing up, putting on your shoes, and walking around the block. Then gradually increase your pace. Little by little, you'll see your confidence and ability grow as you move toward that bigger goal.

Here's the key: *focus.* It's not about doing everything at once but taking consistent small steps as a team. Improving by just 1% every day really adds up—by the end of the year, you'll both be nearly 38 times better.

*Formula:* $(1 + 0.01)^{365} = 37.78.$

But if you get 1% worse each day, you'll end up with just 2.55% of your potential by year-end

*Formula:* $(1 - 0.01)^{365} \approx 0.0255.$

So, next time you and your partner face a big goal, break it down into smaller tasks together. This way, you'll both feel less overwhelmed and see yourselves making progress much faster than you expected.

Big goals aren't meant to be achieved overnight. They're meant to be broken down into bite-sized pieces and celebrated along the way. Keep the big picture in mind, but focus on the small, actionable steps that will move you both forward. Because *small steps, taken as a team, lead to big, lasting change.*

## Make Room for Mistakes

Let's be real, nobody gets everything right on the first try, espe-cially when it comes to money! Think of your financial journey like learning to ride a bike: you're going to wobble, maybe even fall, but that's how you figure out what works for you. The im-portant thing is to give yourself permission to make mistakes and treat them as learning moments, not failures.

As a couple, it's important to remember that mistakes aren't the end of the road. If you or your partner overspend one month or forget to put money into your savings, don't see it as a failure, but as a chance to regroup and learn. It might even spark a conversation about what went wrong and how you can support each other next time. Remember, you're already making great progress by identifying where you are, recognizing what you need to work on, and actually taking the first step towards a solution. So give your partner a high five for getting started, because this is a huge achievement!

Mistakes are a natural part of any financial journey. We all ex-perience setbacks. Maybe you invested in something that didn't pan out, or you took a financial risk that was higher than you'd like to tolerate. It happens to everyone. What matters most is that you and your partner don't dwell on the mistake. Instead, help each other get back on track. Supporting your loved ones through setbacks not only strengthens your financial habits but also strengthens your bond as a couple.

Keep reminding yourselves: progress isn't about being perfect. It is about showing up, learning, and getting a little better every day. So, dust yourself off, give each other a hug, and keep walk-ing your path to financial freedom!

## Stay Focused and Supported

Sticking with your financial goals gets a lot easier when you stay focused and have a strong support system behind you. Think about it: any big change, whether in your money or your life, happens one small step at a time. It's not about giant leaps, but about the steady habits and small actions that add up over time.

One of the best ways to keep going is by focusing on your most important goal. Imagine that the next step is the only thing standing between you and your final goal. Would you rather take that step or put it off? The key is to just get started and let the momentum carry you forward.

As a couple, cheer each other on every step of the way. Acknowledge both of your efforts and be there for support through the ups and downs. If you ever feel stuck, lean on your love for encouragement or reach out for help from a trusted friend or a professional. Remember, you are not alone. Having your partner with you makes all the difference. With steady focus and a strong support system, you will keep making progress, one step at a time.

## Celebrate Progress

Every step forward matters, no matter how small. Progress isn't always smooth. Chores, life changes, and unexpected events can make it feel like you didn't get much done. But that's not true! Be sure to notice and celebrate every win, especially the little ones. Whether it's sticking to your budget for a tricky category like food or shopping, putting aside a small amount for emergencies, setting up automatic investments, or finally reviewing your insurance or investment statements—it all counts!

As a couple, celebrate your progress! Treat yourselves to something fun within your budget, or simply share your victories together. These moments of celebration build motivation and remind you both that *every little victory brings you closer to your bigger goals*. Whether it's saving for a down payment, paying off debt, or planning for your future, the journey will be more rewarding when you recognize how far you've come, especially when things get tough. Remember, real change happens one step at a time, so make sure to celebrate each and every one!

By learning to embrace mistakes, stay focused on your goals, and celebrate your wins together, you and your partner will build a strong foundation for lasting financial success and a deeper connection. Keep moving forward hand in hand, and you'll find that every small step makes you stronger, brings you closer, and helps create the life you want.

## Now, It's Your Turn!

As you've seen, change doesn't happen all at once; it's a journey that unfolds step by step. But here's the exciting part: you're already on your way! Now, it's time to take action and dive deeper into your own transformation. You've already begun thinking about what you want and how to align your goals with your deeper desires. Now, we're going to get clear on where you are and what changes you want to make in your life and finances.

# Exercises for Chapter 5:
# Master Money Basics

## Exercise 5-1: Happiness

1. Set a timer for two minutes each.

2. Share with your partner: A recent moment I felt truly happy was . . . .

3. You'll each take turns to share and listen. Decide who goes first. The listener pays full attention, keeping eye contact and not interrupting or taking notes. It's okay to use sounds like "um" or "wow" and body language.

4. Once the narrator finishes, the listener shares their feelings with: "When you said (repeat their specific words), I felt (an emotion) in (a part of my body)."

   For example:

   - "When you mentioned how you appreciated my help in solving that problem, my shoulder felt relaxed."

   - "When you got excited talking about our trip, I felt pumped in my legs."

5. Switch roles and repeat the process.

## Exercise 5-2: Stress

1. Again, set the timer for two minutes each.

2. Take turns to open up and share with your partner: Recently, what has been stressing me out is . . . .

3. Decide who goes first. The listener pays full attention, keeping eye contact and not interrupting or taking notes. It's okay to use sounds like "um" or "wow" and body language.

4. Once the narrator finishes, the listener shares their feelings with: "When you said (repeat their specific words), I felt (an emotion) in (a part of my body)."

   For example:

   - "When you shared your concern about our busy schedule, I noticed my jaw tighten."

   - "When you mentioned your frustration at work, I felt your stress in my neck."

5. Switch roles and repeat.

## Exercise 5-3: Financial Freedom

1. Take two minutes each to share: What would it feel like to be financially free?

2. Decide who goes first. The listener pays full attention, keeping eye contact and not interrupting or taking notes. It's okay to use sounds like "um" or "wow" and body language.

3. Once the narrator finishes, the listener shares their feelings with: "When you said (repeat their specific words), I felt (an emotion) in (a part of my body)."

   For example:

   - "When you mentioned how you appreciated my help in solving that problem, my heart warmed."

- "When you mentioned building wealth for our family, I sensed pride in my back."

4. Switch roles and repeat.

## Exercise 5-4: Financial Wellbeing Flowchart—Where are You?

1. Share with your partner: Which step are you on in the Financial Wellbeing Flow Chart?

2. Decide who goes first. The listener pays full attention, keeping eye contact and not interrupting or taking notes. It's okay to use sounds like "um" or "wow" and body language.

3. Once the narrator finishes, the listener shares their feelings with: "When you said (repeat their specific words), I felt (an emotion) in (a part of my body)."

   For example:

   - "When you described paying off a little more debt each month, I sensed relief in my breath."
   - "When you mentioned increasing retirement contributions, I felt proud in my chest."

4. Switch roles and repeat.

## Exercise 5-5: Money Basics

1. Take two minutes each to share: In the Financial Wellbeing Flowchart, which step(s) are you planning to work on or further strengthen?

2. Decide who goes first. The listener pays full attention, keeping eye contact and not interrupting or taking notes. It's okay to use sounds like "um" or "wow" and body language.

3. Once the narrator finishes, the listener responds with a statement of feeling, and then guides the narrator to answer these two questions: When do you plan to take the first step? Who can help you?

4. Switch roles and repeat.

# Your Reflection

Take a moment to jot down your thoughts and experiences
from the exercise. Use this space to capture any insights,
feelings, or ideas that came up.

_____

_____

_____

_____

_____

_____

_____

_____

_____

_____

_____

_____

_____

_____

# CHAPTER 6

# The Hidden Secret to Freedom

———— ♥ ————

*"If you don't know where you are going, you'll end up someplace else."*

**— Yogi Berra**

I'll never forget that moment in early 2022 when my net worth tracker revealed I had hit my financial freedom goal. The satisfaction was immediate, but it soon disappeared. Years of spreadsheets, number crunching, and a decade working in finance had paid off. Yet, as someone who could model billion-dollar business plans but had missed the vast richness of personal financial planning, I realized my focus had been too narrow for too long.

For years, I was obsessively tallying assets, chasing "my number," and running investment returns, but I didn't grasp the full expanse of financial planning. Now, after several years of ongoing education, teaching, and guiding others as a planner, I see both the depth and breadth of *comprehensive financial planning*. I've witnessed stress fade away when people understand their options and gain clarity and confidence by seeing the bigger picture. With a good financial plan, they know exactly where they stand, where they're headed, and how all the moving parts—investments, taxes, insurance, retirement, other life goals, and estate plans—all fit together. **Holistic planning is the hidden secret to financial freedom.**

Looking back, I wish I had had this big picture vision in 2017 when I felt like a zombie working a job that didn't fulfill me but provided stability and balance. Or in 2021, during team shortages and unexpected challenges at work. And in 2022, juggling multiple roles: working full-time, teaching at Arizona State University, hosting a YouTube channel and podcast, growing my business, while striving to be an engaged mom. I reached my financial number, but the fear of uncertainty and failure drove me to burnout. If I had had the freedom and insight to pull the trigger to quit my job earlier than March 2023, I would have made different life choices, been much happier, and made my loved ones around me happier. I know everyone has their own journey, but it never hurts to have a map in hand while you're at it.

This chapter is for you to explore the full financial landscape. You can do much more than simply plug away at wealth accumulation. You can be more efficient, confident, and truly enjoy your journey and where it's heading, without derailing (at least not too far), no matter what life throws at you.

**Comprehensive financial planning gives you:**

- Peace of mind that you're ready for "what ifs."
- The ability to see and seize opportunities at every stage of life.

- Powerful tools and tech to model scenarios and make informed choices instead of winging it.

In this chapter, you'll find the **Three Investment Phases:**

- Phase One: The Building Years
- Phase Two: The Growth Spurt
- Phase Three: The Fun Ride and Beyond

You'll also learn about these financial strategies:

**Tax Planning & Tax-Advantaged Accounts:** Learn how strategies like Roth conversions and tax-advantaged accounts, such as 401(k), 403(b), 457(b), IRA, Roth IRA, 529, HSA, and FSA, do more than save taxes. They empower your long-term plan!

**Three Insurance Principles:** It's not just about full coverage. It's about protecting what matters most without paying extra that you're unaware of.

**Wills, Trusts & Action Guide:** Discover why estate planning is a vital piece of true financial health, with action steps to guide you.

**Modern Planning Tools:** See how technology makes visualizing your entire financial life easier than ever, helping you confidently make decisions at every turn.

In short, comprehensive financial planning means seeing the whole picture and understanding the future consequences of your choices. You might realize you are richer and better positioned than you ever imagined. You'll be empowered to take actions to make your life even better. This process transforms your financial journey from a numbers game into a source of clarity, calm, and even excitement, no matter where life brings you.

## To Start Off, You Might Be Richer Than You Think

When you think about your financial future, it's normal to feel overwhelmed. But here's something to brighten your outlook: you might be richer than you realize, especially when you factor in your human capital. This is a powerful, hidden asset that's often overlooked in financial planning.

In simple terms, human capital means the value of your skills, experience, education, and the ability to earn income in the future. It's one of your biggest financial assets, even if it's not visible like savings or investments. Let me explain more about why this matters.

## Your Earning Potential

Let's start with a simple example: imagine a couple who earns a combined $100,000 after taxes each year and plans to retire at age sixty-five, which is the average retirement age in the US. If they both keep working for thirty more years—from age thirty-five to sixty-five—their combined earnings over that time could add up to about three million dollars.

Of course, how much of this money you have available in retirement depends entirely on how much you save and invest along the way. Your salary is just the starting point. The real power comes from protecting and growing your investments wisely.

## The Power of Saving and Investing

When it comes to saving and investing, if this couple puts away 15% of their income (which, in this case, equals $15,000 per year), and if they earn an average annual return of 7% (after inflation), their investments will grow to approximately $1.4 million by the time they retire in thirty years.

But that's not all. If they own a home and continue paying down the mortgage, that home will likely be fully paid off by retirement, adding more financial stability to their situation. This doesn't even account for potential bonuses, salary increases, or any gifts or inheritance that could come their way.

## Living Costs and Making Intentional Choices

When you're planning your finances together, it's important to consider your living costs as a couple. In some areas, $85,000 can cover most essentials like housing, food, healthcare, utilities, and transportation. But if you're living in a high-cost city, that same amount might not go as far, so being intentional with your spending is key.

Work together to focus on what truly matters to both of you. Maybe you decide to prioritize living in a great neighborhood over having extra space, or you choose community-based child-care instead of more expensive options. Shopping second-hand or renting occasionally used items can be a smart way to save. Whether it's clothes, furniture, or even baby gear, you can often find what you need without the high price tag.

Instead of making last-minute travel plans or booking getaways on a whim, which can easily lead to overspending and even credit card debt, consider exploring local destinations together. You might be surprised by how much you can experience close to home without the extra costs of flights and hotels. Also, don't forget to utilize public resources like libraries, where you can borrow books, movies, and even e-readers. Tool libraries let you borrow things like drills and ladders instead of buying them.

As a couple, planning your purchases together can help you avoid impulse buys and ensure you're spending on things that really add value to your lives. Cutting back on non-essentials, such as extra subscriptions, frequent takeout, or luxury goods can free up money for your shared goals. Small, intentional choices can add up, helping you build the life you want together while staying financially secure.

## Getting Creative with Spending and Saving

Living below your means is not about scraping by. It's about making smart, intentional choices that align with your values. It's not about depriving yourself, but about focusing on what matters most to you while making sure your financial future is secure.

Some people take this idea a step further with geoarbitrage, which means moving to a place where the cost of living is lower while keeping the same or even higher income. This often happens through remote work or other income sources that don't depend on location.

Geoarbitrage can increase your purchasing power, potentially lower your taxes, speed up your savings, and even improve your overall quality of life. This strategy works best for people with flexible jobs or retirement income that is not tied to one place. But if your income depends on a specific location, the benefits of geoarbitrage might be limited.

The key takeaway here is that small, consistent decisions add up. Whether it's saving a percentage of your income, cutting back on unnecessary spending, or making more mindful choices about where you live and how you travel, it all leads to a more secure, fulfilling life. And when you take those small steps now, your financial future will be stronger than ever!

## Social Security: What Couples Need to Know

Now, let's include Social Security benefits in the picture. Using the example of a couple earning a combined $100,000 per year after taxes, we can estimate their Social Security benefits around age sixty-five. The couple plans to retire together when the older partner turns sixty-five and the younger partner is sixty-three. Here's a rough idea of what that might look like:

|  | Spouse 1 | Spouse 2 |
| --- | --- | --- |
| Current Age | 35 | 33 |
| Current Monthly Salary | $5,750 | $4,375 |
| Benefit if Starting at Age 63 (76%) | $1,927 | **$1,602** |
| Benefit if Starting at Age 65 (88%) | **$2,232** | $1,855 |
| Benefit if Starting at Age 67 (100%) | $2,536 | $2,108 |

If we consider average life expectancies, which are seventy-six years for men and eighty-one years for women, the couple could receive their individual Social Security benefits for about eleven years until the first partner passes away. After that, the surviving spouse may receive survivor benefits or their own benefit, whichever is higher, for the remainder of their life, which could be around seven more years, assuming they live to about age eighty-one.

Note: Survivor benefits can be claimed as early as age sixty, but the amount will be reduced if claimed before full retirement age. At full retirement age, the surviving spouse is generally eligible to receive 100% of the deceased partner's benefit. The exact benefit amount depends on the deceased partner's earnings history and when the surviving spouse begins to claim.

Now let's calculate their total benefits:

$2,232 x 12 x 11 (for Spouse 1 for eleven years) = $293,904

$1,602 x 12 x 11 (for Spouse 2 for eleven years) = $211,344

$2,232 x 12 x 7 (for Spouse 1's survivor benefits) = $187,440

Total benefits = $693,517.

## What Does This All Mean?

Here's the bottom line. For most people, your biggest sources of income when you retire will be the money you've saved and invested over the years, plus your Social Security benefits—and any pension you might have on top of that.

At first, these numbers might feel far off or like distant goals. But they are actually realistic milestones on your financial journey with your partner. The earlier you start investing, the more regularly you save, and the more thoughtfully you plan your money, the better you can build the financial resources to support your lifestyle well into retirement.

Remember, you might be richer than you think. By making smart and intentional choices today, you're already laying the foundation for a secure and comfortable future. With consistent, small steps, you'll get closer to your financial goals while enjoying the peace of mind that comes from knowing you have a plan in place.

According to recent data, the average retirement income for couples in the US is about one hundred thousand dollars a year, coming from Social Security, savings, pensions, and sometimes part-time work. Your personal number may be higher or lower depending on your lifestyle and where you live, but setting clear goals and taking action now will make a big difference.

## Where You Want to Be

Now that we've discussed your total resources, it's time to focus on your grand vision—where you really want to be in life. Knowing where you stand is one thing, but now let's dig into how much you need to live the life you've always dreamed of!

We will then put your resources to work in a way that helps you reach your bigger goals with confidence and excitement.

# Wealth Roadmap Part 1 of 5: Wealth Goals

Get ready to map out your dream life and see exactly how much it will cost. Instead of just guessing big numbers, this exercise helps you and your partner figure out the costs for things like your home, car, childcare, college savings, and more.

Don't worry, this isn't about saving up a huge pile of money all at once. It's about making a plan that fits what you really want and making sure you're on track to reach those goals, all while having a good time along the way!

By breaking it down into manageable steps, you'll create a clear picture of your future and start turning your dreams into achievable plans.

I've put together a system to make it super easy, and I'll share a handy **QR code** to the template below so you can jump right in.

## Steps to Get Started:

1. **Essential Annual Spending & Lifestyle Costs**: Start by filling in your **annual living expenses** in **cell C5**—things like rent or mortgage, food, healthcare, and utilities. Then add your **lifestyle costs** (like travel, hobbies, dining out) in **cell C6**. Go ahead, be kind to yourself here!

2. **Your Dream Homes**: What does your dream home look like? Pick your ideal primary residence and vacation home. Don't stress about the exact numbers right now— let your imagination run wild!

3. **Vehicle Costs**: What's your car situation? Add the value of any additional cars you might own (think: RVs, trailers, or boats). If you already have a car, plan for your next one—how much would you like to spend?

4. **Kids and Education**: Input the number of kids you want to have, early childcare solution (because, let's face it, childcare isn't cheap!). And don't forget to plan for their college fund—what kind of school are you envisioning for them?

5. **Pet Costs**: Don't leave out your furry friends! Enter the number of pets you plan to have, and remember—pets can be pricey! (Let's set aside $32,000 for the lifetime cost of a cat and $35,000 for a dog).

6. **Lifestyle Upgrade & Giving**: What kind of lifestyle up-grades would you like to invest in? Think about charitable

donations and gifts, too. This would be in addition to what you already put down in step 1 / **Cells C5 and C6**.

7.  **Healthcare After Retirement**: Consider how many people you'll need to help with healthcare after retirement—yourself, your spouse, or even your aging parents if they're not financially independent.

8.  **Location Matters**: Where you live and where you want to live will affect how much money you need to live your dream life. The cost of living can be very different from city to city! If your city isn't listed, choose one from the list with a similar cost of living to get a good estimate. This way, you can better plan your financial goal based on where you want to be.

## The Big Reveal

Once you've filled in all the details, here's what you'll see:

- **Line 7**: How much it costs to live a comfortable life in your current location (Net Assets to Live Happy and Free).

- **Line 23**: How much you'll need to live your ideal life in an average city in the US (Net Assets Needed to Fulfill All Your Financial Dreams).

- **Line 24**: How much it would cost to live a comfortable life in your dream city—adjusted for the cost of living.

- **Line 25**: The amount you'll need to live your **ideal life** in your **ideal city** (Financial Independence Adjusted for Cost of Living).

- If you plan to retire around the average age of sixty-five, use the numbers in **column D**. If you want to retire earlier, look at the numbers in **column E** instead.

## Let's Get Started!

Ready to start tracking your **Wealth Goals**? Scan the **QR code** below to begin! The journey to financial freedom starts with knowing your numbers and taking action. You've got this—the power is in your hands!

## How to Get There

To reach your financial goals, smart investing is key. It is not just about putting money into a savings account or hoping for the best. It means making sure your resources work together: investing wisely, minimizing taxes, protecting yourself with insurance, and planning your estate with wills and other important documents.

All of these pieces work together to help you maximize your financial potential and build a secure, lasting future.

By managing all the important areas in a balanced way, you create a strong foundation. This foundation does more than just keep you and your partner safe; it helps both of you thrive. Now, let's look at how to make the most of your investments, taxes, insurance, and planning for your legacy, so you can live a life that feels truly successful.

## Three Investment Phases

Over the years of helping people build financial success, I've noticed that wealth-building usually happens in three stages based on your net worth. Each stage has its own energy and goals, and all offer their own kind of freedom—as long as you are clear on how to get from where you are to where you want to be.

**Phase One: The Building Years** (Net Worth Below $200,000)

This phase is about hard work, disciplined saving, and creating strong financial habits. It sets the foundation for everything that follows. Having guidance that supports your mindset and habits can make all the difference.

**Phase Two: The Growth Spurt** (Net Worth Between $200,000 and $1,000,000)

Here, you start making smarter money choices while focusing more on your passions. It's about seizing opportunities, building momentum, and growing your wealth steadily and sustainably. Knowing your options early can make a big difference in your life.

**Phase Three: The Fun Ride and Beyond** (Net Worth Above $1,000,000)

At this stage, you have the ability to make bigger decisions and enjoy more options. It's less about long hours and more about living with balance, health, and purpose. Aligning your long-term plan with your values helps you maximize your resources for the life you want and the legacy you wish to leave behind.

Here's a quick exercise to help you identify your current phase based on your net worth:

## Wealth Roadmap Part 2 of 5: Net Worth

- **Go on a Treasure Hunt for Your Assets:** Think of yourself as a treasure hunter searching for all your valuable "loot." List everything you own—cash in your bank accounts, retirement savings, investments, your home, your car, and even collectibles. Add up their current market value to see the full size of your treasure chest!

- **Spot the Sneaky Gremlins (Liabilities)**: Now, find the "gremlins" that are quietly eating away at your riches. These are your debts like student loans, car loans, credit card balances, your mortgage, and any other debts. Add up everything you owe to see what might be draining your earnings and gains.

- **The Big Reveal:** Subtract your debts from your assets. The result is your net worth, your personal scorecard on your financial journey. If you use the template, the math is already done for you, so you get an instant picture of where you stand!

- **Track Your Progress Like a Pro:** Use the Google Sheet template (just scan the **QR code** below to get your own copy) as your personal adventure log. Update it every quarter and watch how your financial world changes over time. Celebrate every victory, big or small!

**Keep the Adventure Going:** Don't stress about ups and downs from market changes. Focus on your long-term plan, stay curious and consistent, and enjoy each step of the journey.

**Challenge Yourself:** Can you grow your treasure and shrink those gremlins before your next update? Review your progress with your partner or a friend. Talking about your wins and goals can keep you motivated.

**Ready to play?** Start building your Wealth Roadmap today by tracking your net worth. The journey to financial confidence begins with knowing your numbers and taking action. You've got this!

**Phase One: The Building Years** (Net Worth Below $200,000)

This phase is all about getting started. As Charlie Munger famously said in the 1990s, "The first 100K is a b*ch!" Well, with inflation over the years, that number has doubled at least! You can't build wealth if you're living paycheck to paycheck and not saving consistently (enjoying life is great too, but you have to start accumulating sooner or later if you don't want to depend entirely on social security in retirement). At this point, your savings rate is the most important factor. Without it, you're not even giving yourself a chance to let your money work for you. One of the easiest ways to boost your wealth is getting your employer match in retirement contributions.

## Grab That Match!

One of my clients, Tyrone, was missing out on a golden opportunity. For years, he never contributed to his 401(k), even though his company offered a dollar-for-dollar match up to 6% of his salary! He came to me worried about debt, cash flow, and still dreaming of real estate investing, even after a few rough deals. He was so nervous about his finances that he hesitated to even claim his free 401(k) money.

So, I gave Tyrone a gentle reality check along with a game plan.

Here's what we did:

- **Free Money Alert!** I showed him that the company match is like a 100% instant return on his investment, plus whatever the market gives him. Who says no to free money?

- **Emergency Fund Check.** He already had a solid six-month emergency fund, so he was in a great spot to start investing for his future.

- **Accessibility Rules Explained.** We talked about how he could tap into his 401(k) if needed, either through a loan or withdrawal following the plan rules. We also covered that he can withdraw the principal (his contributions) portion from his Roth IRA at any time without taxes or penalties, as long as the account has been open for more than five years. However, any earnings withdrawn early may be subject to taxes and penalties.

- **Real Estate Ready.** We created a backup plan so he'd be ready if a great real estate deal came along, but not at the expense of his retirement.

- **Level Up!** I encouraged him to take advantage of his employer's offer to cover a professional certification, and to start networking like crazy.

- **The Big Move.** He cranked up his 401(k) contribution to 12%. And for him, that meant he'd reach the annual allowed limit of $23,500 (for 2025), maxing out both his company match and his own retirement savings in one bold step. Even though it felt a little scary at first, it's a huge leap toward long-term financial security, especially with early retirement in mind.

- **And here's the bonus:** Because he's single and in a high tax bracket, every dollar he contributes now lowers his taxable income, saving him thousands in taxes this year. That means more money working for him in the market. With compounding returns and smart tax planning, he's not just building a nest egg, he's setting himself up for a confident and comfortable early retirement.

Tyrone now has a clear strategy that aligns with his long-term vision. That mindset shift was huge! His story is proof that with the right plan and a little encouragement, even the most daunting financial decisions can become empowering and fun.

## Home Ownership: Building Wealth

One of the biggest early boosts to wealth is homeownership, but only if you're planning to stick with it for the long haul. Buying a home is one of the most powerful ways to build equity over time, but it requires careful planning and strategy. Let's dive into how you can make homeownership a reality and why it's such a smart move in the long term.

## How to Fund Your Down Payment

There are many ways to gather the funds for your down payment, and getting creative here can make all the difference:

- **Side hustles and extra work**: Take on freelance gigs, part-time jobs, or odd jobs to earn extra cash.

- **Save bonuses and windfalls**: When you receive unexpected money, like a work bonus or gift, don't spend it—save it for your down payment.

- **Couch surfing or living with family**: If it works for your situation, consider staying with a friend or family member temporarily to save more aggressively for your home.

- **Use public transportation or bikes**: Cut back on transportation costs to save more.

- **Borrowing from family or friends**: If you go this route, make sure to set up proper documentation and offer a fair interest rate to avoid any awkwardness.

- **Down payment assistance**: Many local, state, and federal programs offer grants or favorable loan terms to first-time homebuyers—look into these!

- **Withdrawal from an IRA**: First-time homebuyers can withdraw up to $10,000 from an IRA without paying the 10 percent early withdrawal penalty. But be aware that withdrawal may still be subject to income taxes and it does reduce retirement savings.

- **Avoid private mortgage insurance (PMI)**: If you can't afford to make a 20% down payment on your home, you will likely have to pay PMI. This insurance protects the lender but is an added cost to you. To avoid PMI, look for loan programs that offer lower down payment requirements without needing PMI. If you still can't avoid PMI, it might be a good sign to wait until your financial situation is more stable before buying a home.

Additionally, you can consider borrowing up to 50% of your vested 401(k) balance (up to $50,000) to fund your down payment. You'll need to repay this loan on a monthly basis, but it's like borrowing from yourself, which can be a smart option if done responsibly. Just be careful not to withdraw funds from your 401(k) before the age of fifty-nine and half, as this would trigger a 10 percent early withdrawal penalty plus ordinary income taxes.

## Why Homeownership Is Still a Good Idea

Despite some of the costs and responsibilities, homeownership remains one of the best ways to build long-term wealth. Here's why:

- **Leveraged Return**: Let's say you put down 20% on a house worth $400,000—that's an investment of $80,000. If the house appreciates by 5% per year, that's a $20,000 increase in the first year, which means you just made

25% on your initial investment of $80,000. Yes, there are expenses like taxes, interest, home insurance, and maintenance. But you're also saving on rent while building equity, so it's like making money while paying yourself instead of your landlord.

- **Forced Savings**: Every time you make a mortgage payment, part of that payment goes toward paying down the loan balance and building equity in your home. Think of it as a "forced savings plan." It might be harder to access compared to cash savings, but with the right property, you are investing in something that can increase in value over time.

- **Income Potential**: Owning a home gives you the freedom to be creative with how you use your living space. You can rent out a room or part of your home to help pay your mortgage. A popular and smart strategy is house hacking, where you buy a multi-unit property, live in one unit, and rent out the others. This approach can greatly reduce your living expenses and invest more. This is exactly how my husband and I got started with home ownership back in 2016!

- **Stability**: Unlike renting, where you're at the mercy of your landlord's decisions (rent hikes, improvement restrictions, etc.), homeownership provides stability. You don't have to worry about rent increases, or whether you'll be forced to move. You have the control to make changes, invest in the property, and build long-term security.

When you think about homeownership, don't just focus on the immediate challenges or expenses. Instead, think of it as a **long-term investment** in your financial future. With the right planning and commitment, it's one of the most effective ways to build wealth while living the life you truly want.

If you're thinking about buying a home, take the time to weigh the pros and cons. Understand your financial situation, compare the potential return on the property with other options, and make sure you're ready for the responsibility that comes with owning a home. With careful planning, homeownership can be a strong step toward building your financial future.

## Avoiding Car Loans

When your net worth is under $200,000, your car is likely the next biggest purchase after your home. Here's a tip that can make a big financial difference: delay buying a new car as long as possible, especially if you live in a city with good public transportation or bike-friendly options.

If you need a car, consider saving to buy a used one. When purchasing a used car, avoid spending all your money on the upfront cost. Set aside cash for more frequent maintenance and repairs later. Used cars typically cost 20 to 45 percent less than new ones, which saves you money upfront. They usually come with lower insurance premiums and registration fees as well. Choosing a used car reduces the need for a large loan and frees up money for other important expenses like buying a home. Just be sure to check the car's history and condition carefully before buying as maintenance can be higher with used vehicles.

On average, routine maintenance and repairs can cost about $900 per year, depending on the make and model. It's wise to budget $100 to $150 monthly to cover oil changes, new tires, and unexpected repairs.

Here's an important insight: having a car loan can reduce how much you qualify for when applying for a mortgage. For instance, every $100 in monthly car payments can lower your home-buying power by around $25,000. Without a car loan, lenders see fewer monthly debts, making it easier to get approved for a larger mortgage.

Additionally, carrying less debt often helps improve your credit score, making it easier to get approved for loans, especially mortgages. So, if you plan to buy a home soon or want to build a stronger financial future, delaying a car loan or buying a used car with cash can be a smart financial decision.

## Wealth Roadmap Part 3 of 5: Investable Cash Flow

Ready to put your money to work? Let's figure out how much cash you can actually invest each year. This is your investable cash flow, the fuel for growing your wealth. If you already have a clear picture of your finances, great! Just add up your savings, retirement contributions, and employer match. If you're not sure yet, don't worry. Getting started is the first step, and here's a simple guide:

1. **Start with Your Income:** List all the money coming in, including salary, bonuses, company stocks, side jobs, rental income, and any other sources for a complete view of your total income.

2. **Subtract Your Essential Expenses:** Calculate your necessary bills like rent or mortgage, utilities, groceries,

transportation, insurance, loan payments, and taxes. You can find your total federal tax on line 16 of your latest tax return (Form 1040), and your state tax from your state income tax form.

3. **Include Your Fun Money:** Life is for living! Set aside a reasonable amount for entertainment, dining out, shopping, hobbies, travel, personal care, gifts, and donations. Don't forget to include money for financial planning. It's an investment in your future.

4. **Calculate Your Investable Cash Flow:** Take your total income and subtract your essential and lifestyle expenses. The amount left is your investable cash flow, which is the money you can comfortably save and invest for future growth without affecting your daily life. If you use the template, this calculation happens automatically in **cell B66**. If the number seems too high, double-check your expenses because small costs can add up. You can also use tools like Empower Retirement or Monarch Money to track your spending and stay organized.

   *Formula:*

   Investable Cash Flow =

   Total Income – Essential Expenses – Lifestyle Expenses

5. **50/30/20 Rule:** In **cells B67 to B69**, you'll see your spending as a percentage of your after-tax income split into essentials, discretionary, and investing. The 50/30/20 rule is a simple budgeting framework: spend 50% on essentials, 30% on wants, and save or invest 20%. If you're aiming for early retirement, you might consider shifting to 40% essentials, 25% wants, and 35% savings and

investing. This rule helps balance your needs, lifestyle, and financial goals while building good saving habits.

6. **Update and Adjust:** Life changes, and your finances will too. Update your Wealth Roadmap whenever there is a major change—like a raise, a new family member, additional income, or new expenses. If you don't have a Wealth Roadmap yet, scan the **QR code** below to get your own copy. Reviewing your progress regularly will keep you on track. Ask yourself: Are we saving at least 15 percent of our income? If not, it might be time to reduce spending or find ways to increase income.

7. **Celebrate Consistency:** Consistency is the key! Small and regular investments add up over time. Keeping your investable cash flow positive and growing, especially early on, will build the resources you need to reach your financial goals. The more you invest now, the brighter your future will be.

Ready to start? Keep building your saved Google Sheet or scan the **QR code** below to create your **Wealth Roadmap** and clarify your investable cash flow today! The journey to financial freedom starts with knowing your numbers and taking action. You've got this.

**Phase Two: The Growth Spurt** (Net Worth Between $200,000 and $1,000,000)

As your net worth grows, your main focus shifts from just saving money to investing it wisely. When your net worth is between $200,000 and $1,000,000, investment returns become the most important factor for growing your wealth, even more than how much you save. At this stage, you begin to see the powerful effect that assets like real estate and a smart investment strategy can have on your financial progress.

It's time to take a deeper look at how your investments are allocated. Your focus now shifts from just saving and accumulating to investing strategically and making sure that each dollar is working efficiently for you. The goal is to create a portfolio that maximizes growth while balancing risk, and understanding the different asset classes and how to allocate them is key.

## Understanding Your Asset Classes

When building wealth and uncovering the hidden secrets to financial freedom, it's important to know where your assets are and how they work together. Assets can be grouped into major categories, each with different roles and characteristics.

Here's a simple breakdown of the main asset classes. I'll save equities for last, as they are often the key to your portfolio's growth, and there is much to learn about them.

## Liquid Assets

These are the funds you can easily access and use right away. Liquid assets include your cash savings, checking accounts, high-yield savings account, CDs, money market funds, treasury bills, and ultra short-term bonds that are easy to sell or cash out. Having a healthy liquid asset cushion allows you to weather emergencies without dipping into your long-term investments. As of May 2025, expect a return of around 3.5% to 4.5% from this class.

## Real Estate

Real estate is a powerful asset, but it's important to understand how to make it work in your favor. Essentially, the value of your property minus any mortgage debt is your home equity. For instance, if your home is worth $400,000 and you owe $250,000, your home equity is $150,000. Real estate typically appreciates over time, making it an important long-term asset. However, there are a couple of things to consider:

- **Liquidity:** Real estate is not a liquid asset, which means it's not as easily accessible as cash or stocks. Selling a home involves time, selling costs, and sometimes market conditions that are beyond your control.

- **Transaction Fees:** The fees involved in selling a property, like agent commissions and closing costs, can be substantial—usually around 6 percent of the sale price. So it's smart to hold on to your property for a while so that it can appreciate. If you sell soon after buying, these transaction fees can eat up your returns and make it much harder to come out ahead.

- **Leveraging Your Real Estate Investment:** Leverage in real estate means using borrowed money, like a mortgage, to buy a property. It allows you to control a larger asset with less of your own cash. The loan-to-value ratio (LTV) shows how much of the property's value is financed through debt. Using leverage can increase your returns because when the property's value grows, your profit is based on the full value, not just the cash you invested. However, leverage also adds risk if property values drop, so it should be used carefully.

Let's break this down:

| Market Value | Mortgage | Home Equity | LTV | Return | Leveraged Return |
|---|---|---|---|---|---|
| 400,000 | 250,000 | 150,000 | 63.3% | 5% | 13.3% |

In this example, the owners are earning a 13.3% return on their home equity through leverage, compared to 25% when the loan-to-value ratio was 80% as mentioned earlier in this chapter. As they pay down their mortgage together, their equity grows, but their leveraged return decreases because they are borrowing less of the home's value. Simply put, the less they owe, the smaller the boost they get from leverage. However, paying off the mortgage also brings peace of mind, financial security, and relief from monthly payments. This can reduce stress for both partners and give them greater control over their shared finances and future.

- **Buy vs. Rent:** You might wonder, "What about the mortgage payments? How do they impact my return?" To keep things simple, let's say your monthly mortgage payment is about the same as what you'd pay in rent for a similar home nearby.

In the Midwest, homes usually have a price-to-rent ratio of about 15:1. This means buying a home costs roughly

15 times what it would cost to rent it for a year. Typically, this makes buying more affordable than renting. However, the expected yearly increase in home prices in this region is lower, generally around 3 percent.

Now, compare that to cities like Seattle or San Francisco, where the price-to-rent ratio can be 30:1 or even 40:1. That means buying is much more expensive compared to renting, but these areas also tend to have higher expected appreciation.

Deciding whether to buy or rent is a big choice that affects your financial future. While this isn't a deep dive into real estate investment analysis (that's a whole other topic), the main takeaway is clear: real estate is a powerful way to build wealth over time. By using a mortgage to leverage your investment and benefiting from your home's appreciation, you can significantly increase your returns.

Even though recent market conditions have moderated home price growth to historical norms of about 3% to 5% annually, real estate still offers opportunities to build equity and net worth. Using leverage allows you to control a larger asset with less cash, potentially increasing your returns, but it also adds risk if property values decline. Although real estate is an important part of many investors' portfolios, it is usually one piece of a diversified wealth-building strategy rather than the sole path to riches.

## Bond

Bonds and fixed income investments are like loans you make to a government or company. In exchange, they pay you a set amount of interest on a regular schedule and return your principal at the end of a defined period. These investments usually experience less price volatility than stocks, making them generally safer and providing steady income, especially government bonds. Adding bonds to your investment mix helps reduce overall portfolio risk and create more stable returns over time. In 2025, a well-diversified bond portfolio can generally expect annual returns between 3 percent and 5 percent, depending on the mix of government, corporate, and high-yield bonds.

Government bonds come in several types, generally categorized by issuer, maturity, and purpose. The most common types include:

- **Treasury Bills (T-Bills):** Short-term government bonds with maturities up to 52 weeks, sold at a discount and redeemed at face value at maturity.

- **Treasury Notes (T-Notes):** Medium-term bonds maturing in 2 to 10 years, paying fixed coupon interest semi-annually.

- **Treasury Bonds (T-Bonds):** Long-term bonds with maturities from 20 to 30 years, also paying semi-annual interest.

- **Treasury Inflation-Protected Securities (TIPS):** Bonds indexed to inflation, where principal adjusts with inflation while paying fixed interest.

- **U.S. Savings Bonds:** Non-marketable bonds like Series EE and Series I, often with fixed or inflation-adjusted interest.

- **Municipal Bonds:** Issued by local governments or states to fund public projects, including general obligation bonds backed by taxes and revenue bonds backed by project income.

Corporate bonds come in different types based on various factors like credit quality, security, maturity, and special features. Here are the main types:

- **Investment-Grade Bonds:** These bonds have high credit ratings (like AAA to BBB) and are issued by financially stable companies. They offer lower risk and typically lower yields.

- **High-Yield Bonds (Junk Bonds):** Bonds rated below investment grade (BB or lower). They carry higher risk of default but offer higher yields to compensate investors.

- **Secured Bonds:** Backed by specific collateral such as company assets, reducing risk for investors in case of default.

- **Unsecured Bonds (Debentures):** Not backed by collateral but based on the company's creditworthiness.

- **Convertible Bonds:** Can be converted into a predetermined number of the issuing company's shares, allowing potential equity participation.

- **Floating-Rate Bonds:** Have variable interest rates that adjust periodically based on a reference rate or formula.

- **Zero-Coupon Bonds:** Do not pay periodic interest but are issued at a discount and redeemed at face value at maturity.

- **Callable Bonds:** Can be redeemed by the issuer before maturity, giving companies flexibility but adding reinvestment risk for investors.

- **Putable Bonds:** Allow investors to sell the bond back to the issuer before maturity at specified times or prices.

Corporate bonds also differ by maturity length (short, medium, long term) and industry sectors, such as utilities, transportation, industrials, and finance.

These varieties allow investors to select bonds that fit their risk tolerance, income needs, and investment strategies.

A key concept in bond investing is duration, which measures how sensitive a bond's price is to changes in interest rates. Duration is expressed in years and represents the weighted average time until the bond's cash flows, including interest payments and principal, are received. Bonds with longer durations are more sensitive to interest rate changes, which means they have greater price volatility and risk. For example, a bond with a duration of five years typically sees its price move about 5 percent if the increase rate changes by 1 percent, but in the opposite direction. If interest rates decrease, the bond's price increases; if rates increase, its price decreases. Bonds with shorter durations are less sensitive to rate changes and generally carry lower interest rate risk.

Besides interest rate risk measured by duration, bonds also face credit risk—the risk that the issuer may default on payments—and inflation risk, which reduces the real purchasing power of fixed payments. Government bonds typically have lower credit risk compared to corporate bonds. Additionally, bonds with higher durations tend to have greater price risk compared to those with lower durations.

Understanding duration and these other risk factors helps investors manage risk and create a bond portfolio aligned with their financial goals and market outlook. This combination of features makes bonds valuable components of diversified investment strategies, offering a balance of income, stability, and risk management compared to stocks.

## Vehicles

When you're just starting out, your car is often one of your biggest assets, and it's super handy for getting around. But here's the twist: cars lose value pretty fast! Think of your car like a shiny new phone that gets a little less impressive every year. On average, a new car loses about 16–20% of its value in the first year and another 12% in the second year. That means after two years, your car is usually worth around 70% of what you paid for it.

So, while your car is awesome for road trips and errands, it doesn't really help your wealth grow. When you look at your net worth, remember: your car's value is slowly driving away over time. Enjoy the ride, but keep in mind it's not speeding up your financial growth—it's more like gently tapping the brakes!

## Other Assets

This is where you may store your more speculative investments, like cryptocurrencies, venture capital, precious metals, and commodities. These can be highly volatile but also present opportunities for high returns if managed carefully. As these assets carry more risk, be mindful of how much of your overall portfolio is tied to them. Here's a quick list of what to expect:

| Asset Class | Estimated Annual Return | Key Notes |
|---|---|---|
| Crypto-currencies | 15% to 30%, but highly volatile | Bitcoin's average annual return over the past decade is around 25%, with large ups and downs. Other cryptocurrencies vary widely in performance and risk. |
| Venture Capital | 13%–22% (median to top quartile) | Average VC fund annualized returns are around 15% per year; top funds can achieve 22%–28%; early-stage targets can be higher, but risk is very high. |
| Precious Metals | 3%–7% | Gold's long-term annualized return is 6%–7%; broader precious metals average 3%–7% depending on holding period and metal. |
| Commodities | 3%–7% | Broad commodity indices (like GSCI) have averaged 3%–7% per year over the long term, but with high volatility and periods of negative returns. |

## Equity

Equity is the backbone of long-term wealth growth. When it comes to building wealth over the long term, equity investments—which includes stocks, ETFs (exchange-traded funds), mutual funds, and even company stock—typically form the foundation of your financial portfolio. These assets provide significant opportunities for capital gains (profits from selling investments at a higher price) and dividends (regular payouts from companies to shareholders). Equity investments allow your money to grow over time, especially when reinvested and compounded.

Equity investments are often considered growth assets because they can increase significantly in value over time. Historically, broad market indexes such as the S&P 500 have returned about 10% to 13% annually on average. This means investing in a diversified mix of stocks can help your wealth grow faster than inflation, supporting your long-term goals like retirement.

## The Importance of Diversification

Diversification means spreading your investments across different stocks, sectors, and countries. This strategy reduces the risk that a downturn in one sector, such as technology, or a market, such as the United States, will significantly harm your overall returns. When done well, diversification lowers your overall risk without reducing your long-term returns. It helps protect your money during market downturns and gives you a better chance to capture gains from different parts of the market.

*Sample stocks in a diversified portfolio might include:*

- **US Large-Cap Stocks:** Companies like Microsoft, Apple, and NVIDIA. These are the big players in the market that have a proven track record of success.

- **US Mid-Cap Stocks:** Medium-sized companies with steady growth and less risk than small caps. Examples are UnitedHealth Group, Best Buy, and DocuSign.

- **US Small-Cap Stocks:** Smaller, up-and-coming companies with potential for higher growth, but also carry higher risk.

- **International Stocks:** Investing globally gives you exposure to markets that might be doing well when the US market is struggling.

A good diversified portfolio might include stocks across different industries (tech, healthcare, consumer goods, etc.), geographies (US, Europe, emerging markets), and market sizes (large, mid, and small-cap companies).

The goal of diversification is to spread out your risk, so if one area of the market takes a hit, other parts of your portfolio may still be performing well. This helps smooth out the ups and downs of the market over time and minimizes the chance of your losing big.

## The Power of Passive Investing for Couples

Now, you may be wondering: "How do we choose the right stocks, ETFs, or mutual funds for our family?" The good news is, you don't have to pick individual stocks to make money—and you don't need to be a financial expert to get started. That's where passive investing comes in.

Passive investing means buying and holding a broad market index like the S&P 500 or the Total Stock Market Index through ETFs or mutual funds. Instead of trying to outsmart the market, you simply buy a small slice of hundreds or thousands of companies in one go. This approach tracks the performance of the overall market, so your investments grow (or shrink) with the economy as a whole. The beauty of passive investing is that it's typically low-cost, easy to manage, and doesn't require constant research or market timing.

## Why Low Fees Matter

Just like dividends and reinvesting help your money grow, fees do the opposite by shrinking your returns. When you invest, paying lower fees means more money stays working for you over time.

For example, index funds like the Vanguard S&P 500 ETF often have very low fees, at around 0.03%. On the other hand, actively managed funds can charge fees over 1%. Plus, if you use a wealth manager or advisor, expect to pay an additional management fee of about 1% to 1.5% on top. These fees add up and can significantly reduce your investment growth.

In 2025, average fees for balanced mutual funds range from 0.25% to 0.50%, while target date funds usually charge between 0.40% and 0.60%. Some low-cost index funds charge as little as 0.015% to 0.05%, and some funds like Fidelity's "ZERO" funds don't charge any fees at all!

If your investment fees exceed 0.5%, consider whether those costs are really worth it. Choosing low-fee funds helps your money grow faster and keeps you on track to meet your goals.

Now, imagine investing $1,000 each month. If your investments grow at 10% annually, you'll end up with a much larger future value than if your return is 8.5% (10% minus the 1.5% fees). Even a small difference in returns can make a big impact over time:

| Years to Invest | Total Investment | Future Value at 10% Return | Future Value at 8.5% Return | Difference |
|---|---|---|---|---|
| 10 | $120,000 | $204,845 | $188,138 | -8.2% |
| 15 | $180,000 | $414,470 | $361,786 | -12.7% |
| 20 | $240,000 | $759,369 | $626,999 | -17.4% |
| 25 | $300,000 | $1,326,833 | $1,032,058 | -22.2% |
| 30 | $360,000 | $2,260,488 | $1,650,706 | -27.0% |

## Long-Term Approach to Equity Investing

One of the key things to remember is that equity investments are long-term. The magic of compound growth takes time, and even though stock prices may fluctuate in the short term, they generally tend to appreciate in value over longer periods. This is why starting early and staying consistent with your investments is so important. The longer your money stays invested, the more it can benefit from the power of compounding.

## Start Young, Grow Strong

Passive investing is a simple way to help kids learn about money and how it grows over time. In our family, whenever our children get cash gifts for birthdays or holidays, we put that money into low-fee index ETFs instead of just leaving it in a piggy bank.

Our eight-year-old son is excited to see his account grow into thousands of dollars over the years. Seeing his savings increase over time helps him learn about patience, the magic of compounding (where money earns more money), and the idea that building wealth takes time, not luck.

Even our four-year-old daughter, who doesn't fully understand investments yet, says "Put it in my bank!" when she gets gift money. Her "bank" is actually invested in a total-market ETF. By making investing a regular family habit, she's picking up smart money skills early, just by copying what her brother does.

This routine makes money lessons real for our kids. It shows them why saving and investing regularly is important, and why thinking long-term pays off. Besides growing their savings, we're also giving them tools, confidence, and smart habits they'll use as adults.

Best of all, these early steps in passive investing will later spark family conversations about money, insurance, taxes, and other important topics when they are ready, helping set them up for lifelong financial well-being.

With the new Trump Account rules in place (more details later in the chapter under Gifting), we are considering moving their money into individual Trump Accounts once they become available, to benefit from the tax-deferred growth.

## Get Started, Stay Consistent

So, how can you make the most of equity investing? It's simple—start early, stay diversified, and keep costs low. Whether you're investing in ETFs, mutual funds, or individual stocks, make sure your portfolio reflects your long-term goals. Consistency and patience are the keys to making these investments grow over time.

Remember, the best part about equity investments is that you don't have to be a stock-picking genius to succeed. By following these simple principles and staying committed, you'll be well on your way to growing your wealth and achieving your financial goals!

## Weighted Average Return

At **Phase Two**, your financial picture now includes a mix of different assets. It's time to look at how all these pieces work together. This is where your Weighted Average Return (WAR) comes in.

Weighted Average Return helps you see the big picture by showing the average return on your investments, based on how much of your net worth is in each asset class. Rather than looking at each asset in isolation, WAR lets you understand how your entire portfolio is performing and how each category—like cash, real estate, bonds, and stocks—contributes to your financial growth. It's a practical, high-level way to check if your portfolio is on track and spot areas that might need a tweak.

Let's get hands-on and learn how to calculate your Weighted Average Return (WAR) and use it to design an investment plan that matches your goals. First, open your Google Spreadsheet from Wealth Roadmap Part 2 of 5: Net Worth. If you haven't finished that step, hit pause for now and complete it first. Just scan the **QR code** below to make your own copy. We'll keep building from there, so every step connects and makes sense as you build your financial game plan!.

Ready? Let's dive in and calculate your Weighted Average Return as the next step on your Wealth Roadmap!

# Wealth Roadmap Part 4 of 5: Weighted Average Return

This exercise is all about calculating your Weighted Average Return (WAR)—the average return on your investments based on how your total net worth is allocated across different asset categories. This is by no means a precise calculation, but a fast and high-level estimate of your asset situation. Here's how you can figure it out:

1. **Categorize Your Assets**. In the template, your assets will be sorted into these categories:

   a. Liquid: cash, savings, CDs, treasury bills, money market funds, etc.

   b. Real Estate: Property value minus mortgage debt.

   c. Bond: Fixed-income investments.

   d. Equity: Stocks, mutual funds, ETFs, etc.

   e. Vehicle: Current market value of your car minus car loan.

   f. Other: Anything else, like crypto, collectibles, etc.

2. **Calculate Return for Real Estate**. For your real estate assets, input the market value of your property and outstanding mortgage balance. Look up the long-term return for your property (you can check sites like Redfin for a five-year estimate and sales history). The leveraged return is automatically calculated in cell M7, which feeds into your total weighted average return in cell D11.

3. **Calculate Return for Vehicles.** For your vehicles, enter the market value and estimate the remaining useful years (the lifespan of well-maintained vehicles is typically ten to twenty years, depending on the type). The depreciation rate is automatically calculated in cell J13 and contributes to your overall return in cell D11.

4. **Bond.** For bonds or fixed income, input the total dollar amount of bonds in your retirement and brokerage accounts. As we assume your investments and retirement accounts are mostly in bonds and equities, this will directly reduce the equity percentage of your total assets.

5. **Confirm Expected Long-Term Returns**: For each category, except for real estate and vehicles, input the expected long-term annual return rate. The spreadsheet provides default numbers, but feel free to update them based on your personal situation.

6. **Set Your Target Allocation**: You can see how your WAR changes as you adjust the percentage of each asset in your total portfolio, primarily in **cells D17, D19, D21, and D22**. For example, you might want to shift some of your assets away from cash and into more growth-focused investments. Watch how your target allocation affects the overall return. This is a simple way to start thinking about how reallocating assets could help you achieve your financial goals.

By calculating your Weighted Average Return (WAR), you'll gain valuable insights into how your assets are performing overall. This will help you make better decisions about where to allocate your money to reach your goals. Whether you need to adjust your portfolio, focus on specific investments, or simply understand your current situation, WAR helps you start thinking about your next steps.

Ready to dive in? Keep building on your saved Google sheet or **scan the QR code** below and create your copy today! The journey to financial freedom starts with knowing your numbers and taking action. You've got this—the power is in your hands!

**Phase Three: The Fun Ride and Beyond** (Net Worth Above $1,000,000)

Congratulations—your net worth has crossed the $1 million mark! At this stage, the financial game shifts. Now, time becomes your most valuable asset. The key to success here is simple: stay in the game and let compounding work its magic. Remember, 99% of Warren Buffett's wealth was built after he turned sixty-five. He did it not by chasing the highest returns, but by letting time and steady growth do the heavy lifting. Think "slow and steady wins the race;" preserving your wealth is just as important as growing it.

Even if you're not a millionaire yet, keep following the roadmap. You might get there faster than you think if you stay focused and take intentional actions. Here's a quick look at what's ahead, and how the first four parts of the **Wealth Roadmap** come together to realize your financial dream!

# Wealth Roadmap Part 5 of 5: Roadmap to Wealth

This is the final step of your Wealth Roadmap! You've already done the hard work by setting goals, tracking your assets, and understanding your cash flow and rate of returns. Now it's time to bring everything together and create your personalized roadmap to wealth!

This is where things get fun—let's put the pieces together and visualize the journey to your financial freedom!

Here are the building blocks we've gathered to build your roadmap:

- **Wealth Goals**: From Part 1, you've identified your essential and "essentials plus" goals.

- **Initial Investment**: From Part 2, you've calculated your current net worth.

- **Annual Investment**: From Part 3, you've figured out your investable cash flow—the money you can comfortably invest each year.

- **Rate of Return**: From Part 4, your weighted average return is ready to guide you forward!

## Here's How It Works:

You'll notice that if you haven't filled in any of the numbers yet, the real return (**cell B5**) starts as a negative number. Don't panic! This simply reflects the reality that without investing, inflation will erode the value of your money over time. But when you plug in your net worth and rate of return, this number will adjust to show how much you're really earning after inflation is taken into account. By using real return in your projections, you won't need to adjust your goals for future prices—it's already built in.

1. **Retirement Age**: To start, pick your retirement age: is it the typical sixty-five? Do you want to retire early? Or maybe you love your work and plan on working for as long as you can? Your goal here is to make sure that you're building a financial foundation that gives you options— so work becomes a choice, not a necessity.

2. **Your Road Ahead**: Now, it's time to compare your projections with your goals. How long will it take to reach your Essential Goal (maintaining your lifestyle in your ideal city) and your Essentials Plus Goal (living your ideal life in your dream location)? This is where the fun begins!

3. **See the Impact**: In columns D through H, you can experiment with different scenarios—change your savings amount per year, adjust your real return rate, and see how it all impacts your journey! You might discover that the impact of your savings has a smaller impact than you thought, or that starting with a strong foundation allows you to lower your return expectations and take fewer risks as you approach retirement.

**Ready to dive in?**

Let's get started! Use the **Google Sheet** you've been building, or **Scan the QR code** below and create your very own **Wealth Roadmap** today! Your financial freedom journey starts with knowing your numbers and taking action. You've got this—the power is in your hands!

**Limitations of the Model**

It's important to understand that the Wealth Roadmap is designed primarily as a mindset tool. Think of it like the map you glance at before a road trip. You'll see the general route and destination, but it won't tell you every single turn, traffic jam, or coffee stop along the way.

It's here to help you see where you are now and where you're heading financially, in the simplest way possible. But it's not meant to replace a detailed decision-making model or a comprehensive financial plan.

To keep the model easy-to-use and approachable, some big (and somewhat tricky) items were left out. For example, healthcare costs in early retirement and long-term care expenses are not explicitly included, even though they can significantly impact your financial plan. We also count equity in your real estate as part of your total net worth, but most people don't sell their homes right after retirement. That means your equity in real estate might not be as liquid or readily available as other investments.

If you're ready to dive deeper, or if you have advanced financial modeling skills, I highly recommend exploring specialized software like Boldin. Powerful tools like this dig into the nitty-gritty details, taking into account things like medical costs, taxes, inflation, investment risks, and much more. This granular analysis can give you a clearer, more complete picture of your financial future.

Later in this chapter, in the section titled "**Modern Planning Tools: Using Technology to Maximize Your Financial Journey**," I'll share more about these advanced tools and resources.

But if detailed financial modeling isn't your thing, and you are facing a major decision like planning for early retirement or building your dream home, it is a great idea to work with an independent financial planner. Many offer comprehensive, personalized plans and some provide flat-fee options starting at $2,500. Others charge by the hour, typically ranging from $200 to $400 per hour. Trust me, investing in expert guidance like this is well worth it for the peace of mind and clarity you will gain, on top of a much better aligned personal strategy for investment, tax, insurance, retirement, and estate planning. (Read more on how to hire a good financial planner later in this chapter.)

For now, think of the **Wealth Roadmap** as your financial compass—a simple, clear guide to point you in the right direction with confidence. Just remember, it's a starting point, not the final word on every financial decision you make.

## Protect What You've Built

As your money grows, it's just as important to protect it as it is to grow it. One big mistake some investors make is putting too much money into just one investment or type of asset. When you have more to lose, a big loss can really hurt. That's why diversification, or spreading your investments around and staying on track with a sound investment strategy should be your top priority.

Smart investors don't just chase the next flashy investment with high rewards. They know it's safer to have steady, reliable income streams than to bet everything on a "sure thing" that's really a gamble. Instead, they build a balanced mix of investments that can ride out market ups and downs without wrecking their financial future.

## The Three-Bucket Strategy

Now that you're in a stronger financial position, it's a good time to revisit the Three-Bucket Strategy first introduced in Chapter 5. This strategy helps you organize your money based on when you'll need it, balancing accessible cash, steady income, and long-term growth.

If you're still working and saving, your short-term bucket should mainly cover emergency funds and near-term planned expenses like vacations. The mid-term bucket might not be necessary unless you're approaching retirement or need money soon for things like children's college tuition (ideally funded through 529 plans). Most of your savings belong in the long-term bucket, invested in a diversified, low-cost portfolio designed to grow your wealth over time.

If retirement is near, it's important to increase your funds in both the short-term and mid-term buckets to prepare for withdrawals and spending. That's where the liquidation strategy comes in, ensuring you have steady cash flow and don't have to sell long-term investments during market downturns.

The Three-Bucket Strategy provides a practical and flexible way to manage your money through different life stages. By maintaining cash for short-term needs, balanced investments for intermediate expenses, and growth-focused assets for the long term, you reduce risk and can confidently plan for financial goals at every stage.

## Liquidation Strategy

To keep your portfolio balanced and liquid, it's important to refill your short-term bucket as you use it for spending. In a bull market, you typically sell (or liquidate) investments from your long-term bucket first to refill your short-term (and mid-term, if needed) buckets. In a bear market, you go for the mid-term bucket to protect your long-term growth potential.

Figure 11: Buckets in Action—Smart Withdrawals for Bull & Bear Markets

THE HIDDEN SECRET TO FREEDOM

This approach keeps your portfolio flexible and ensures you always have the cash you need, no matter how the market behaves. The chart below shows how this strategy works during both bull and bear markets:

## Retirement Planning: How Much Do You Really Need?

For those already retired, the numbers shift a bit. Let's say you plan to spend about $90,000 per year (don't worry about taxes for now, we'll talk about them soon), and $42,000 of that is covered by Social Security. This means your annual cash need is $48,000 ($90,000 – $42,000).

You'll want to set aside $96,000 in a safe, easily accessible place, to cover two years of expenses. The next eight years of cash needs, or $384,000, should be placed in a blend of bonds and equities ETFs. This gives you some security, while still allowing for growth. The rest of your portfolio can be fully allocated to equities for optimal growth.

## Time is Your Ally

When your net worth is over $1,000,000, time becomes your greatest asset. Your focus shifts from just accumulating wealth to protecting it, leveraging the power of compounding, and making smarter, risk-aware decisions—just like Warren Buffett did. It's about letting time and consistent growth work for you over decades to come.

Investing wisely and staying focused on your long-term goals will make all the difference. With your financial foundation set, your next step is to keep growing your wealth while confidently navigating life's changes.

To truly maximize your earnings, it's important to take advantage of tax-friendly accounts like retirement plans, IRAs, and Roth accounts. Smart tax strategies can lower your tax bill and help your money grow faster after taxes.

Don't worry; I'll break down how to use these tax tools so you'll know exactly how to protect your wealth and make it work hard for you!

A strong investment plan means staying diversified, balancing liquidity and growth, and letting time and compounding do the heavy lifting. Focus on stability, tax efficiency, and your long-term goals. Remember, the path to lasting wealth is built on smart, steady progress.

Now, let's explore tax planning—an essential step to help you keep more of your investment earnings and safeguard your financial future.

## Three Tax Planning Principles

Maximizing your after-tax returns starts with understanding how to make your earnings and investments as tax-efficient as possible. There are three core principles every smart investor should know: not all income is taxed the same, tax planning is a lifetime process, and incorporate tax strategies into your legacy goals. Let's break these down so you can start weaving them into your financial strategy.

## 1. Not All Taxes Are Equal

When it comes to taxes, not all types of income are taxed the same way. Understanding the difference can help you keep more of your money and make smarter financial decisions.

## Ordinary (Regular) Income

Think of it as your "everyday money." This covers your paycheck, bonuses, rental income, interest from your bank, and even those quick wins from selling stocks you've owned for less than a year. The government takes a slice of this pie using regular tax brackets—so the more you earn, the bigger the bite! For example, in 2025, if you're married and filing jointly, once your taxable income goes over $206,700, you'll pay 24% on the next dollar, and 32% once you cross $394,600. And if your state has income tax, there's an extra bite being taken!

## Tax-Advantaged Pre-Tax Accounts

You can reduce your taxable ordinary income by contributing to tax-deferred retirement accounts. The money in these accounts grows tax-deferred, meaning you don't pay income taxes on earnings or contributions until you withdraw the funds, ideally after age fifty-nine and a half to avoid penalties. Here's a bit more detail on each:

- **401(k)**: An employer-sponsored retirement plan where employees contribute pre-tax income, lowering taxable income now. The funds grow tax-deferred until withdrawal during retirement.

- **403(b)**: Similar to a 401(k), this plan is for employees of public schools and nonprofit organizations, offering pre-tax contributions and tax-deferred growth.

- **457(b)**: Available to state and local government employees and some nonprofits, this plan allows pre-tax contributions with the advantage of penalty-free withdrawals upon separation from service, plus special catch-up options near retirement.

- **Traditional IRA**: An individual retirement account that may allow tax-deductible contributions depending on your income and participation in other plans. Earnings grow tax-deferred until withdrawal.

Each of these accounts helps reduce your current or future tax burden while allowing your investments to grow more efficiently, catering to different employment situations and savings objectives.

## Tax Tip:

You can stash ordinary income in tax-deferred accounts like 401(k)s and IRAs (there's an income limit for deductible IRA contributions though). That means you don't pay taxes on that money now—it grows tax-deferred until you take it out later (ideally after age fifty-nine and a half to dodge early withdrawal penalties). This can be a smart move if you think you'll be in a lower tax bracket in retirement or plan to move somewhere with lower (or no) state income tax.

## Long-Term Capital Gains

Now, let's talk about the "slow and steady" money. If you buy an investment—like stocks, real estate, or mutual funds—and hold onto it for more than a year before selling, you get a sweet deal: long-term capital gains tax rates. These are much lower than ordinary income rates! In 2025, married couples filing jointly pay:

- 0% if your taxable income is up to $96,700

- 15% if you're between $96,700 and $600,050
- 20% if you're above $600,050

If you're a couple earning more than $250,000 per year, you may owe an additional 3.8% Net Investment Income Tax (NIIT) on certain investment income. This includes interest, dividends, rental income, and capital gains—but it does not apply to withdrawals from retirement accounts. The NIIT kicks in when your modified adjusted gross income (MAGI) exceeds $250,000 for married couples filing jointly.

The tax applies to the lesser of your net investment income or the amount your MAGI exceeds the threshold. This means if you have investment income and your income is above the limit, you pay 3.8% on the smaller amount between those two.

## Tax Tip:

Want to pay less tax? Hold your investments for at least a year before selling. That way, you'll earn more and pay less to Uncle Sam!

## Tax-Free Assets

Tax-free assets are like finding a secret treasure chest in the world of investing! With these accounts, your money grows and you don't have to pay taxes on the gains, forever. Some of the best examples are:

- **Municipal bonds**, which pay interest exempt from federal income taxes.
- **Tax-exempt mutual funds and ETFs** that hold municipal bonds.

- **Roth IRAs and Roth 401(k)s:** You pay taxes up front on your contributions, but all your growth and future withdrawals are totally tax-free (as long as you follow the rules).

- **Health Savings Accounts (HSAs):** Triple tax advantage! You get a tax deduction for contributions, your money grows tax-free, and withdrawals for qualified healthcare expenses are also tax-free.

- **529 Plans:** Perfect for education savings—your money grows tax-free and you can use it for qualified education expenses without paying taxes on the gains.

- **Life insurance policies** with cash value, providing tax-deferred growth and tax-free death benefits (more on insurance later in the chapter).

## Tax Planning Principle #1 in a Nutshell

- Everyday money like salary, bonuses, interest, and short-term capital gains (from assets held a year or less) are taxed at your ordinary income tax rates. To save on taxes, try using tax-deferred accounts, like retirement plans, or hold investments for at least one year to qualify for lower tax rates.

- Investments held for more than a year get special tax treatment called long-term capital gains, which usually mean much lower taxes.

- Tax-free accounts, like Roth accounts, are the VIPs in your financial life. Use them wisely, follow the rules, and your future self will thank you!

Taxes don't have to be scary. Play the game smartly, and you'll keep more of your hard-earned money in your pocket.

## 2. Tax Planning Is a Lifetime Process

Just like your financial goals and investments span a lifetime, effective tax planning should be ongoing and comprehensive too. Instead of focusing on a single tax year, build a strategy that covers your entire financial life. This helps you avoid decisions that save taxes now but could lead to higher costs later.

Long-term tax planning gives you clarity and control, helping you keep more of your money throughout all stages of life. Key strategies include Roth conversions, choosing the right accounts for your investments, and planning withdrawals carefully.

Using these strategies together helps you optimize your after-tax income, preserve your wealth, and prepare for a prosperous financial future.

## Roth Conversions

Roth conversions are a valuable tax strategy where you move money from pre-tax retirement accounts (like a traditional IRA or 401(k)) into a Roth account (such as Roth IRA). When you do this, you pay income taxes on the amount converted in that tax year, but all future growth and withdrawals from the Roth account are tax-free.

The key to maximizing the benefit of Roth conversions is timing. It's best to convert during years when your taxable income is lower, which helps reduce the tax impact of the conversion. For example, if you retire early, take a break from work, or experience a year with lower income, that could be an ideal time to convert.

Also, if the market is down, performing Roth conversions then can be advantageous because you convert accounts when their value is lower. As the market recovers, the growth in the Roth IRA will be tax-free, potentially increasing your long-term savings.

Finally, Roth conversions can help reduce your taxable income later in retirement by lowering future Required Minimum Distributions (RMDs) and possibly reducing taxes on Social Security benefits, Affordable Care Act (ACA) health insurance subsidies, and Medicare premiums like IRMAA, which are all based on income.

## How It Works: Case in Point

Meet Kelly and Sam from Chicago. Kelly was born in 1975, and Sam in 1974. They plan to retire together when Sam turns sixty-five in 2039.

When they first retire, they expect to live mostly off their savings, so their taxable income (and their tax rate) will likely be low at the start because they won't be taking money out of their retirement accounts right away.

According to current US rules, people born in 1960 or later must start taking Required Minimum Distributions (RMDs) from their pre-tax retirement accounts at age seventy-five. For Sam, that means his first RMD will be in 2049, when he'll need to withdraw about 4.1% of his account balance. Kelly will start her RMDs the following year. The amount they must withdraw will increase each year, which also means their tax bills will rise over time.

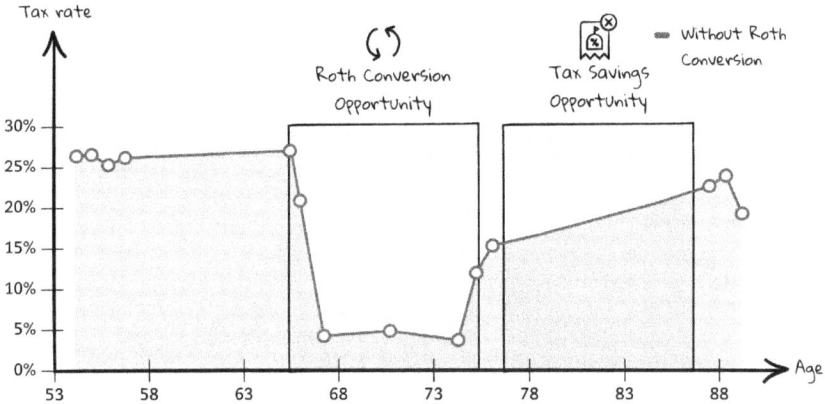

Figure 12: Watch Out for the Retirement Tax Spike!

The great news? Between retirement and when RMDs start, Kelly and Sam have a golden opportunity to do Roth conversions. They can move money from their pre-tax retirement accounts into Roth IRAs, where it can grow tax-free and future withdrawals won't be taxed. Doing this before RMDs begin can help lower their overall tax burden later.

If they retire as planned and start Roth conversions immediately, their tax rate in early retirement might be around 22%. Over time, this could drop to around 15% in later years, and eventually fall close to 0% near the end of their retirement.

Keep in mind that this example looks only at the tax impact of Roth conversions. Your situation could be different depending on several factors, including when you plan to retire, other sources of income during retirement, the size of your pre-tax retirement accounts, and important income-based factors such as Affordable Care Act (ACA) health insurance subsidies and Medicare premiums (IRMAA), which were mentioned earlier. Because Roth conversions increase the taxable income for the year you convert, they may affect your eligibility for these programs and could lead to higher premiums. For this reason, careful planning is very important.

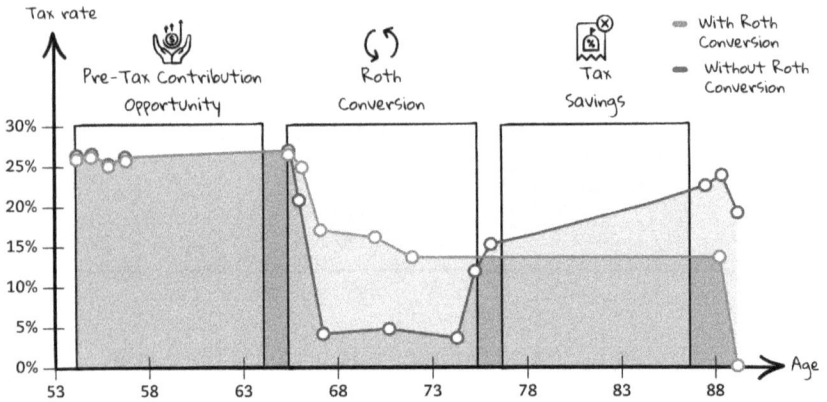

Figure 13: Roth Conversions Could Save Taxes

## Quick Takeaway

Roth conversions let Kelly and Sam pay some taxes earlier, so they can enjoy lower taxes and more financial freedom in later years. It's a smart way to plan ahead and reduce taxes and stress later on.

## Asset Location: Where Your Investments Thrive Best

Think of asset location as finding the most comfortable, most tax-friendly home for each of your investments—because not all investments (or homes) are created equal!

**High-growth assets**, like stocks and high-growth ETFs you expect to soar, love living in Roth IRAs or Roth 401(k)s. Why? Because in these tax-free accounts, all that growth and any qualified withdrawals are completely tax-free. It's like your money is living in a cozy, tax-sheltered mansion where Uncle Sam can't knock on the door!

**Dividend stocks** do well in taxable brokerage accounts because they often generate long-term capital gains and qualified dividends. That means even outside of a fancy tax shelter, these investments get a nice little tax break! Plus, when you inherit appreciated assets, such as stocks and ETFs in a brokerage account, or real estate, the cost basis of the assets gets "stepped up" to their fair market value on the original owner's death day.

For example, if your parents bought stocks for $20,000 and they are worth $50,000 when you inherit them, your new cost basis is $50,000. When you sell later for $80,000, you only owe tax on the $30,000 gain. It's a neat way to save on taxes, and your heirs benefit too!

**Tax-inefficient assets**, such as taxable bonds, REITs, and high-turnover mutual funds, prefer the protection of tax-deferred accounts, such as traditional IRAs or 401(k)s. These investments throw off lots of ordinary income, which gets taxed at higher rates. By tucking them into a tax-deferred account, you shield those frequent payouts from annual taxes and only pay up when you withdraw (hopefully in a lower tax bracket!). If you inherit a tax-deferred account from anyone other than your spouse, you'll most likely have to withdraw all funds within ten years, and pay tax at your ordinary income tax rates. There's no step-up in tax basis here. Every dollar withdrawn is taxed as ordinary income.

## Why is asset allocation important?

Matching the right asset to the right account can help you keep more of your returns and pay less in taxes over the years. It's like hosting the ultimate party for your investments—everyone's in the spot where they thrive best!

*Here's a quick and simple guide to asset location:*

- **High-growth assets**, like fast-growing stocks, are best held in Roth accounts because your earnings can grow completely tax-free.

- **Dividend stocks** fit well in taxable accounts because their long-term capital gains and qualified dividends are taxed at lower rates than ordinary income. Plus, when heirs inherit these assets, the cost basis steps up to the market value at that time, helping reduce taxes. This makes taxable accounts a smart place for dividend stocks.

- **Tax-inefficient assets**, such as bonds and other income-generating investments, belong in tax-deferred accounts. These accounts protect you from paying taxes on earnings each year until you withdraw the money.

By thoughtfully placing your investments in the right "locations," you help your money grow more efficiently and reduce unnecessary taxes down the road.

If this feels overwhelming, working with a comprehensive financial planner who understands taxes (like myself) can make navigating these decisions much smoother. The right professional can help you align your strategy with your goals, without any pressure or sales pitch, just clear guidance to let your money work smarter for you.

THE HIDDEN SECRET TO FREEDOM

## Withdrawal Strategy

Now, let's talk about how to take money out of your accounts, because where and how you withdraw is just as important as where you put your money in the first place. Here's a simple example:

Let's say you need $48,000 per year to supplement your Social Security income of $42,000. How you get that $48,000 matters:

- If you take them from a tax-deferred account (like a traditional IRA or 401(k)), you'll need to withdraw about $56,470. Why? Because $8,470 of what you pull out will be owed in taxes (assuming an effective rate of 15% for federal and state tax).

- If you need $48,000 after taxes and take it from a taxable brokerage account invested in long-term assets, you could sell just $48,000 worth. With only Social Security and the stock gains, you might remain in the 0% long-term capital gains tax bracket, meaning you pay no taxes on that sale.

- If you take $48,000 from a tax-free account such as a Roth IRA or Roth 401(k), you get the full amount without any tax, regardless of your income level.

And here's one more tip: You can mix and match withdrawals from these accounts to optimize your household taxes and manage your withdrawals for minimum impact on your retirement income. This can also help avoid higher IRMAA premiums, keeping your healthcare costs lower as well.

## 3. Integrate Tax Planning with Gifting and Legacy Goals

Coordinating your tax planning with estate planning is one of the smartest moves you can make to ensure that your wealth is transferred efficiently to your heirs or charitable causes. A proactive approach to tax and estate planning helps reduce unnecessary taxes, ensuring that more of your wealth reaches the people and causes you care about. Here are some strategies to integrate tax and estate planning that can help you maximize the impact of your wealth transfer.

### Donor-Advised Funds and Smart Gifting

Let's talk about Donor-Advised Funds (DAFs), a super-efficient way to give back while optimizing your taxes. If you're looking to make a charitable impact while saving on taxes, DAFs are a fantastic tool. Basically, a DAF is a charitable investment account where you can contribute money, stocks, or even real estate, and get a tax deduction right away. Plus, all the assets you contribute can grow tax-free within the fund.

What's even better? You get to choose where and when to distribute the funds. For example, you could make a big contribution to a DAF in a high-income year, get a tax break, and then distribute the funds over the years as you see fit. This strategy allows you to take advantage of the tax deduction now and spread your charitable donations out over time, giving you flexibility and control.

### Gifting Appreciated Assets: A Win-Win Strategy

Here's another tax-savvy strategy: gifting appreciated assets. These are investments like stocks, real estate, or business ownership that have increased in value over time. Why is this so smart? Well, if you were to sell these assets, you'd have to pay capital gains tax on the increase in value. However, when you gift these appreciated assets to your heirs or charitable causes, they inherit your cost basis. This means they pay capital gains tax when they eventually sell the asset, probably at a lower tax rate than yours, or perhaps they will even be exempt from paying taxes.

This strategy also avoids the capital gains tax you'd have paid if you sold the asset yourself. It's a win-win scenario for both the giver and the receiver.

**Tax Tip:** If you give assets to your children under 18 (or full-time students under 24), watch out for the kiddie tax. In 2025, unearned investment income over $2,700 is taxed at the parents' tax rate, which can increase their overall tax burden.

**Trump Account Supplement:** Trump Accounts, established under the One Big Beautiful Bill Act (OBBBA), are new tax-advantaged savings accounts available for children under 18. Parents, employers (such as family businesses), and others can contribute up to $5,000 per year per child, with this limit indexed for inflation starting in 2027. Contributions are made with after-tax dollars and are not tax-deductible, but the earnings grow tax-deferred. Employer contributions are allowed up to $2,500 annually per child. Trump Accounts offer a strategic way to save for children's futures and may help manage the impact of the kiddie tax by growing savings outside the child's taxable investment income.

## Gifting: A Smart Way to Reduce Estate Taxes

Gifting is a smart way to reduce estate taxes. It is not just about charity but also a powerful method to pass wealth to your loved ones. In 2025, you can give up to $19,000 per person without triggering gift taxes. If you're married, you and your spouse can elect "gift splitting" and give up to a total of $38,000 per recipient per year, all tax-free.

If you give more than $19,000 to any one person in a year or elect gift splitting as a couple, you'll need to file IRS Form 709 to report the gift. However, this does not mean you owe taxes right away. The extra amount simply counts against your lifetime gift and estate tax exemption, which is $13.99 million per person or $27.98 million for a married couple in 2025. You only pay gift or estate tax if your total gifts over your lifetime (above the annual limits) and your estate together exceed this exemption.

**Tax Tip**: If you're planning on making large gifts, it's important to stay up to date on the latest tax laws, as they're constantly changing. Consulting a tax professional is a great way to stay ahead of any adjustments in the rules.

## Integrating Estate Planning with Tax Planning

When you plan your estate, it's crucial to include tax strategies to maximize how much wealth you pass on and minimize taxes owed. Without this, taxes can significantly reduce your legacy.

Start by evaluating your assets, investments, and long-term goals. This ensures you transfer wealth efficiently and lower tax burdens. Effective estate planning combines:

- Smart investment choices focused on tax efficiency

- Using tax-advantaged accounts like Roth IRAs, Traditional IRAs, and 401(k)s

- Employing gifting strategies, such as annual exclusion gifts, to reduce taxable estate

- Creating trusts that can provide control, protection, and tax benefits

Because tax laws and your personal situation may change, regularly reviewing your estate plan with a qualified financial advisor or estate attorney is key. This keeps your strategy aligned with your goals and helps avoid unexpected tax consequences.

Taking a comprehensive, integrated approach protects your wealth and supports a smoother, more tax-efficient transfer to your heirs.

## Putting It All Together

Effective tax planning means being proactive and strategic throughout your lifetime. To make the most of your money, maximize tax-advantaged accounts, invest smartly, and align your tax strategies with your legacy and financial goals.

By taking a big-picture approach, you can coordinate withdrawals, plan Roth conversions, and choose the best places for your investments. This will reduce your lifetime tax burden, increase your charitable giving power, and optimize your retirement income.

Consider strategies like gifting, using donor-advised funds, giving appreciated assets, and thoughtful estate planning. This all works together to create a system that helps your wealth grow efficiently and reflects the values you want to pass on.

Smart planning helps you enjoy the rewards of your hard work with less tax stress. It also lets you leave a lasting impact on your family, community, and the causes you care about most.

When you plan ahead and stay focused on your goals, your money works harder for you and your legacy.

## Three Insurance Principles: Protecting What Matters Most

I get it—insurance is one of those topics that either makes your eyes glaze over or makes your heart race, depending on your experiences with it. But the reality is it's a crucial part of our financial toolkit, even if it's sometimes misunderstood or over-complicated. Let's break down the three key principles I use to guide my approach to insurance. These principles can help you shield your financial wealth without getting sidetracked by unnecessary products.

## Principle 1: Insurance Is for Protection, Not Investment

The first rule is simple: insurance is meant to protect you from financial disasters, not to build wealth. It is designed to cover major unexpected expenses—like accidents, serious illness, or a house fire—that could otherwise wipe out your savings and threaten your family's future.

Permanent life insurance may look attractive because it offers coverage for your entire life and has a cash value that grows over time. However, most other investment options tend to deliver better returns with lower costs.

As a fee-only financial planner, I often review permanent life insurance policies that promise protection, long-term growth, and tax advantages. Despite this, I do not own any, nor plan to buy. This is because insurance's true purpose is protection, not investment.

Some Indexed Universal Life (IUL) and Variable Universal Life (VUL) policies are heavily marketed due to the high commissions sales representatives earn. Even well-meaning friends or family might recommend them. These policies tend to be complicated and costly, making them less suitable for most people.

Be cautious about sales pitches promoting ideas like "infinite banking" or "being your own bank." These usually involve permanent life insurance policies that build cash value over time. However, the cash value growth in these policies often lags behind what you could earn with low-cost index funds. Many people find that after paying premiums for ten years, the cash value is still less than what they have paid in. This means the money could have grown more efficiently if invested elsewhere.

**Pro Tip:** Choose term life insurance for reliable protection. Then, invest your extra money in higher-return assets. This approach saves you money on premiums and fees while avoiding locking your money in expensive and low-performing insurance products.

## Principle 2: Cover Low-Probability, High-Impact Risks

Think of insurance as your safety net for the big stuff—things that don't happen often, but could devastate your finances if they do. I'm talking about risks like a house fire, a serious car accident, or health issues. Insurance is meant to cover these types of life-changing events so that you can rebound financially, leaving you space to manage the emotional and logistical side of things.

On the flip side, don't waste money insuring against things that happen frequently and are easy to handle on your own. Extended warranties, cell phone insurance, and trip delay insurance are often unnecessary and can end up costing you more than the actual benefit. Instead of paying premiums for these low-cost, high-frequency incidents, consider self-insuring. That means setting aside a small emergency fund to cover these minor mishaps when they happen.

## Principle 3: Increase Your Deductibles

If you want to lower your insurance premiums, consider increasing your deductible. The deductible is the amount you pay out of pocket before your insurance starts to cover expenses. Choosing a higher deductible, like $2,000 or higher, usually means your monthly or annual premiums will be significantly lower. This simple change can save you hundreds of dollars each year.

The catch? You'll need to have enough savings to cover the higher deductible in case something happens. This is why a healthy emergency fund is important! Having a financial cushion set aside to cover these costs gives you peace of mind while still saving on premiums.

When I first started, I chose lower deductibles to keep out-of-pocket costs low in case of a claim. As I saved more money (and improved my driving skills), I increased my deductibles on all my insurance policies. This change lowered my premiums, which freed up extra cash that I was able to invest and grow over time.

With high-deductible health plans, you can also contribute to a Health Savings Account (HSA). In 2025, couples or families can contribute up to $8,550. If you are 55 or older, you can add an extra $1,000 as a catch-up contribution. As I mentioned earlier, HSAs offer triple tax benefits: contributions are tax-deductible, earnings grow tax-free, and withdrawals for qualified medical expenses are tax-free. This makes an HSA a powerful way to save on taxes while preparing for future healthcare costs.

## Final Thoughts: Insurance as Your Defense, Not Your Offense

Insurance is the final safety net. It is what catches you when everything else fails. It's like the airbag in your car. You hope you never have to use it, but it is there when the unexpected hits hardest. This way of looking at insurance helps you understand that you are not simply buying peace of mind, you are protecting everything you have worked for. Picture what it would be like to face a catastrophic event with proper insurance: your financial foundation remains stable, your family is cared for, and recovery is possible. Now imagine facing the same event without insurance: uncertainty, potential devastation, and a much harder road to recovery. That contrast makes the value of coverage real and urgent, not just an abstract idea.

Insurance is not the star player on your financial team but rather the defensive lineman. It protects you from life's unexpected hits, but it should not be your primary tool to build wealth. By following three principles—protect what matters, cover the big risks, and increase your savings and deductibles—you can make smart choices that save money and guard your wealth over time.

Remember, it is all about striking the right balance between risk and protection, understanding your true needs, and obtaining coverage that fits your life stage. By focusing on the essentials and avoiding unnecessary insurance products, you can protect what you've worked so hard for without wasting any resources.

Take time to reassess your insurance needs with these principles in mind. Doing so will help you make informed decisions and keep your financial future secure.

If you are unsure whether you have the right insurance products, consult an independent advisor or insurance broker who can guide you through the options and help you find the best path for your situation. A customized approach that prioritizes your goals is always the best choice.

## Will and Trust Principles: Protecting Your Legacy and Loved Ones

No one likes to think about what will happen after they're gone, but having the right will and trust in place is essential to ensure that your wishes are followed, your loved ones are protected, and your family doesn't face unnecessary stress or confusion if something happens to you. But let's be honest, talking about your wishes can feel overwhelming. The good news? Starting the conversation now will save your family a lot of headaches down the road, and trust me, it's worth the effort!

### Benefits of Having a Will and Trust

**Control Over Your Assets:** Think of having a will or trust as your way to call the shots, even after you're gone. It's like having "superhero strings" from the great beyond! With a will, you get to say exactly who gets your stuff and who will take care of your kids. A trust is like the deluxe version: you can set special rules for how and when your money and property are handed out, and even add protection for younger or vulnerable family members. In short, you're the director of your own legacy, making sure everything goes just the way you want!

**Avoiding Probate:** One of the biggest advantages of having a trust is that it helps your family avoid probate court, which can be a long, costly, and public legal process. While a will usually goes through probate, a properly funded trust allows assets to transfer directly to your heirs without court involvement. This keeps your financial affairs private, speeds up inheritance, and makes things easier for your loved ones during a difficult time.

**Reduce Family Conflict:** Clear instructions in a will or trust can prevent misunderstandings or conflict about your wishes. When your family knows exactly what you want, they're much less likely to fight over your estate, ensuring peace of mind during an already difficult time.

**Special Situations:** Trusts can be used for a variety of special situations, like tax planning, protecting assets from creditors, supporting loved ones with special needs, or making charitable gifts. They're versatile tools that help you accomplish a lot more than just distributing wealth.

## Strategic Trusts and Wealth Transfer

Trusts are powerful tools in estate planning that help you transfer your wealth smoothly and reduce taxes. A revocable living trust acts like a relay baton. You keep control of your assets while you're alive, but when the time comes, your assets pass directly to your heirs—no courtroom hurdles, no probate delays!

For greater tax benefits, irrevocable trusts act like a secure vault outside of your taxable estate. Once you place assets into an irrevocable trust, you give up control, but those assets are no longer counted as part of your estate for tax purposes. This can reduce or even eliminate estate taxes, especially once you have used up your lifetime gift and estate tax exemption.

What makes trusts really powerful is they can be customized to fit your specific goals. Whether it's providing for a loved one with special needs, saving for future generations' education, or making sure your wealth is shared just as you want, trusts offer flexibility and control.

Using revocable and irrevocable trusts strategically allows you to protect your wealth, ensure it passes according to your wishes, and minimize the tax burden on your family.

## The Medical Power of Attorney (POA)

A Medical Power of Attorney (POA) is a separate legal document from your will or trust, but it's just as important. This document lets you appoint someone (in a couple, it's often your spouse) to make medical decisions for you if you can't make them yourself. This might happen if you're seriously ill, injured, or otherwise unable to communicate. Your trust doesn't cover medical decisions, and your will only takes effect after you pass away.

Without a Medical POA, your loved ones could face a long and stressful legal process to gain permission to make those decisions for you, adding unnecessary emotional turmoil during difficult times. It's important to pick someone who knows your values and healthcare wishes and is ready to take this responsibility seriously. Just like your finances, your health decisions are a vital part of protecting your future and giving your family clear guidance in a crisis.

Deciding when control passes to your appointed person usually happens when a doctor confirms you cannot make or communicate your own medical choices. At that point, the person you named as your Medical POA steps in.

If you want your healthcare wishes respected, make sure you have a Medical POA in place!

## How to Get Started: Planning for Your Legacy Made Easy

Talking about wills and trusts isn't exactly dinner-table conversation. But trust me, the sooner you get started, the easier it'll be for you and your loved ones down the road. I know it's not the most fun topic, but here's the thing: not having a plan is the worst plan. When there's no plan in place, families often end up scrambling to figure out what to do next, facing months (or even years) of stress in probate, and dealing with the financial burden while grieving. Do the hard work now, and you'll save your family a ton of hassle later on!

How do we get started? Let's break it down.

## Step 1: Start the Conversations

The most important step is to talk with your family. It might feel a little awkward at first, but once you get going, it gets easier. Take some time to think about your wishes and share them openly with your loved ones. Let everyone know where your estate plan documents are kept, and keep the lines of communication wide open.

Active listening is your secret weapon, and you've been practicing it throughout this journey! Honest, early conversations help reduce stress and confusion later on. So, grab some snacks, gather your loved ones, and start talking. This is the best way to ensure your plan truly supports your partner, your family, and reflects what you want.

## Step 2: Get It in Writing

Once you've had the talk, put everything on paper and make it legally binding. This may require witnesses or notaries, depending on your state. No need to overthink it! But, if your estate is complicated—blended families, business ownership, property in multiple states—you'll need personalized guidance. I highly recommend consulting with an experienced estate attorney to get things right.

## Step 3: Know Your Options

Online templates are tempting, but when things are complex, an online template may not be clear or customized enough for your needs. If you're dealing with family dynamics, special assets, or anything that could cause confusion or dispute, it's important to have legal advice. An estate plan isn't a one-size-fits-all deal. Get the right advice to ensure your assets go exactly where you want.

## Top Five Mistakes People Make with Estate Planning

Let's make sure you avoid some common pitfalls:

### 1. Not Having a Will or Trust

Many people think they'll get to it "later" or that they don't need it at all. But without a will or trust, the state decides who gets your stuff. That's a gamble you don't want to take.

### 2. Not Updating Your Documents

Life happens—marriages, divorces, babies, deaths. Any big change should trigger an update to your plan. Keeping your documents up-to-date avoids confusion and protects your wishes.

### 3. Not Coordinating Beneficiary Designations

Retirement accounts, life insurance, 529 plans, and bank accounts pass directly to the beneficiaries you name on those accounts, regardless of what your will or trust says. This means that if you don't coordinate these beneficiary designations with your overall estate plan, your wishes may not be carried out as intended.

### 4. Choosing the Wrong Executor or Trustee

Picking someone who isn't organized or trustworthy can cause delays and drama. Instead, choose someone reliable who can and is willing to handle the responsibility.

## 5. Not Communicating Your Plan

If no one knows where your will or trust is, or what your wishes are, your plan won't be very helpful. Make sure your loved ones know exactly where to find your important documents and that they understand your wishes clearly.

## Summary: Plan Today for Peace of Mind Tomorrow

An estate plan isn't just about dividing your assets. It's your chance to make sure your wishes are honored, your partner is cared for, and your legacy lives on. Avoid common mistakes like procrastination and keeping your plan a secret. By communicating openly, you set yourself and your family up for a smoother, less stressful future.

Here's the thing: the best time to start planning is *now*. Get organized, identify what you want, put it on paper, and let your loved ones know what needs to be done. You'll make life easier for everyone, and you'll have peace of mind knowing your legacy is safe and sound in the hands of those you care about most.

Don't put it off any longer—mark a date on your calendar to get started! You've got this!

## Using Technology to Maximize Your Financial Journey

Technology is not just making financial planning easier. It is making it smarter, more interactive, and even more inspiring. Today's financial tools do more than show you numbers. They help you understand the bigger picture, explore your options before making decisions, and give you the encouragement to move forward.

THE HIDDEN SECRET TO FREEDOM

And honestly, by the time you finish this book, these tools might have already improved even more!

## 1. Comprehensive Financial Planning Platforms

Think of these as command centers for your money. They pull together all your accounts, run powerful "what-if" scenarios, and create clear visuals to show you where you're headed.

**Advisor-Led Tools:** Platforms like eMoney, RightCapital, and MoneyGuidePro are often used by financial advisors to design detailed roadmaps for your future. Together, you can:

- Consolidate all your accounts and investments in one secure dashboard

- Explore "what if" situations (What if we retire early? What if we travel the world? What if the market dips?)

- Run advanced simulations like Monte Carlo analysis to see the likelihood of having enough money to hit all your goals

- Get easy-to-read summaries that give you clarity and confidence in your plan

**Consumer-Led Tools:** Platforms like Boldin and Empower Retirement give you the ability to take control of your financial planning, even when working independently. With these tools, you can:

- View all your financial accounts and assets in one con-solidated dashboard

- Stress-test your financial plan using built-in recession simulators and scenario modeling

- Explore personalized "what-if" scenarios, such as large expenses or unexpected windfalls, and instantly see their impact on your goals and timeline

When couples use these softwares together, they gain a clear, shared understanding of their finances. This visibility helps facilitate productive conversations about money grounded in real numbers and visuals, turning potentially tense discussions into collaborative decision-making and aligned strategy. Making major financial choices together is easier when everyone can see the big picture clearly.

## 2. Expanding Financial Literacy and Access

Thanks to cool mobile apps, digital wallets, online learning tools, and fact-based AI models, financial know-how isn't just for experts anymore. It's for everyone! These handy helpers close the gap between complicated professional plans and everyday money tips, so you can take charge with confidence.

The AI models that reference credible resources and avoid hallucinations are designed with advanced algorithms that cross-reference claims against verified data sources to ensure accuracy and reduce false information generation. They make getting up-to-date, personalized insights super easy. I use Perplexity myself for quick tax and finance questions as well as detailed research! Some of my peers also swear by Gemini 2.5 Pro for similar help.

The best part? There's always more to learn, and exploring topics you're curious about can make your money journey even more fun and powerful. However, AI tools have limitations. They are not specialized tax or financial planning software, and the accuracy depends on the data they access. Users should still carefully vet AI-generated information before acting on it.

### 3. Interactive AI Conversation Bots: Your Thinking Partner!

Want to converse with some of the greatest minds about your money and life goals? Platforms like Delphi AI, Potential AI Hub, and Picasso IA bring this concept to life!

Imagine brainstorming your next big idea with a virtual Steve Jobs, gaining motivation insights from Arnold Schwarzenegger, or exploring ethical questions with Socrates. All from your phone or laptop!

These AI chatbots are designed and trained to emulate the thinking and speaking styles of these iconic figures, blending timeless wisdom with practical financial and motivational advice. Many even personalize the experience by addressing you by your first name, creating an engaging, personalized think tank of legends at your fingertips. However, it's important to note that some platforms may include embedded advertisements during interactions, so always stay mindful of marketing content while using these services.

### Bring It To Action

As you work through this chapter, I encourage you to experiment with these tools, add screenshots to visualize your process, and write down tips to boost your understanding. The more you engage actively with your financial planning, the more empowered you'll feel to make choices that align with your values, goals, and lifestyle.

## Work with a Financial Planner

As your wealth grows, many couples start thinking about hiring a financial planner. At this stage, it's crucial to find a comprehensive planner whose values align with your own. A lot of people make the mistake of paying 1% of their portfolio just to have their assets managed and a meeting once a year. This is not worth it—you deserve more than that.

Make sure you're doing regular check-ins with your planner to ensure your asset allocation is still in line with your risk tolerance and life goals. However, avoid the temptation to make changes every time the market shifts. Have at least four key meetings a year to focus on:

- **Portfolio performance**
- **Tax planning**
- **Life goals**
- **Anything else that's keeping you up at night**, as it likely impacts your finances as well.

## See My Work in Action

Curious how a holistic financial planner can help you transform your financial future? Check out real cases from couples, small business owners, and individuals I've had the privilege to work with. These are people just like you who want to align their money with what truly matters.

On my website, **www.ensofin.com**, you'll find detailed stories showing how we tackle everything from overcoming debt and growing investments to setting clear goals and making intentional moves that turn dreams into reality. These aren't cookie-cutter plans. Each strategy is customized to bring clarity, confidence, and peace of mind.

Whether you're ready to take control of your finances or just wondering about how the process works, these real-life examples reveal the true power of comprehensive, thoughtful financial planning. The secret to financial freedom? Knowing your options and feeling confident every step of the way.

Financial freedom is deeply personal, and every client's story reflects their unique journey. Interested in learning more about how we work together? Visit my website for case studies and practical resources that can help spark your path to success.

## Now, It's Your Turn!

Are you ready to dive in and take your financial journey to a whole new level? These simple, fun exercises are designed to help you and your partner grow closer, dream bigger, and build a money plan that feels exciting and totally doable. Let's make financial planning an adventure you both look forward to!

# Exercises for Chapter 6:
# The Hidden Secret to Freedom

## Exercise 6-1: What Lights You Up? (Flow)

1. Set a timer for two minutes each.

2. Share with your partner a recent moment when you felt energized and happy, where time just flew by.

3. You'll take turns to share and listen. Decide who goes first. The listener gives their full attention, maintaining eye contact, with no interruptions, and then shares how the story moved them.

   For example:

   - "When you shared how you lost track of time painting, I felt so inspired and happy for you!"

4. Switch roles and repeat the process. This is your moment to take note and celebrate what makes each of you shine!

## Exercise 6-2: What's Holding You Back? (Obstacle)

1. Again, set the timer for two minutes each.

2. Take turns to open up about a money challenge or something you've been avoiding, what's nagging you, or the hard decision you keep putting off.

3. The listener responds with empathy, expressing what feelings the story sparked.

   For example:

- "When you talked about feeling overwhelmed by bills, I felt tightness in my shoulders."

- "When you admitted feeling stuck, I felt a cold heaviness in my limbs and a dull ache in my head."

4. Switch roles and repeat. Facing obstacles together makes them easier to overcome!

## Exercise 6-3: Map Your Journey (Wealth Roadmap)

This dynamic exercise shows you where you are now, where you want to go, and the exciting path you'll take to get there!

1. Grab the Wealth Roadmap worksheet (you can make a copy and customize it for your own situation).

2. Together, fill out each section—Wealth Goals, Net Worth Tracker, Investable Cash Flow, Weighted Average Return, and Roadmap to Wealth.

3. Get your worksheet here: www.shorturl.at/AUqG6

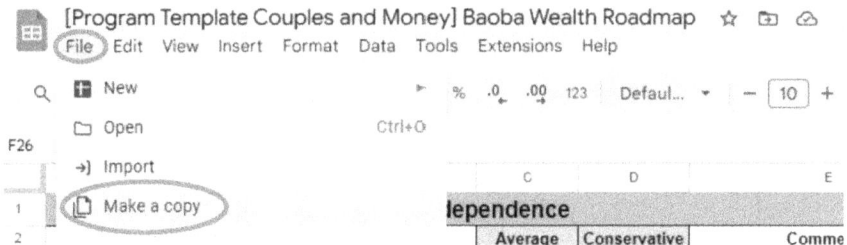

4. See an example here: www.shorturl.at/wxjf1

## Exercise 6-4: Walk the Talk

1.  Take two minutes each to share which part of your road-map feels like the biggest challenge or the one needing the most action.

2.  The listener provides time and space for you to think out loud:

    -   What is one small thing you can do about it?

    -   When will you start?

    -   Who can cheer you on or help along the way?

3.  Switch roles and repeat. This is where your plans start turning into real progress!

## Exercise 6-5: Make It Stick

1.  Write down ideas for meaningful habits that make finan-cial planning a joyful and natural part of your life. Maybe it's a weekly check-in, rituals to celebrate small wins, or pairing it with something you already love doing. Any other ideas?

| Make It Consistent | Make It Fun | Other Ideas |
|---|---|---|
|  |  |  |

2.  Share your ideas and choose one to start right away!

## Keep It Consistent, Keep It Fun!

Remember, the real magic happens when you take small steps every day and stay consistent. Celebrate every win, stay curious, and enjoy the amazing journey you're on together. You have already made powerful progress toward your dream financial future. Keep that energy flowing and watch how quickly things start to change!

Go ahead and give each other a big high five. You absolutely deserve it! Exciting things are coming your way!

# Your Reflection

Take a moment to jot down your thoughts and experiences from the exercise. Use this space to capture any insights, feelings, or ideas that came up.

_____

_____

_____

_____

_____

_____

_____

_____

_____

_____

_____

_____

_____

# CHAPTER 7

## Keep Going—
## Momentum for Life

Saturday morning sunlight poured through the kitchen window as I typed the last lines of a new chapter. My coffee sat cooling beside me, the house unusually peaceful. The kids were playing nearby in the open media room, their laughter echoing softly just steps from the kitchen. Two years into my journey as an entrepreneur, I felt deeply connected with my husband. Together, we had spent countless evenings dreaming together, mapping out our future, cheering each other on, and growing stronger side by side.

But as I recounted stories of authors dropping $60,000 on ghostwriters or $20,000 on publishing and promotion, I noticed a shadow flicker across his face. He set down his mug, eyes searching mine.

"Are you writing this book as a passion project, or is it really a business?" he asked, voice low but edged with worry. "And how much have you spent on it already?"

His words landed like a splash of cold water. For me, this book was both a mission and a business—my heart and hustle rolled into one. I'd thought we were united, but suddenly it felt like we were speaking different languages. The conversation spiraled, tension thickening the air as we circled around our fears and hopes, never quite meeting in the middle. The room felt smaller, the silence heavier, until the kids' gymnastics class gave us a merciful break.

As I drove my kids to the gym, my eight-year-old son broke the silence from the back seat: "Was Daddy giving you a hard time?" His innocent curiosity made me smile despite myself. "Yes," I admitted, "but that's okay. It must be something really important to him. We'll figure it out."

## Coming Back to the Table

The weekend passed in a haze—me replaying our conversation, him quietly thinking it over. Monday morning came, and after he dropped the kids off at school, we finally sat down together, just the two of us. This time, we dug deeper. I shared my fears about working abroad for a year starting summer 2026, since we had agreed to live in Asia so our kids could experience the culture and connect with their roots. I worried about what it would mean for my business. He opened up about his worries over our long-term security and whether I was sticking to the rule of "paying myself first."

We agreed to sit down again in the spring, before we moved back to the US, to revisit our financial goals and plans. We promised to face whatever comes next, together.

Then he looked into my eyes, soft and steady, and said, "I love you, and I have no doubt you'll be successful."

Tears came to my eyes. In that moment, I felt truly seen, deeply supported, and more inspired than ever.

What followed was a quiet but powerful shift in our routine. That Monday conversation cleared the air and gave us a fresh sense of purpose and partnership. We realized that keeping momentum in our financial journey wasn't about never having doubts or disagreements. It was about coming back to the table, again and again, with honesty and openness.

We decided to set regular check-ins, our own "money dates" to review our progress, talk through any worries, and celebrate even the smallest wins. These moments became less about spreadsheets (we'd still get excited about updating our Net Worth Tracker every quarter, though) and more about staying connected, supporting each other's dreams, and making sure our plans reflected the life we wanted to build together.

Momentum, I learned, isn't a sprint. It's built on small, steady actions: reviewing our goals, tweaking our routines, and showing up for each other—even when conversations get tough. Every honest talk, every shared decision, and every step forward (no matter how small) added energy to our journey.

As we moved forward, I felt more confident than ever that we could handle whatever came next, not because everything was perfect, but because we chose to keep growing together as a team.

## The Power of Regular Check-ins

You've weathered a money challenge, worked things out, and maybe even shared a hug. So why keep talking about money? Because lasting love and financial success come from regular effort, not just one big breakthrough. Open and honest communication about money is like tuning a finely crafted instrument. It takes care and attention, but when you get it right, the harmony is beautiful.

Checking in regularly about money keeps your relationship strong and flexible, like a choreographed dance that gets smoother each time you practice. The more you do it, the more natural it feels. Soon, you and your partner will be perfectly in sync, ready to face life's twists and turns, especially the moments charged with emotion and financial impact.

## Strategies for Keeping Money Alive and Real

### 1. Find Your "Why": The Soul for Your Money

Everyone's values and priorities are different, and they shift as life moves forward. The turning point? When your "why" becomes crystal clear, and the pressure to impress other people melts away. Suddenly, you're living for what matters to you (and your loved ones), not for what looks amazing on social media.

- **Make money meaningful** and connect it to your shared dreams. Think about the kind of life you want to build together. Is it a cozy beach house, a foodie adventure around the world, more family time and less stress from work, or lazy mornings snuggled in a paid-off home? Your "why" is both your compass and your motivation. It should inspire you and keep you grounded when everyone else seems to be running in different directions.

- **Stay grounded by thinking long-term.** Don't get swept up by what friends or influencers say you *should* want. Take a moment to ask: "Does this fit our real values?"

For major spending or life decisions, pause together and ask: "Does this get us closer to our vision—our personal life goals?"

- **Mix and Match: combine your quirks.** If one of you craves adventure and the other feels best with security, make joint money goals that respect both! For example: Create a "freedom fund" for spontaneous travel *and* keep an emergency stash to make rainy days feel less scary. You'll both feel heard and your goals will actually feel exciting.

## My "Why" Story

Not long after I graduated, I got an amazing job in private equity working in West Africa. Suddenly, I was around big-time business people—mine owners, real estate tycoons, and business brokers. These were the kind of folks who drove fancy cars, showed off the newest phones, and wore sharp Italian suits with expensive diamond Swiss watches. They really cared about appearances and didn't hesitate to let me know that my outfit didn't quite match their "elite" world.

The comments would swirl around me:

*"You're making a good salary. Why not treat yourself? Why not upgrade your wardrobe or buy an expensive phone? After all, you are the face of your company, you know!"*

I'd smile, thank them, and go right back to saving. I knew my goal wasn't about fitting in. I was dreaming bigger. Sure, my phone wasn't new and my bag wasn't on a waitlist, but every month my savings grew and I slept soundly, knowing I was funding my dreams rather than status symbols.

A couple of years later, I announced my plans to travel across Africa and Europe and then move to the US for my MBA, funded by my own savings and a generous scholarship from the University of Notre Dame. As a proud Domer, I'm deeply grateful for the opportunity that changed my life. That's when the same people who once doubted me finally understood what I'd been quietly working toward. Their judgment turned into admiration; they were impressed by the priorities and discipline that had guided me all along.

As life has evolved and my family has grown, so have my priorities. No longer is it just about "socking money away" or growing a massive nest egg. Now, time and flexibility matter most. I want the kind of life where I can keep growing professionally, but also take weeks off in the summer to travel, visit family across states or continents, let my kids build memories with their cousins, and share long, lazy days with grandparents. That's the true reward: the ability to choose your lifestyle, connection, and experiences instead of accumulating things merely to impress others.

## The Takeaways

- Your "why" will change as you grow. The key is to pause, check in, and realign.

- Be fearless about being different. Ignore outside pressure if it means staying true to what's most important to you.

- Money isn't about having the *best things* today—it's about building the *best life* for yourself and those you love, for the long haul.

So celebrate the goals that matter most to you, and don't hesitate to go against the grain to make them happen!

## 2. Nurture New Habits and Narratives

Money conversations don't have to be tense or boring. Turn them into something you actually look forward to, like a quarterly "net worth party." Grab some drinks, put on a playlist you both love, and spend a couple of minutes updating your spreadsheet (it's literally that quick). Then . . . celebrate!

Toast to your progress, no matter how small, high-five each other, and soak up the peace of mind that comes from knowing you're on track. There's nothing like the feeling of working as a team toward the same goal.

Your money "dates" don't have to be fancy. They could be a coffee together, a walk around the block, or a cozy pajama chat about dreams, choices, bumps, and wins. The important part? You're making talking about money a habit instead of a crisis-of-the-moment drama.

**Why it works:** The more you get used to talking about money, the smoother and more comfortable the conversations become, much like dating. When you have these conversations, you won't be caught off guard by surprise bills, and you won't bottle up your worries until they explode.

## 3. Celebrate Wins like It's Game Night

On your money dates, celebrate every win—big or small—as if you were heading out for your best game night ever. Cheer each other on and enjoy the moment after every victory.

Celebrate achievements like:

- Tracking down that credit card balance and interest rate
- Finding creative ways to save money
- Adding an extra $100 to your emergency fund
- Sticking to your budget for a whole week (that definitely deserves a high-five!)
- Any move that brings you closer to your shared dreams

Try a quick gratitude round at the end:

- What's one thing you appreciate about your partner right now?
- What tiny money win did you score this week?
- What surprised you or went better than you expected?

**Why it works:** Celebrating and practicing gratitude turns money from a stressor into a shared win. It rewires your relationship with money, transforming it from a challenge to a powerful tool that helps you succeed together.

## How Nicole's Money Dates Went

Remember Nicole from Chapter 4? She had been quietly juggling money on her own, not wanting to stress out Scott, her husband. But the growing credit card debt soon became impossible to ignore.

When Nicole and Scott hired me as their financial planner, we crafted a plan together, like preparing for a big date night but with dollars and cents:

- Replaced costly permanent life insurance with a simpler term policy, saving hundreds monthly

- Put savings and tax refunds toward paying off debt, cutting $850 in interest a month
- Set clear short-term and long-term savings goals
- Tweaked their investments to fit their 15-year retirement goal
- Most importantly, established spending and saving habits together, because cash flow is like the heartbeat of your financial relationship; without it, things get shaky.

Nicole took a brave step: inviting Scott into the process through a shared spending app and weekly "money dates." These mini dates were their time to connect, communicate feelings, and celebrate wins over Nicole's favorite ice cream.

Sure, some weeks were tough, but by teaming up, they built trust, regained control, and felt hopeful again. Their savings grew, debts shrank, and retirement accounts started growing, all while strengthening their partnership in building a good life together.

## 4. Keep Money Fears in Check

Every couple faces money worries, and that's normal. What really matters is how you handle them. When a wave of anxiety or fear hits, give yourself or your partner permission and time to feel it. Create a safe space where it's okay to vent, laugh, or just share the "yikes" moments without judgment.

You've practiced switching roles in the money exercises, where one of you listens and supports, and the other shares openly. This skill doesn't just help with money conversations; it helps you notice when your partner needs support and know when it's your turn to step in.

Here's the truth: it's okay not to have all the answers right away. The true power comes from knowing that together you will figure things out eventually. Some challenges take time to solve, and the key is standing side by side through it all.

When negative thoughts sneak in with, "We're doomed!" or "We'll never recover!", pause and ask yourself:

- What is actually happening right now?
- What is the real challenge, not the scary story my mind is telling?
- How did we address a similar emotion before?
- How do we respond as a team?

If those "what-ifs" keep creeping back, fight them with facts and a reminder of *what you do control.*

## 5. Be Intentional: Use Money to Grow Relationships That Matter

Money is a tool to create the life and connections you want. Intentional spending and planning help you build memories, share experiences, and deepen bonds. When you put your money toward what truly lights up you and your loved ones, it keeps your financial journey real, enjoyable, and meaningful.

I've always believed that money is just a tool, not the final prize. The real win is building a life you love with meaningful relationships. Over time, I've learned how powerful it is to use money on purpose, shaping it around what really matters to you and taking care of the people you love. It's different for everyone, even for folks in the same family! That's why a little intentional planning and honest conversation go such a long way.

Sure, money can't buy close relationships. But it can buy time, adventures, shared experiences, and professional help, making more opportunities for bonds to grow and memories to bloom.

Take my mom and dad, for instance. They're total opposites when it comes to travel and activities. For years, my mom talked about seeing new places . . . but she never pulled the trigger. With a bit more flexibility in my work and schedule, I decided to make those trips actually happen for her.

Here's how we make it work: Whenever I travel for work to a place my mom hasn't been before (she's very clear—no repeat destinations!), I invite my parents to come along. My dad usually bows out, but when my mom comes, I take my daughter out of daycare so she can travel with us. This way, they get quality time together while I'm busy working. Every trip ends up with plenty of laughter, adventure, and great memories!

Last summer in China, I organized a ten-day side trip away from my parents' usual hometown routine. Traveling with my mom can be an adventure in itself! Sometimes she gets separated from the group (several times a day!), or she'll say, "I'll never travel with you again!" when we disagree on something. But I've learned to greet these moments with humor and patience. Rather than reacting, I focus on the fun we're having and the progress we're making. Because honestly, she's always up for joining the next trip, despite what she says when she's angry!

One afternoon, while exploring a bustling market, she disappeared into the crowd. The kids and I joked, "Here we go again," as we searched for her. When she finally reappeared, carrying one bag of fresh lychee and another heaped with giant mangos, proudly showing off a trinket she had bargained for, we all burst out laughing. That moment captured our trips perfectly—chaotic, unpredictable, but full of surprising joys.

By the end of the trip, we weren't just sharing sights but stories and inside jokes only we understood. Those memories brought us closer and gave my kids moments they will treasure forever. Even when things get a little bumpy, I remind myself these adventures with my mom are worth every detour.

Traveling with family has taught me something priceless: even when the moments aren't perfect, intentionally making time to be together helps deepen bonds and open hearts. Watching my mom explore new places with my kids has brightened her days and helped me see her in a whole new light.

I've also learned to embrace her quirks and set gentle boundaries, such as when she repeats stories about my dad and their relationship. It all becomes part of the journey and makes our time together richer.

Here's a bonus: giving my mom space to have her own adventures has improved her relationship with my dad, too. She's less wrapped up in his moods and has more mental space to focus on what really matters. Meanwhile, my dad has started thinking about his own dreams, something he rarely did before. I keep reminding them both that the resources they've accumulated are there for bringing joy, not just for safety.

*Money isn't just about dollars and cents. It's a tool to create time, energy, and joy for you and the people you love.* When used with intention, it opens the door to new experiences, strengthens your bonds, and sparks new dreams for everyone.

## 6. Rally Your Financial Cheerleaders

Money can be tricky, and when navigating it as a couple, the right support can make all the difference. Think of your mentors, role models, and even trusted professionals—like financial planners, tax experts, or coaches—as your personal *financial dream team*. And the real MVPs? **You two**.

Mentors and role models give you a glimpse into how other couples make money work for them. They share real-life lessons, shortcuts, and encouragement to keep you motivated and moving forward as a team. Paid professionals bring expert advice tailored to your unique situation, helping you make confident decisions, communicate better, and avoid common pitfalls.

Here's the magic of being a couple: 1 + 1 > 2. You have each other's backs, which means you're not just sharing money—you're doubling your perspectives, strength, and support. You get to celebrate the wins, face down the setbacks, and keep each other motivated in ways no solo journey can match.

With your financial cheerleaders on your side, you're never going it alone. They keep you grounded, honest, and growing your money skills as a team. This turns financial goals into shared adventures, and challenges into opportunities to strengthen both your relationship and your wealth.

## When Advice Becomes a Sales Pitch

When it comes to money, our first instinct is often to ask people we know: friends, family, or even a cousin's "investment guy." And while they may mean well, the moment the conversation turns into a sales pitch, especially for something that pays them a high commission or big fee, it's your signal to slow down.

They might truly believe what they're offering is great, but financial products that pay high commissions are usually not the best match for you. Sometimes, they simply fit the seller's wallet better than yours.

A smarter move is to do your own research first. If you decide to get professional help, choose advisors who are independent. That means they aren't paid by insurance companies or brokerage firms to push certain products. Think of it like hiring a personal trainer who actually cares about your health, not about selling you their favorite protein powder.

By taking time to check facts, compare options, and ask tough questions, you'll make decisions because they're right for your goals, not because someone you know made them sound convincing over coffee.

## Knowledge Point: What Is the Fiduciary Standard?

In the US, a financial advisor who follows the *fiduciary standard* is legally required to put your best interests ahead of their own. This means they must recommend what truly benefits you, even if it means they earn less money. Fiduciary advisors often include Registered Investment Advisors (RIAs) and independent financial planners. This is different from the *suitability standard*, where advisors only need to recommend products that are "suitable" for you but not necessarily the best or lowest-cost option. Advisors under this standard often include broker-dealers, stockbrokers, and insurance agents, many of whom can earn higher commissions by selling certain products, even if those choices aren't ideal for your situation.

In Canada, the fiduciary standard exists but is less common and often less strict than in the US. Advisors there may follow a duty-of-care or suitability standard depending on where they work.

Across Europe and other developed countries, rules vary by country, but most have strong protections to make sure advice is suitable and transparent. Many require advisors to disclose fees and conflicts of interest and encourage independent advice, though the specific fiduciary duties differ.

If you live in North America, it's important to educate yourself: watch out for high-commission products, which are often found in insurance policies, certain annuities, and some mutual funds. These products can create conflicts of interest for the advisor. Always do your own research and verify any advice before making financial decisions.

## How Money Addresses Our Needs

You're heard me saying it in many different ways now: *money isn't just about numbers or accumulating wealth; it's a resource that helps us meet different needs in life, from the basics to our deepest dreams.* Think of it like climbing a staircase, where each step unlocks new possibilities and comforts.

**1. Survival** (food, shelter, safety)

At the most essential level, money helps cover your basic needs so you and your family can survive and feel safe. This means paying for shelter, food, utilities, healthcare, basic insurance, and building an emergency fund. Without this foundation, it's hard to focus on anything else.

**2. Stability** (security, consistency, independence)

Beyond survival, stability is about maintaining a predictable, nice life. Money frees you from high-interest debts and financial stress. Free from bad and risky debt and having a stable cash flow gives peace of mind, reduces anxiety, and lets you breathe easier about your life.

**3. Growth** (achievement, savings, investments)

With stability, money can be used to grow your future through savings and investments. This step is about building wealth slowly and steadily to fund bigger life goals: buying a home, retiring comfortably, educating your kids, or starting a business.

**4. Flexibility** (options, adaptability, freedom)

As your financial foundation grows stronger, money creates flexibility and freedom: the ability to say yes to experiences, adventures, and choices that enrich your life. This could be traveling, hobbies, changing careers, or spending more time with loved ones without constant worry.

**5. Meaning** (purpose, belonging, impact)

At the highest level, money becomes a powerful tool to align with your values. It involves purpose, belonging, and contributing to something larger than oneself. It's about using your resources to support causes that matter, give back to the community, nurture relationships, or invest in experiences that bring lasting joy and fulfillment.

## Expanding the Perspective

When it comes to meeting our needs, whether it's putting food on the table or chasing our boldest dreams, our minds often jump straight to if we can afford it. We tend to assume that bigger goals require bigger budgets, and that the higher the aspiration, the more financial resources we *must* have.

But here's the truth: while money can open doors, not every higher-level need depends solely on how much we spend or own. Many of our deepest ambitions: connection, purpose, joy, are often more about creativity, relationships, and values than about dollar signs.

## Possessions vs. Outside Resources

Most of us are naturally wired to collect *possessions*: a house, car, gadgets, or education—things we own outright because we paid for them. These possessions feel very real, personal, and concrete. Private ownership has been a driving force behind the growth and success of our society. While money can buy these things, it's not the only way to meet our needs or fulfill our dreams.

Here's an important insight: there's a whole other set of valuable resources outside your direct ownership. Outside resources are things you don't personally own, but can still use, enjoy, and benefit from. Examples include helpful friends and neighbors, business partnerships, community programs, co-working spaces, public services, open-source tools, and most importantly—the goodwill of people who believe in and support you.

Understanding the difference between possessions and outside resources can broaden how you think about wealth. Possessions provide a solid foundation that you control entirely. Outside resources expand your reach and create opportunities beyond what you own individually. Together, they give you a more powerful and flexible path to achieving your goals and living well.

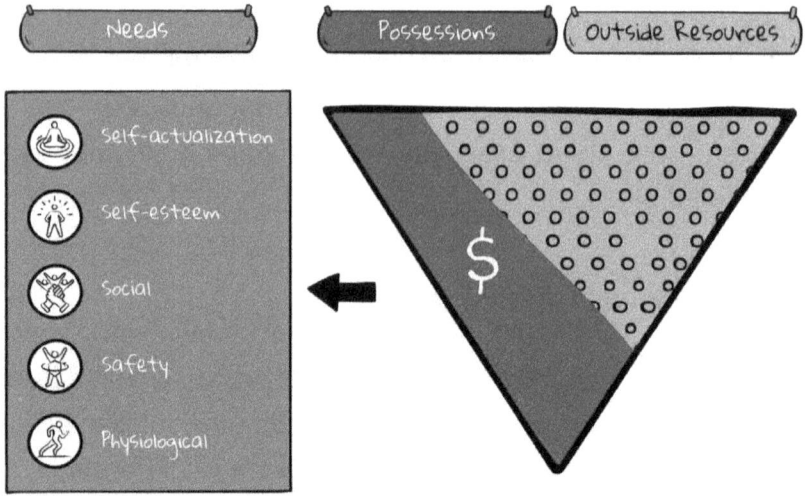

Figure 14: How to Fill Your Cup—It's Not Just Possessions!

When we tap into these outside resources, we can often achieve the same results or even better without spending much of our own money or owning a lot ourselves. It's like borrowing super-powers instead of buying a cape. Some of life's best resources don't have a price tag at all if we are open to them.

By broadening our view beyond ownership and direct purchase to focus on access and collaboration, a whole new world of possibilities opens up.

It's not about whose name is on the account, contract, or title. It's about whether you can actually use that resource to meet your needs. A borrowed tool, a shared workspace, a community program, or a friend's expertise can be just as valuable—sometimes even more so—than something you paid for.

Money is a powerful tool, but it is only one tool in the toolbox. Life becomes more creative and often more fun when you realize you have many other tools at your fingertips. These tools include your relationships, your community, your skills, and your willingness to collaborate and problem-solve.

Creative problem-solving does not rely solely on money. It depends on using what you have wisely and resourcefully to overcome challenges and seize opportunities. The best solutions often come from thinking outside the box, asking for help, and tapping into the strengths all around you.

## True Abundance

When you can see the full picture—the things you own, the possibilities you can tap into, and the outside resources you have access to—you realize something powerful: you already have what you need to meet your needs at many levels.

That's *true abundance*.

It means feeling connected to the people, opportunities, and resources that surround you. It's the confidence that, with your relationships, creativity, and resources, you can handle whatever life brings your way.

This kind of abundance comes from shifting your mindset from scarcity to generosity and trust. When you believe there's enough to go around, you become more open to opportunities, more resilient in facing challenges, and more willing to take smart risks.

Money is a tool that fuels your journey, but it's not the whole story. True wealth includes your health, your relationships, your passions, your community, and your sense of purpose. When all these come together, you create a rich, meaningful life filled with joy, growth, and freedom.

*True abundance includes:*

- **Access to resources** beyond ownership. This might be community support, shared tools, networks, or public services that help you thrive without needing to buy or own everything yourself.

- **Meaningful relationships** where giving and receiving flow naturally, creating a safety net of emotional and practical support.

- **The freedom to collaborate and innovate** in how you solve problems, meet needs, and pursue your dreams. When you tap into the collective power around you, abundance multiplies.

- **A mindset of gratitude and generosity** that opens doors to unexpected opportunities and connections, making life feel wonderful and worth living.

In couples and families, especially those blending different cultures, backgrounds, and financial beliefs, true abundance is about combining these elements. It's recognizing that more than money, it's the connections, creativity, and shared values that create lasting wealth and happiness.

Instead of chasing an endless pile of stuff or bigger bank balances, start celebrating the abundance you already have—the people, opportunities, and partnership that enrich your life every day.

True abundance is a journey of discovery, cooperation, and joy. It invites you to think bigger, lean on each other, and redefine wealth in ways that nourish your heart and your dreams.

When you see money as just one form of wealth, you naturally open up to talk about finances more openly. Those money conversations become shared strategy sessions where you build trust, make plans, and steer your life together toward a shared horizon.

## Financial Openness

Nobody is born knowing how to talk about money. It's a skill that many couples learn over time, often through trial and error. But here's the encouraging part: every honest money conversation you have together is like leveling up in a video game. Each discussion builds trust, strengthens your bond, and adds new tools to your relationship toolkit to handle whatever life throws at you.

The goal is not perfection or having all the answers. The true power comes from being open, inviting your partner into your financial journey, and showing up for each other—even when money talks feel uncomfortable. That is where your relationship superpowers shine: ***love + money = success.***

Regular money talks with your partner are like binge-watching a favorite TV series. With every new "episode," your story grows richer, your understanding deepens, and your teamwork improves. Over time, you will reach your own "season finale"—a place of financial harmony where both of you feel secure, supported, and free.

Research shows couples who openly communicate about money experience less stress, greater financial satisfaction, and stronger relationships. Scheduled money conversations reduce tension, prevent surprises, and help partners work together toward shared goals confidently.

To level up your money talks, set aside dedicated time, be honest but respectful, and approach discussions as a team. Your future selves will thank you!

## Now, It's Your Turn!

Congratulations on making it this far! Now let's bring everything together! Think of this moment as your relationship's power-up round or a money gala. These exercises are all about keeping your energy high, staying connected, and building on the progress you've made together. Same as in previous exercises, you'll take turns as the empowered narrator (the one sharing) and the empowering listener (the one holding space and listening). The magic here is in really listening and being in sync with your partner. It makes each of you feel seen, valued, and motivated.

Remember, *momentum* is your secret power bank. The continued adventure toward a stronger partnership and brighter financial future still goes on. Every micro action, every chat, high-five, and shared plan makes you grow closer, dream bigger, and thrive together!

# Exercises for Chapter 7: Keep Going—Momentum for Life

## Exercise 7-1: Small Wins (Celebrate)

1. Set a timer for two minutes each.

2. You'll take turns to share and listen. Describe to your partner a recent win you're proud of, big or small; it all counts.

3. The listener gives full attention, keeps eye contact, and when the story ends, reflects how they felt.

   For example:

   - "When you shared how proud you were of tackling that project, I felt so happy and inspired by you!"

   - "When you mentioned your excitement about our progress, I sensed hope in my breath."

4. Switch roles and repeat the process. Every win is a step forward, so celebrate them all!

## Exercise 7-2: Setback (Support)

1. Again, set a timer for two minutes each.

2. Take turns to open up and share about a recent challenge or something you've been avoiding.

3. The listener gives full attention and then shares what emotions hearing the story sparked.

For example:

- "When you talked about feeling stuck, I felt an urge to help you in my stomach."
- "When you mentioned being stressed, I could feel the tension in my shoulders."

4. Switch roles and repeat. Facing challenges side by side makes difficulties easier to overcome.

## Exercise 7-3: Gratitude (Appreciate)

1. Take two minutes each to share something you've felt grateful for recently.

2. The listener listens closely and reflects their emotional response.

   For example:

   - "When you said you're grateful for how we've been working as a team, I felt warmth in my face."
   - "When you said thank you for listening to your worries, I felt accomplished in my heart."

3. Switch roles and repeat. Gratitude strengthens your bond instantly.

## Exercise 7-4: Reflection (Grow)

1. Looking back on your guided journey together with this book, take two minutes each to share one thing about yourself that's changed the most.

2. The listener reflects back the feelings the story brought up.

For example:

- "When you shared how much you've grown in understanding money, I felt proud in my spine."
- "When you talked about your personal growth, I felt a deep sense of joy for you in my smile."

3. Switch roles and repeat.

## Exercise 7-5: Momentum (Drive)

1. Take two minutes each to share how you want to keep growing and moving forward from here.

2. The listener reflects back the inspiration or feelings they experienced while listening.

   For example:

   - "When you said you're driven to reach those goals, I felt excited about our future together."
   - "When you mentioned your commitment to growth, I felt proud in my chest."

3. Switch roles and repeat. Your vision is your fuel, so keep it alive!

## Keep the Spark Alive

Give yourselves a big high five! These exercises are designed to help you keep the momentum going and strengthen your partnership going forward in life. This is your opportunity to grow together, learn from the bumps, and celebrate all the wins, both big and small, as a team.

Every little action you take, whether it's talking about your dreams, setting a new goal, or showing up for your "money date," brings you closer to the future you want to build together.

Keep going, stay playful, and cheer each other on. The best part? The journey is just getting started, and you are doing it side by side. Let's make your next move the most exciting one yet!

# Your Reflection

Take a moment to jot down your thoughts and experiences from the exercise. Use this space to capture any insights, feelings, or ideas that came up.

_____

_____

_____

_____

_____

_____

_____

_____

_____

_____

_____

_____

_____

_____

# CHAPTER 8

# Two Sides, One Coin

It was a lazy Sunday morning, ten years after we'd said, "I do." Sunlight spilled softly through the kitchen window, wrapping the room in gold. My husband handed me the coffee he'd just made. The quiet hum of togetherness filled the air, making it feel warmer than it already was.

I looked over my mug and asked, "Remember back when we were living together, before we got married? I used to buy that nice coconut water in a little glass bottle, and you told me it was too pricey and I shouldn't waste money on it?"

He chuckled, the years crinkling in the corners of his eyes. "Yeah. It was $4 a bottle! And you didn't even have a job then, just living off your savings."

I grinned. "Well, I eventually found a job. But by that time, that coconut water didn't bring me joy anymore."

With a thoughtful tap on the table, he said, "You should always adjust your lifestyle based on your income. Otherwise . . . if the money runs out, what then? Ask your parents for help?"

I gasped, half-joking. "Wow, that's a strong statement! If you'd said that back then, we might have had such a fight we wouldn't even be here today!"

He shook his head with a laugh. "Of course I didn't say it. I knew better than to start that argument when you were so stressed, looking for a job. I was confident you'd find one."

Beneath that easy exchange lived layers of history: nerves, pride, love, and all the little ways we learned from each other over the years and grew together.

I still remember the original conflict from ten years ago so vividly: standing by the cooler at Mariano's, just downstairs from our tiny 500-square-foot studio on East Randolph Street in Chicago, $4 coconut water in hand, feeling small but stubborn. A few days later, my husband quietly bought me a couple of bottles as a gift. They sat in the fridge untouched for a while because, honestly, I was still upset.

What he didn't know was that this drink wasn't just an indulgence; it was a bridge to another chapter of my life. It carried the warm ocean breeze from my first solo trip to Thailand in 2010, a trip I had paid for with my own hard-earned money. It held the memory of cold winter nights spent on the first floor of Hesburgh Library, where the scent of books mingled with the bakery aromas drifting in from the Panera tucked inside. Between long hours of study, in a foreign country where I knew no one, that short walk to Panera and that small bottle of coconut water became my refuge, a small piece of freedom I could always count on.

Sometimes it's not about the price tag or the brand, but about the meaning tucked inside life's little comforts. For me, that coconut water was more than a drink. It was a small piece of security and hope, something steady to hold on to while everything was changing. Whether it's your mom's favorite tea, a worn-out jersey from home, or even just a familiar snack, we all cling to simple things that remind us who we are when the world feels big and uncertain. Those tiny rituals bridge distances between countries, families, and even between two sides of a marriage, making us feel a little less alone and a little more at home, wherever we are.

My husband knew exactly how much I was struggling back then, in those stressful months after graduating and still searching for a job. From the very beginning, our relationship with money and work had been worlds apart. He paid his own way through college, flipping burgers every summer. I, on the other hand, hadn't really worried about money until my last couple of years at university, mostly because my parents made quiet sacrifices behind the scenes (even though, compared to the US, higher education in China didn't cost nearly as much). But everything changed fast when they told me they couldn't support my plans for grad school abroad. Suddenly, I was on my own for the very first time, stepping into a whole new kind of adventure.

Despite this, before leaving China, I gave my parents $20,000, which was half of my savings after working for three years. True to their lifelong habit of careful saving, they tucked the money away and never spent it. In fact, in 2012, the household savings rate in China was around 40%, and I'm sure my family's was even higher than that.

Today, I fully agree with my husband: adjusting your lifestyle to your income is wise. But back then, I was still betting on the future, trusting it would rise to meet me. And that's the thing about a couple with different upbringings, instincts, and dreams.

Yet when put together, they form a whole, like two sides of the same coin.

## Broader Challenges for Culturally-Diverse Couples

For many couples, navigating differences is part of the journey. But for couples crossing cultures or borders, the layers run deeper and the stakes often feel higher. We face unique complexities that test our communication, planning, and understanding on a daily basis. Some of the key challenges include:

- **Cultural Differences:** Couples may come from backgrounds that are either more self-oriented (prioritizing individual goals) or family-oriented (prioritizing collective family needs). These differences shape expectations on everything from decision-making to caregiving and celebrations. Open communication, understanding, and respecting traditions are crucial for harmony.

- **Geographic Distance and Travel Strains:** Living apart from extended family due to immigration means more long-distance travel, which is costly and strains limited vacation time. This can create stress around holidays, caregiving, and important family milestones that can't be easily attended.

- **Socioeconomic and Social Welfare Differences:** Different countries have different social safety nets and economic expectations. In some families, immigrants may face the expectation to financially support relatives back home, adding pressure on top of building a new life from scratch by themselves. Others may struggle navigating unfamiliar healthcare, legal, or welfare systems.

- **Navigating Legal, Banking, and Cross-Border Complexities:** Immigrant couples may contend with different legal systems surrounding marriage, inheritance, and property rights. Banking and cross-border financial planning can be complicated by currency differences, tax laws, and documentation requirements, demanding special knowledge and careful coordination.

Despite these challenges, many couples find strong, loving ways to manage cultural differences and financial complexities. Some effective approaches include:

- **Open and Honest Communication:** Regular, empathetic conversations about values, expectations, and priorities help build trust and prevent misunderstandings. Address difficult topics (like spending or family obligations) early, and keep dialogues ongoing as situations evolve. In other words, all the skills you've been learning through this book would be highly useful and relevant.

- **Budgeting with Flexibility:** Creating a financial plan that allows room for unexpected costs like international travel or supporting family abroad is critical. Flexibility helps couples adapt without stress when life throws curveballs.

- **Understanding and Respecting Traditions:** Learning about each other's cultural norms and family rituals fosters connection and reduces conflict. Finding ways to blend traditions or celebrate both backgrounds builds shared meaning.

- **Navigating Legal and Financial Systems Together:** Seeking expert advice for cross-border financial planning, legal issues, or immigration matters relieves uncertainty.

Many governments and nonprofit organizations, such as Consumer Financial Protection Bureau[13] and Immigrant Rising[14], offer free or low-cost resources, so you don't have to figure it out alone. Planning together for tax, estate, and banking questions ensures both partners feel secure and informed. When you're on the same page, it's easier to make smart decisions as a team.

These solutions may not make every challenge disappear, but they can lay a strong foundation for a life built together. Like two sides of the same coin, each partner's background and experiences stay beautifully unique, yet fit perfectly together to create something whole. Every difference becomes a chance to learn, every challenge a shared victory, every compromise a deeper thread in the story you're writing as a team. Over time, those very differences that once felt like obstacles can become the glue that holds you closer together, forging an unbreakable bond.

No matter where we came from—our culture, upbringing, personal experiences, or the environments we grew up in—we all face life's challenges in unique ways. How we handle stress, adversity, and change can look very different from person to person. Yet, beneath these differences lies a powerful truth: emotions, core values, and the desire for connection are universal. This shared humanity is what brings couples together across cultures and circumstances.

---

[13] www.consumerfinance.gov/complaint
[14] www.immigrantsrising.org

## How We See Wealth

Our relationship with wealth isn't just about numbers; it's deeply tied to how we see ownership, responsibility, and belonging. For some, wealth feels personal and individual, something that "belongs" to me alone. For others, it is shared broadly across the nuclear family. Others may see wealth as a communal resource for the extended family, spanning generations and branches.

- **Individual Ownership:** In many cultures or personal outlooks, wealth is viewed as the individual's to earn, manage, and enjoy. This perspective aligns with ideas of personal achievement, independence, and self-reliance. Often seen in more individualistic societies, it shapes financial decisions that prioritize one's own needs and goals first, then the immediate family's second.

- **Nuclear Family Orientation:** Many people relate wealth primarily to their household, the nuclear family. Here, wealth is a resource shared between partners and their children to meet collective needs, provide security, and plan for the future. Financial decisions tend to focus on the immediate family's wellbeing, such as buying a home, saving for children's education, or protecting family income.

- **Extended Family and Multigenerational Approach:** In contrast, cultures and families with strong multigenerational ties see wealth as belonging to the extended family network. Wealth preservation and accumulation are often viewed as a shared family responsibility, transcending the nuclear unit. This view motivates pooling resources to support grandparents, cousins, and future generations, as well as investing in family businesses or real estate that benefit the larger kinship group. This extended approach is common among families across the socioeconomic spectrum, whether out of economic necessity in lower-income households or intent to steward legacy in affluent ones. It highlights interconnectedness and long-term thinking about family prosperity.

When couples see money and ownership differently, especially in cross-cultural or immigrant relationships, it can affect how they understand each other's financial values. Noticing whether one partner sees money more as "mine" or more as "ours" makes it easier to communicate, build trust, and balance both viewpoints—like two sides of the same coin.

## Navigating Conflict Styles in Relationships

Every couple and every family handles conflict in their own unique way. Relationship experts often point to four classic conflict styles: competing (trying to win at all costs), accommodating (giving in for the sake of peace), avoiding (sidestepping tension entirely), and collaborating (working together to find the best solution for everyone). While it's not unusual to see a blend of these within a single family, each style has its strengths and pitfalls.

## Competing

The competing style is great at getting things done quickly and showing confidence. People who use this style often say things like, "This is what needs to happen right now," or "That's the way it's going to be, end of story." It helps bring important issues out in the open and prevents problems from dragging on.

However, competing can come off as aggressive or dismissive when someone says, "I don't care what you think, I'm right," or "I know what's best, so I'm going to do it my way." This style creates winners and losers, which can harm trust and leave others feeling unheard.

## Accommodating

Accommodating promotes peace and kindness. Those who use it often say, "I don't mind, whatever works best for you," or "No worries, it's not that important to me." This shows flexibility and a desire to maintain good relations by putting your partner's needs first. It can be very helpful in smoothing over small disagreements and keeping the relationship calm.

On the downside, accommodating can quietly build frustration when your own needs get ignored or suppressed. When you constantly say, "It's okay, let's do what works for you," or "I just want to keep the peace," important issues might never get addressed, leaving feelings bottled up beneath the surface. This can eventually create imbalance and feelings of being unappreciated.

## Avoiding

Avoiding helps people sidestep tension with phrases like, "Let's not talk about this right now," or "Can we talk about this later?" It can give space to cool off and for reflection before engaging in difficult conversations. Sometimes, it can prevent unnecessary arguments, which is useful when timing isn't right.

But avoiding problems often doesn't make them disappear. They tend to grow beneath the surface and cause misunderstandings or emotional distance. When you get into a pattern of saying, "It's fine, really. It's nothing," or "If I ignore it, maybe it'll just go away," important concerns might remain unresolved, which can harm closeness and lead to long-term tension. Avoiding too much makes it harder to build true connection and trust.

## Collaborating

Collaborating is considered the healthiest conflict style because it seeks win-win solutions that satisfy everyone's true needs. People using this style might say, "Let's figure this out together so we're both happy," or "What do you need, and here's what I need. How can we make this work?" This encourages open communication, collaboration, and mutual respect, which helps build trust and fosters deeper connection between partners.

Despite its strengths, collaborating takes time, effort, and willingness to be vulnerable, which some may find frustrating or uncomfortable. Phrases like, "It might take longer, but I want us both to feel good about this," reflect its deeper commitment. If people aren't used to being open about their true feelings, this style can feel awkward or challenging at first, but is often the most rewarding.

When I look at myself, I know I've often slipped into the avoidant camp, hoping tension will fade on its own. My husband tends to be more on the competing or collaborating side; he's not afraid of direct conversations and prefers to put things on the table. My parents, raised in a culture where open disagreement felt risky, usually leaned toward avoiding or accommodating, keeping peace but often leaving things unspoken.

Since intentionally allocating time to communicate and connect with my husband and parents, I see things getting much better, more collaborations are now possible with my progress on inner work, and more possibilities start to emerge. I've seen the same results in my groups and clients: when partners communicate more openly, they have more meaningful conversations, deeper bonding, and more creative solutions and joyful moments together.

## Turning Conflict into Connection

When conflict shows up in relationships, the goal isn't always to "win" or to "solve the problem." It's important to understand each other and find a better path forward as often as you can. Here are three strategies that help turn disagreements into opportunities for growth, not roadblocks:

## 1. Focus on Interests, Not Positions

It's easy to get stuck debating who's "right" or "wrong," defending positions like "I want to travel" versus "We need to save money." But the real progress comes when we dig deeper and ask, why does each person care so much about their view? Focusing on underlying interests, such as the desire for adventure, the need for security, or the wish for connection, helps everyone feel seen and opens the door to creative solutions that address both people's real needs.

## 2. Separate People from the Problem

When tempers flare, it's common to take things personally ("You never listen" or "You just want your way"). But what if the issue isn't the person, but the problem itself? By viewing the problem as something you're tackling side-by-side, not something between you, it gets easier to discuss things thoughtfully and avoid blame. Swap "you vs. me" for "us vs. this challenge," and watch conversations become more supportive.

## 3. Brainstorm Creative Options Together

Don't settle for just one "winner"—open the door to new ideas! When you both work together to brainstorm solutions, you're more likely to discover an approach neither of you considered before. What starts as a tug-of-war can turn into a team strategy session: "What if we both put aside a little for travel and boost our savings with a side gig?" The best answers often come from thinking outside the box, together.

Conflict doesn't have to be something couples avoid. When handled the right way, it can actually help you understand each other better, bring you closer, and strengthen trust. It's not about winning or losing—it's about finding solutions that put you on the same team.

What really makes the difference is focusing on why something matters, not just what the argument is about. When you look beneath the surface, separate the problem from the person, and get creative together, even hard talks can turn into break-throughs. Conflict isn't always the enemy. In many cases, it's the thing that sparks growth and transforms a relationship.

## Beyond the Numbers

I've had the pleasure to work with Sameer and Amanda, a couple whose money habits couldn't be more different. Sameer is extremely diligent, always monitoring their finances and feeling a big responsibility for the family's security. Meanwhile, Amanda is more easygoing and places a high value on providing comfort and quality for everyone they love. To everyone's surprise, when we completed their financial plan, we learned they were in a better position than they had thought: Sameer could even take a 50% pay cut and still have enough to support their needs.

But as we talked further, the full picture emerged. Sameer wasn't just looking out for his own household and their two children, he was also providing lifelong support for his mom and disabled brother, who, as foreigners, have no access to social welfare or government assistance. On top of that, he wanted to set aside a cushion for Amanda's parents, who had faced significant challenges managing money in the past. All of this meant his single income was carrying the weight of six people and preparing for any future unknowns.

From Amanda's view, she deeply admired Sameer's hard work and the responsibilities he carried, but she wished their life felt a little lighter. She wanted him to have less financial stress and for their family to enjoy more comfort, ease, and happiness—not just pressure and sacrifice. Her dream was to use their money not only for security, but also to create moments of joy, care, and peace together.

When these bigger motivations came into focus, the respect in the room grew even stronger. It became clear that Sameer's caution and concern came from a place of deep love and a strong commitment to caring for both of their families. Together, we made a plan to put protections in place for his assets and income, highlighting his health and wellbeing, while also brainstorming creative ways to leverage his skills and diversify their income over time, so the weight on his shoulders could gradually ease. Amanda expressed hope, saying, "If we can work on this as a team, I know we'll get to a place where we both feel secure and happy."

Their journey is ongoing, and I genuinely admire them throughout every step. Watching the two of them come together, communicate openly, and build a future that supports everyone around them, especially when formal support systems are limited, is truly inspiring. I feel grateful to be part of their story.

## Let Go of the Old Rulebook

One of the biggest lessons I've learned, both in my own life and in working with culturally diverse clients, is that the ways our parents or grandparents managed life and money don't always work well today. Even our own past wins or habits might not fit our current reality. We carry cultural assumptions and lived experiences like invisible rulebooks in our minds, telling us what's "right" or "expected," even when the world around us has changed.

I've felt this first-hand in my family's financial journey. My husband and I helped my parents buy a home here in the US. It's one of those unforgettable milestones filled with gratitude and pride. But looking back, I realize what came next was telling: for the entire first year, I quietly paid their utilities and handled all the bills myself, out of love and a deep sense of responsibility.

Last fall, I made a deliberate change: I stopped paying their bills for them. Instead, my parents, who have more than enough financial resources, began paying their own expenses directly. This shift was significant not just practically, but emotionally. It gave them full control and reinforced their financial independence. It was a key step in honoring their ability to manage their own lives and resources, while also respecting the cultural journey they are on.

The next step? Encouraging them to actually use their resources for their own dreams and life goals. That's much harder for them than it might sound. They grew up in a tradition where each generation was expected to save as much as possible to pass down to the next. It's part of an unspoken cultural code. Having lived through periods of extreme hardship in China, like the famine and economic chaos of the Great Leap Forward in the late 1950s and the political turmoil of the Cultural Revolution in the 1960s and '70s, they are hard-wired for safety and security, obligated to save, and not spend, even though we all know that's not sustainable. In Chinese, there's a proverb: 富不过三代 ("wealth does not last beyond three generations"), because the first generation builds it, the second preserves it, and the third squanders it.

Even when my husband and I reassure them that we don't need their money, and that our children's education is on track to be fully funded, they still hesitate. Spending feels like breaking the rules. Recognizing their roots helped me understand the emotional and cultural complexity behind their hesitation. It's not just about money; it's about deeply-held values, memories, and a lifetime of lessons learned under very different circumstances.

Supporting them through this shift means honoring those experiences while gently helping them embrace the freedom to live fully now, without guilt or fear. We will keep encouraging them to see it differently, that joy and comfort now are just as important as saving for the future. And we are being patient, knowing that shifting long-held beliefs takes time.

That's the real takeaway: what looks like a simple financial move can actually be about permission—permission to let go of outdated "rules," to spend, to enjoy, and to redefine traditions in ways that serve today's realities, not yesterday's.

The truth is, we can respect where we came from without letting it hold us back. When we let go of the old "rules" about money and tradition, we give ourselves space to think differently, set new boundaries, and make choices that match who we are today, and who we want to be in the future. In this case, our family history is one side of the coin; our new family's future is the other.

## Moving Beyond Old Money Stories

Just like cultural habits and family patterns, old investment experiences and money mindsets sometimes need a second look. Many people carry the echoes of past market booms or busts, some painful, some rewarding, that shape their current attitudes toward money and risk. But relying on those old lessons without reevaluating the current situation can hold you back or cause unnecessary stress.

For example, many Chinese investors who lived through the real estate boom at home eagerly bought properties overseas, in places like Hong Kong, Canada, or Australia, hoping to secure stable assets and steady income. But with interest rates rising sharply in recent years, those same investors are now feeling the squeeze as mortgage costs climb. This shift is forcing them to take a hard look at past choices that made sense in a very different economic time.

Similarly, consider those who lived through the global economic crisis of 2008. Many were deeply shaken by the stock market crash and the turmoil in financial systems worldwide. Even years later, they remain hesitant to re-enter the stock market, cautious about repeating past losses despite the many opportunities that long-term market growth can offer.

Don't let old wins or past mistakes steer the wheel. The secret is to zoom out, focus on the big picture, and aim for your long-term goals. Just like life, markets are always changing. When you look at investing with fresh eyes, do your research, and make choices that are right for today and tomorrow, you replace fear with confidence and step into a brighter financial future.

For couples, especially those balancing cross-cultural influences and complex family expectations, this means having open discussions about money experiences, fears, and aspirations. Making informed, patient decisions together allows you to build financial resilience without being tethered to outdated assumptions.

## The Power of Education, Mentors, and Role Models

Navigating financial decisions wisely means more than just avoiding bad advice; it's also about surrounding yourself with trusted sources of inspiration and learning. While being cautious of conflicts of interest and high-commission sales is crucial, the journey is much richer when you seek out mentors and role models who genuinely care about your growth and success. These guides, whether experienced professionals or supportive personal contacts, offer a deeper kind of guidance, one rooted in knowledge, encouragement, and shared experience.

Growing up in rural China, my dad made the big move to the city when I was in second grade, so I could have a better education. It's a gift that set the course for everything that followed. When

I first arrived in the US, I was lucky to be embraced by the incredible resources and alumni network at the University of Notre Dame, which opened doors and broadened my horizons.

Along the way, mentors came into my life who changed the trajectory of my career and goals. My first boss in the US, a Wharton graduate with decades of experience in corporate finance, took a chance on me and taught me technical skills and business knowledge without reserve. It's an opportunity I still deeply appreciate today. The idea of buying my first home, a two-flat owner-occupied unit in Wicker Park, was inspired by a close friend from my MBA program. Even this book and my YouTube channel had roots in a thoughtful conversation with a professor at Arizona State University who encouraged me to share my story and insights.

As I transitioned into entrepreneurship and began living my passion, I was incredibly fortunate to learn from many generous mentors. These mentors didn't just offer occasional advice; they allowed me to shadow their work firsthand, giving me a window into their processes and how they approach challenges and opportunities. Even now, some dedicate time with me each month in check-in sessions, sharing insights, sparking new ideas, and providing invaluable guidance.

Their willingness to invest time and wisdom in me has been a gift beyond measure. I'm immensely grateful for their support, not just for what I've learned professionally, but for the understanding and motivation they've helped me build along the way.

Just like the mentors who guided me and helped me grow, your spouse is your lifelong guide too—the best thinking partner, honest feedback provider, and motivation to be better every day. Together, you learn, grow, and inspire each other to build a life richer than either could alone.

This blend of education, guidance from diverse mentors, and the encouragement of a loving partner forms a powerful foundation. It reminds us that success and growth often come from the people we meet and the wisdom we choose to embrace, and that supporting each other through this journey called life is one of the greatest experiences a couple can share.

## The Principles Apply to Both Sides of One Coin

Throughout this book, we've explored the emotions that money stirs up and how to talk about them openly, how to dream big about a life free from financial stress, and how to take those first steps toward making it real. We've shared principles and best practices that work and remain just as relevant for cross-cultural and immigrant couples as they are for anyone else.

Along the way, we've explored the powerful habits and mindset that really make a difference in financial success. This includes knowing where your money goes, spending less than you earn, investing wisely and consistently with a long-term view, understanding your entire financial picture, and using your money to support what truly matters to you. These timeless habits are the foundation of real financial well-being.

No matter how different our backgrounds, accents, or life stories may be, these essentials unite us. They're the "one coin" that every couple can hold: two sides, each unique, yet part of the same story. When you build your financial life on these habits together, you create more than security. You create trust. You create freedom. You create a shared life you're both excited to wake up to, every day.

Our traditions, experiences, and expectations may not look the same, but the money wisdom at the heart of this book is universal. That's the beautiful truth: in love and in money, we are partners first. And with every mindful choice, every honest conversation, every goal set side by side, we are writing a life that is uniquely ours—stronger, freer, and more connected than ever.

So take what we've explored here, put it into practice, and step boldly into the future you've imagined together. Your best chapter is yet to come!

# Exercises for Chapter 8: Two Sides, One Coin

Give each other a big hug, maybe a kiss . . . or, if you're feeling generous, a massage. You've worked hard on your money, now go enjoy the fact that your life and your finances are united, and thriving!

Sometimes the best investment is in each other. And this one pays instant dividends. Have fun!

# Your Reflection

You made it to the end of the book, and that's truly something to celebrate! Use this space to jot down your thoughts and experiences, and capture any insights, feelings, or ideas that came up along the way.

_____

_____

_____

_____

_____

_____

_____

_____

_____

_____

_____

_____

# ABOUT THE AUTHOR

Prudence Zhu, CPA, CFP®, CFT™, is deeply passionate about helping couples and families transform financial stress into lasting success and harmony. As founder of Baoba USA and Enso Financial, she guides people through important money decisions, fosters meaningful communication, and helps couples build strong financial foundations based on trust and shared values.

Originally from central China, Prudence began her career in West Africa before moving to the United States on her own in 2012, with a full scholarship and big dreams. Nine years later, she achieved financial freedom through smart money choices, personal growth, and resilience. This life-changing journey inspired her mission to help others find both financial peace and personal fulfillment. After a successful career in private equity and corporate finance, Prudence became an entrepreneur dedicated to helping people align their money with their values and build stronger, closer relationships.

Prudence holds an MBA from the University of Notre Dame and an MS in Entrepreneurship and Innovation from Arizona State University. She is also an advocate for financial education and has taught at Arizona State University, equipping students with practical skills and confidence. Her expert advice has appeared in well-known publications such as Kiplinger, Investopedia,

Bloomberg, US News, and AARP, and she has been featured on podcasts including the New Planner Podcast, and others covering topics from money and taxes to real estate, business, and mental health.

When she is not working, Prudence enjoys traveling, spending intentional time with her family, and engaging in personal growth activities that keep her inspired.

Prudence believes that when couples work openly and intentionally on their finances, they build not only greater wealth but also stronger, more fulfilling relationships. She hopes this book sparks meaningful conversations, fuels your dreams, and inspires you and your partner to build a life you truly love—together!

Photo: Prudence, her husband and their children

**LinkedIn:** /in/prudencezhu

**Website:** InvestWithPrudence.com

# ACKNOWLEDGMENTS

There are so many people I want to thank for helping bring this book to life. And yes, I'll inevitably forget someone (my apologies in advance), but please know my gratitude runs far deeper than these pages can capture.

First, to my husband, family, and friends: thank you for stepping in with my children whenever I disappeared into "book mode." Your love, patience, and backup parenting made this whole project possible.

To Hitendra Chaturvedi, Professor C, thank you for planting the seed back in 2022 and telling me I would one day publish a book. At the time, I smiled politely, but inside I was thinking, "Me? Really?" Turns out, you knew better. That spark carried me through the rocky stretches.

To authors like Tony Steuer, Doug Nordman, and Echo Huang, I'm grateful for your openness in sharing your paths. Your roadmaps gave me hope and proved that book publishing doesn't require superpowers, though a steady drip of coffee came close.

To Patrick Kelley, my motivation coach: somehow you always knew when I was running on fumes and had the uncanny ability to recharge me like a human espresso shot. Thank you for the energy and encouragement. I couldn't bottle it, but I sure appreciated it!

To my publishing team:

- Katrina Sawa at Jumpstart Publishing, thank you for holding me accountable when procrastination nearly staged a takeover.

- Kristen Hugins at Joyfull Communications, for untangling my words and polishing them until I thought, "Wow, did I really write that?"

- Tasrif Ahmed, for perfectly capturing "yes, that's the one!" in a book cover.

- Silvia Staneva, your art made complex ideas look so effortless, which we both know is its own kind of brilliance.

To my peers and colleagues in worlds of financial coaching, financial literacy, fee-only and advice-only financial planning, life planning, and financial therapy—you've shaped not only my business but also my growth as a human who's still learning every day.

I'm continually inspired by role models like George Kinder, Rick Kahler, Sheryl Garrett, and Barry Michels. Your courage and resilience keep reminding me that perseverance isn't just for certain seasons of life; it's for all of them.

To my clients: thank you for trusting me with your stories, dreams, and challenges. You are the reason I bring my best every day. And I'll admit, you often end up teaching me.

And to everyone who's read my LinkedIn posts, newsletters, early drafts of this book, or tuned into my webinars: you probably don't realize how many times your comments and feedback became the boost I needed to keep creating, instead of giving in to the seductive pull of endless online videos.

This has truly been a collective journey, stitched together by so many supportive hands. Seeing it on paper feels both surreal and exhilarating. And honestly? I can't wait to see what comes next!

# JOIN THE PROGRAM

**Couples and Money: Seven-Step Group Coaching Program for Financial Alignment and Wellness**

If you loved the book and want more coaching and support, this seven-month online program is for you. It helps couples communicate, align financial goals, and thrive together.

*A Couple's Guide to Money* is just the start. To truly put these skills into action and achieve financial freedom, additional learning, coaching, and a supportive community are essential.

This program goes beyond the book to cover all you need for emotional and financial harmony. It offers:

- ✓ Seven group coaching sessions (up to 90 minutes each) with real conversations and expert guidance
- ✓ Group skills training to build confidence and teamwork
- ✓ Cohort offering support and fresh perspectives
- ✓ Digital worksheets and written materials for ongoing use

*Money talks are about more than numbers — they build team-work, trust, and clarity. Join us to make money wellness simple, fun, and life-changing.*

*Sincerely,*
*Prudence Zhu*
*www.baoba.us/services#program*

*Questions? Send them our way! Support@baoba.us*

www.ingramcontent.com/pod-product-compliance
Lightning Source LLC
Chambersburg PA
CBHW071542210326
41597CB00019B/3085